THE SUSTAINABLE(ISH) LIVING GUIDE

THE SUSTAINABLE(ISH) LIVING GUIDE

Everything you need to know to make
small changes that make a big difference

Jen Gale

GREEN TREE
LONDON • OXFORD • NEW YORK • NEW DELHI • SYDNEY

GREEN TREE
Bloomsbury Publishing Plc
50 Bedford Square, London, WC1B 3DP, UK

BLOOMSBURY, GREEN TREE and the Green Tree logo are trademarks of
Bloomsbury Publishing Plc

First published in Great Britain 2020
Copyright © Jen Gale, 2020
Chapter opener illustrations by Jessie Ford
Buyerarchy of needs (p19) content by Sarah Lazarovic
Hierarchy illustrations (p19 and p36) by JPSquared

Jen Gale has asserted her right under the Copyright, Designs and Patents Act, 1988,
to be identified as Author of this work

A catalogue record for this book is available from the British Library

Library of Congress Cataloguing-in-Publication data has been applied for

ISBN: TPB: 978-1-4729-6912-5; eBook: 978-1-4729-6913-2; ePDF: 978-1-4729-6914-9

4 6 8 10 9 7 5 3

Typeset by Deanta Global Publishing Services, Chennai, India
Printed and bound in Great Britain by CPI Group (UK) Ltd, Croydon CR0 4YY

The Forest Stewardship Council® (FSC®) is a global, not-for-profit organization
dedicated to the promotion of responsible forest management worldwide. FSC defines
standards based on agreed principles for responsible forest stewardship that are
supported by environmental, social, and economic stakeholders. To learn more, visit
www.fsc.org. By choosing this product, you are supporting responsible management
of the world's forests.

To find out more about our authors and books visit www.bloomsbury.com
and sign up for our newsletters

For our kids and their futures

Contents

Introduction

The world is changing around us. And it's changing at a terrifying rate. In just the last few years, it feels like climate change has gone from being this kind of 'some day' threat to something that we see the effects of every day. We're seeing more and more extreme weather events, air pollution is increasing, and our oceans are drowning in plastic. There is a very real possibility that ours will be the first generation to have kids whose quality of life is worse than our own. Left unchecked, climate change could create something akin to an apocalyptic scenario, **in our lifetimes.** Rising sea levels will lead to a loss of land for both living and farming, our polluted oceans will become less and less able to support life and our polluted waterways will mean a lack of clean drinking water. All coupled with a rising population. It's the perfect storm.

And it terrifies me. It terrifies me almost to the point of paralysis. These issues are so big. So complex. Surely someone somewhere with more power/influence/money than little old me has got a handle on this? Surely the governments of the world, big business bosses and manufacturers have got our backs? How can *I* be expected to create change when the world's leaders don't seem to have either the will or the power to do so?

But in among that terror I cling on to hope. Because it's the only way. We have to hold on to the hope that as a global society we can turn this ship around. That we can put aside our political differences, our personal greed, our belief that money makes the world go round, and come together to fix what is the biggest problem humanity has ever faced.

Not the most uplifting start to a book, is it?

But I think we need to get really clear about the extent of the problem we're dealing with. We've got to stop kidding ourselves that it will all be OK, and that someone else is going to fix this mess without us having to change anything about how we got here in the first place. I'm guessing if you've picked up this book you've got some kind of inkling about the situation we're in.

Times are changing. Maybe too slowly, but change is starting to happen. Even in the process of writing this book, it feels like there has been a real shift when it comes to all things planet, and climate and plastic. The phraseology has changed – it used to be global warming, then we moved to climate change, both of which don't sound too worrying, do they? Well, now we're on to no holds barred climate crisis, and climate emergency – leaving us under no illusion that we need to act. And thanks to the likes of teenage activist Greta Thunberg, the student climate strikes, Extinction Rebellion, and of course national treasure Sir David Attenborough, we're talking about the climate, and the catastrophic impact human activity is having on it, more than ever before.

This leaves lots of us looking for ideas and answers, and it's amazing for someone like me (who's been blogging about this stuff for the last seven or eight years) to go from feeling like I'm banging my head against a brick wall even a year or two ago, to now starting to feel like we're pushing on an open door when it comes to ideas and answers.

I don't have the answers, I'm afraid. But I do have lots of ideas of changes you can make, in your life, in your home, that will make a difference. Changes you can make without having to wait for the government to be pressured into action. Without having to wait for big business to find a conscience. And the good news is I'm not going to tell you that you have to eschew modern society, sell your house to move into a yurt in the woods, and start knitting your own yoghurt. You can absolutely do that if it appeals, but there are other options. There are ways to fit 'sustainable living' into the life you lead. **To change your impact without radically changing your life.** But we all know how hard it can be. What we're talking about here is changing habits. Habits that we've probably built up over years without thinking about what we're doing, or the impact it has. Changing habits is hard work; ask anyone who's been on a diet, or given up smoking. It's about creating a 'new normal' – one that's better for us, better for our cluttered homes, our bank balances, and the planet. And we can do it one simple step, one change, at a time.

I'm not a natural tree-hugger. I was brought up in the middle-class affluence of the 1980s with baby boomer parents whose natural kickback against the austerity of the post-war years seemed to be to buy, and to buy new. At the age of about 12 I decided I wanted to be a vet and spent the next 15 years or so of my life working towards that dream, and the next 10 years realising the dream wasn't all it was cracked up to be. Shortly after graduating, I met my now husband and when we set up house together we gaily spent days traipsing around Ikea, never once thinking that we might be able to get the things we needed secondhand, or that we might not actually need the pack of 100 tealights and the novelty plastic watering can that somehow found their way into the trolley as we wandered through the market hall. And then one evening (seven years, one wedding, and two kids later) I sat reading a magazine article about a lady who was partway through her 'secondhand safari' – a year of buying nothing new. And I somewhat randomly and naively thought it sounded like a fun challenge that we could have a go at too, little knowing that it would genuinely change my life.

We merrily set about buying nothing new, discovering a multitude of alternative retail outlets, and sharing our journey in a blog I called *My Make Do and Mend Year*. As ridiculous as it now sounds, I had never really given a huge amount of thought to the stuff that we bought, other than where we might be able to get it cheapest. I didn't think about what resources had been used to make it, where it had been made, who might have made it, or what would happen to it after we were done with it. Most of my buying decisions were just because – because we needed it, because I saw it in the supermarket while doing the food shop, because I thought the kids might like it, because it was Christmas… And now suddenly I was having to put a lot more effort into finding the things we needed or wanted, and that stopgap, that time to breathe and actually think about what I was buying, changed everything. I started to learn about fast fashion, about resource depletion, plastic pollution, and yes, climate change. I was confronted with the fact that our consumerism is killing the planet. That the choices I was making every day, often without really thinking about them, were having a hugely negative impact on both people and the planet. It was overwhelming. And it was like opening the proverbial can of worms. Once I opened my eyes and started to think and learn about the impacts of my choices, it sometimes felt hard to know the right thing to do. And it felt futile at times too. In the face of all these massive and complex issues, it felt laughable to think that the choices of one person, of one family, could even begin to make a difference.

But my biggest takeaway and learning from that year was that my choices, our choices, your choices matter. Yes, we can only do what we can do, and no, that will never be enough, but it's really, *really* important that we take responsibility for the impact that our choices have on the planet, and that we strive to make better choices wherever and whenever we can.

All quotes potentially become clichés after a while, but that doesn't mean they don't hold true, and this one from the inspirational Dr Jane Goodall sums things up far better than I ever could:

'You cannot get through a single day without having an impact on the world around you. What you do makes a difference, and you have to decide what kind of difference you want to make.'

I firmly believe that's what 'sustainable living' is all about – making different choices. Getting informed, making a start, having a go. It's about embracing the 'ish'. Making changes one baby step at a time, knowing that we won't always get it right, knowing that no one lives a perfectly sustainable life, and that that's OK. But just because we can't be perfect, it doesn't mean that we can't get started and we can't have an impact. We absolutely can. And as each of us makes different choices, makes changes, shows others what we're doing and talks about why, the ripples spread, and more and more people are inspired to act. Momentum builds and all of these small actions add up to change the world. Here's another favourite quote, this time from Howard Zinn:

'We don't have to engage in grand, heroic actions to participate in change. Small acts, when multiplied by millions of people, can transform the world.'

In this book I'm sharing with you some of the things I've learned over the past eight years since that year of buying nothing new. I'm not an environmental scientist, and I'm not perfect by any stretch, I'm just a regular person muddling through, learning as I go. But I do know that we can all make a difference. And I want you to know that **you** can make a difference. Every single day. Without making huge sacrifices, without massively compromising your quality of life, or missing out, or becoming that slightly grubby hippy-ish family down the road that everyone avoids eye contact with in case they get a lecture on the perils of car travel, or eating meat, or wearing clothes.

This book is for you if you're worried about the state of the planet, but you're just not sure where to start or what to do. It's for you if you've got your own reusable coffee cup (whoop!) and know that there's other stuff you could be doing, but it all feels a bit overwhelming. It's for you if you feel a kind of low-level guilt about the things you do every day, knowing that there is a better way, but you're up to your eyes in work and family and life stuff, and it doesn't feel like there's the time or energy to make big changes.

And I'll be honest here, it's probably not for you if you're already well on your way. If you're knocking out beeswax wraps, heating your house with an air source pump (*see* Chapter 7) and have been using a cargo bike as your main source of transport for the last couple of years, you're going to be disappointed by this book. There's nothing groundbreaking in it. There's no amazing new scientific research, it's just me, a very ordinary person, an ex-vet, knackered mum of two, sharing the things that I've learned in what I hope is an accessible and actionable way.

What I want more than anything from this book is for it to make you stop and think. And then for it to make you **go and do**. Because we can have all the knowledge in the world, but unless we act on it, it's useless. It's a bit like a diet. We all know that if we want to lose weight we need to eat less and move more. It's not rocket science, despite what the diet industry might want us to believe. But just reading about losing weight isn't going to help. Getting informed about the perils of being overweight doesn't make the pounds melt away. There is no silver bullet. Creating change needs action. I hope that I can help you to work out the actions that will work for YOU, and then for you to go out and make them happen. And to make it as easy as possible! This isn't a beautiful coffee table book. It's a guidebook. A workbook even. I want you to fold down pages, to annotate and underline, to use the sections at the back of each chapter to create your very own action plan. I want you to be able to look back after a few months and see the changes that you've made; at the difference that you've made. Because it really does add up.

We have very little control over what those around us do (my own kids do their best to prove this to me every day); over what policies our government adopts or doesn't (although it is imperative we make our voices heard to those in power – *see* Chapter 12). But that doesn't mean we are powerless. We have the power to make different choices, more informed choices, better choices, every single day. We can start to create the world we want to live in through the choices we make. I hope this book helps you to do that.

My make do and mend year

What started as a 'fun' and slightly naive challenge in September 2012 genuinely changed my life; not just how and what I buy, but how I see my place in the world too. I found my voice and through blogging every day for a year (no, I have no idea how I managed it either) I discovered a love of writing that I had buried under the need to concentrate on the sciences for my career aspirations.

At the start of the year I was trepidatious – I was worried we had bitten off more than we could chew; that all of the white goods in the house would collude to simultaneously break down as the clock struck midnight on the first day of the challenge. I was anxious about where I would find the things that we might need, and how difficult it was going to be. But I needn't have worried. The white goods all survived the year intact, and it was actually far easier than I thought it was going to be to buy nothing new for the year. What was interesting, though, was quite how unsettling it was to have the safety net of instant consumerism whisked out from under us. Early on in the year we drove up to Scotland to visit my in-laws and previously when we were packing for holidays my concerns about forgetting something vital would be allayed with the knowledge that we could always pick up a replacement version with a quick trip to the nearest town or supermarket. However, on this occasion that wasn't going to be possible – if we had forgotten something, we were going to have to wander aimlessly around a strange town in search of the charity shops and then keep our fingers crossed that the charity shop fairies were looking out for us, and they would have what we needed. It really brought home to me how much we took the quick fix of consumerism for granted. But as the year progressed, and I got familiar with the abundance of alternative retail outlets available for secondhand stuff, my concerns lessened. It was genuinely like a little switch had been flicked in my head, and attention shifted entirely away from new stuff. And there is **so** much stuff out there in charity shops, at flea markets, vintage fairs and car boots. I discovered sites like Freecycle and Freegle (*see* page 27), where you can give and receive unwanted stuff for free, as well as a whole community of amazing people doing wonderful sustainable(ish) things all around the world, through the power of social media.

But what about the rest of the family, who were dragged along by my latest 'amazing idea'? My husband was supportive in a kind of 'anything for a quiet life' way, and once he realised how much money we were saving (we saved around £2000 over the course of the year, so not an insignificant amount), he became a little more enthusiastic. His biggest hang-up was that he couldn't buy newspapers, an issue that led to some heated debate about whether they counted as buying something new. I'll leave you to draw your own conclusions as to who might have won that particular argument... And the kids? Well, they were four and two, so young enough still to not really worry about the difference between a 50p toy car from the car boot, or one from the toy shop. Doing the same thing with teenagers on board would be a different kettle of fish altogether. I do often wonder for how much longer I will be able to impose my values and ethics on them as they grow, and whether or not they will be conscious consumers as they enter their teens and start forming their own set of standards they want to live by. Family and friends were, I think, a little bemused. My parents just didn't get it at all. My brother and his wife had to put up with some embarrassingly bad presents for Christmas and birthdays, which they did with remarkably good grace, and I was never quite brave enough to bounce up to fellow parents at pre-school and ask them if they thought we were a bit weird.

As the year progressed, it felt like I had found my 'thing'; the reality of being a vet didn't match up to the dreams I had as a teenager, and had left me stressed out and, quite frankly, miserable. The blog and the year gave me a new focus, passion and purpose, but I was as surprised as anyone at the media attention and new opportunities that arose. I went on our local BBC radio station to give regular updates on our year, got a double-page spread in *The Sun* newspaper, coverage in the *Guardian*, and even a teeny box in *The Times* when our year ended. I was invited to give a TEDx talk, which was terrifying for someone who had always avoided public speaking at all costs (I kind of love it now!). The fact that it was newsworthy goes to show just how deeply embedded consumption is in our modern society.

Once the year ended, the journey continued. I had learned so much, and it was stuff that couldn't be 'un-learned'. It was impossible to return to such an **un**conscious, **un**thoughtful way of consuming once I knew the impact it was having on the planet. We're less strict now about 'rules' and we do buy new. But when we do it's a much more considered decision, seeking out ethical and sustainable alternatives, which thankfully are becoming easier and easier to find as the world slowly wakes up to the problems our throwaway society is creating.

I get that a year buying nothing new isn't going to appeal to everyone, and I've done that bit so that you don't have to. But I would genuinely recommend a spell of buying nothing new to everybody. A year might be a little extreme, but even a month (or a week if you're a really hardened consumer!) is such a powerful thing to do. Going 'cold turkey' on buying new stuff forces you to stop and think before buying, and that space is what's important. It helps to break the habitual consumption that we can all be guilty of. It could be the start of a life-changing journey, one that will have a positive impact for you and for the planet.

Making sustainable(ish) changes

Making any change can be difficult, especially if it's to long-entrenched habits – if you've ever been on a diet, you'll know this. And making changes to live more sustainably is no different. What we don't want to do is the equivalent of a crash diet where we start off being really extreme, and then crash and burn when it all feels like too much hard work.

Here are some top tips for making changes that are sustainable for the planet and sustainable for you long term:

TOP TIPS

Get motivated
Simon Sinek gives a very famous and very powerful TED talk about the importance of 'starting with why'. Getting clear on why you

want to make the changes you're making is a powerful motivator and reminding yourself of your 'why' periodically will help to keep you going. There're enough scary stats in this book to motivate you (!), or check out some of the films recommended on pages 140–41.

Start with the low-hanging fruit

Go for some quick, easy wins to start with – the hardest thing with any change is often getting started, so once you've made some easy changes you have some momentum behind you to tackle the next ones.

Don't go hell for leather right from the start

If you wake up one morning, promise you're never going to buy anything new ever again, never throw anything away again and never use single-use plastic again, you're setting yourself up for failure. These things are doable if you aspire to them, but they take time, research and commitment. They don't happen overnight.

Go one step at a time

Big goals like 'plastic-free' or 'zero waste' are brilliant, but they are also potentially overwhelming. Break things down into milestones along the journey. And then break each milestone down into the steps you need to take. Every single step, no matter how small, counts.

Aim for progress and not perfection

If you spend any time online and start delving into 'sustainable living', you will see the poster girls and boys of green living. Remember that the curated perfection of their social media feeds might not truly reflect the reality, and that their version of 'perfection' might not be yours. Also remember that they didn't wake up one morning like that – you haven't seen their journey and the detours, wrong turns and slip-ups along the way. Don't let perfection stop you from getting started. All progress is progress.

Be realistic

Work out what is possible and doable for **you** and your unique set of circumstances. We all have our own challenges and our own constraints. Someone else's 'easy' might be your 'super hard' and that's OK.

Top Tips continues overleaf

Be really clear about what you want to change

If you want to reduce your plastic use (yay!), be really clear about how much you want to reduce it by. Give your brain something to work with so you know if you're making progress. In Chapter 3 I talk about doing a plastic audit, and something like this is great for any change you're wanting to make – giving you a baseline to start from and to measure your progress against.

Don't try and do it all at once

'Sustainable living' is a massive and all-encompassing topic. What I don't want you to do is to read this book and then try to change All The Things, all at once. Pick one chapter to make a start on. Give yourself some really specific goals, and identify a couple of changes you could make easily in the first week or so, and then a few you could make in the next month. Once those changes and habits are entrenched and secure, move on to another chapter. And simply rinse and repeat.

Write it down

Write down the change(s) that you want to make and stick this somewhere you'll see it. In addition to this, you could also tell your family/friends or post it on social media. A little bit of public accountability can go a long way.

Don't go it alone

Anyone who has embarked on a fitness regime will know that buddying up with someone else makes the whole thing much more pleasurable and, importantly, much more likely to happen. Get the family on board, recruit a friend, make it into a friendly competition, find your tribe on social media.

Set some deadlines

Once you've decided what changes you want to make, set yourself some deadlines. I'm totally a deadline person, and without them I drift and faff and procrastinate. If you want to reduce the rubbish you send to landfill by half (whoop!), when do you want to do that by? If you want to buy no new clothes (hurray!), how long will you challenge yourself to keep this up?

Accept that you might sometimes slip up

Going back to the diet analogy, we all slip up sometimes, none of us is perfect. But just as scoffing half a pack of biscuits one evening in front of the TV isn't a valid excuse for chucking in the whole diet, forgetting your reusable cup and still succumbing to a takeaway coffee doesn't make you a failure. Think about what went wrong and why, and what you can change to give yourself a better chance next time.

Read and do

This is a book about 'doing'. About changing some of the things we do, the things we buy, and subtly changing the way we live to create a more sustainable future for the planet and for future generations. So what I really want to happen after you read each chapter of this book is for you to make a plan of the things you want to change, and then to do them!

There are checklists (by no means comprehensive but hopefully enough to get you started!) of some of the changes you might want to make at the end of every chapter. Tick off any you're already doing and give yourself a pat on the back. Then identify two or three other changes you want to make and write them down in the space below the checklist.

HERE ARE SOME QUESTIONS OR PROMPTS TO THINK ABOUT:

- Why is this change important to you? To your family? To your community? To the planet?
- What would your '10/10' for this area be? Do you want to be 'plastic-free'? Or reduce your use of single-use plastics by half? Or simply remember your reusable water bottle every day for a week?

- What would be the easiest way to get started? What's the smallest baby step?
- Who do you know who is already one step ahead of you on this journey? How could they help you?

Some definitions

Sustainable living

This will mean different things to everyone, but the Wikipedia definition tallies pretty closely with my own and is:

> '...a lifestyle that attempts to reduce an individual's or society's use of the Earth's natural resources, and one's personal resources. Its practitioners often attempt to reduce their carbon footprint by altering their methods of transportation, energy consumption, and/or diet.'

Carbon footprint

The dictionary definition is this:

> 'The amount of carbon dioxide released into the atmosphere as a result of the activities of a particular individual, organization, or community.'

Nearly every activity releases carbon dioxide (CO_2) and other greenhouse gases that are contributing to climate change. When we eat food, that food has been grown somewhere (using water and possibly fertilisers and pesticides), it's been harvested, processed and transported. All of these steps require energy, which presently largely means fossil fuels. In this book we're focusing on the impact of our choices and actions as individuals, and as individuals we have our own carbon footprint, depending on where we live, what we do, what we eat and more. To really accurately calculate your carbon footprint would probably require you to sit down with an environmental scientist for the best part of a week, delving into

OK. So are you ready? The need for change has never been more urgent. The clock is ticking. But there is still time, and there is still hope. With this book I hope I'll help you to cut through the overwhelm, all the

- Who else could help you?
- What resources or additional things do you need to have in place to give yourself the best chance of success?

your every move and purchase, but the World Wildlife Fund (WWF) have put together a handy 'footprint calculator' (www.footprint.wwf. org.uk) – a five-minute questionnaire running through the biggest impact areas of our lives – that gives you a great idea of the impact of your current lifestyle on the planet. Do it now to give yourself a baseline, and then repeat it periodically to track your progress.

Water footprint

As well as emitting carbon and other greenhouse gases, most of our daily activities require water. It's not just the water that we drink and use for cooking and washing, nearly everything has a water footprint. The clothes that you're wearing needed water to grow the cotton (cotton is a very hungry plant – see page 114), process it into fabric, and dye it, for example.

Greenhouse gas (GHG) emissions

Greenhouse gases such as carbon dioxide (CO_2), methane (CH_4) and nitrous oxide (N_2O) trap heat in the atmosphere, warm the planet and lead to climate change and air pollution. They are emitted by human activities such as burning fossil fuels.

Greenwashing

Greenwashing has lots of definitions, some more confusing than others, but this one from the Cambridge Dictionary is pretty clear:

'Behaviour or activities that make people believe that a company is doing more to protect the environment than it really is.'

Sadly, sometimes we can't always take what businesses, organisations or even governments say at face value, and it pays to do a little digging to see if their actions are matching their words.

different advice, all the noise. And that you'll be empowered to take action on the climate crisis, starting in your own home, with the choices you make every day.

Conscious consumption

It's a message that goes against the grain of everything we're told every day by retailers, and in fact by our governments, with their seemingly set in stone stance that infinite economic growth is possible and must be achieved on a planet of finite resources. But I believe that at the very crux of living more sustainably is the need to consume less, and to consume more thoughtfully. More consciously. Essentially, we need to stop buying crap we don't need. Which sounds dull, I know, but let's get the tough love over and done with right at the start.

There is simply no way we can carry on consuming at the rate we are, and still have a habitable planet left. On current predictions for climate change, we're heading for at least a 3°C rise in temperature before the end of THIS century – if we're not around to see that, our kids probably will be. And that 3°C rise doesn't mean warmer summers and a better tan; it means catastrophic climate collapse, sea level rises, millions of climate refugees, less fresh water, less land to grow food. It's not good. To put it mildly.

But what has this got to do with us upgrading our iPhones, or hitting the high street when we've had a crappy day? I'm glad you asked.

DID YOU KNOW?

Household consumption is responsible for more than 60 per cent of global greenhouse gas emissions.

A study in the *Journal of Industrial Ecology* in 2015 (I read this stuff so you don't have to!) found that household consumption (of everything from food to fashion) is responsible for more than 60 per cent of global greenhouse gas emissions and 50–80 per cent of total land, resource and water use. And another, more recent report from the European Commission found that 'better educated households have generally higher consumption levels, and therefore emissions'. So just because you've got a degree doesn't mean you make better buying decisions, it just means you buy more.

These are pretty shocking stats. But they're also really heartening too – because we are in charge of our own consumption. We don't need to wait for government legislation, or for big business to grow a conscience, this is stuff we can change **right now**. From the comfort of our sofas if we want to. All by doing (buying) LESS.

Sounds simple, doesn't it? As I said at the start – we just need to stop buying crap we don't need. Easy. Or is it? It should be, but, as I'm sure many of us can vouch for, it really isn't quite that simplistic.

You see, shopping has become about more than simply fulfilling a need for the thing we're buying – it's become a complex cocktail of pleasure, reward and guilt, with a double shot of clever manipulation by advertisers. We buy stuff when we're happy, when we're sad, when we're bored, when we're out with friends on a Saturday. We buy stuff because we're sold the story that our lives will be infinitely better, richer, more fun, more fulfilling when we have a new sofa/phone/car/pair of shoes. We all *know* that stuff doesn't make us happy (beyond that initial endorphin hit), yet we still seem to maintain the hope that it will. It's that definition of insanity – doing the same thing again and again and being surprised when nothing changes. Except our homes are becoming more cluttered, and our bank balances are declining. Just a couple of days after buying that must-have top, or going crazy and treating ourselves to some sexy new pants, our lives are no different – we are no more beautiful or alluring, and we're just left with a massive wedgie and wanting our granny pants back.

How to stop impulse buying

Tara Button, founder of the website Buy Me Once (www.buymeonce.com) and an advocate of buying well and buying to last, has some great advice to help us shop more consciously. She recommends doing a bit of detective work and taking a long hard (honest) look at your bank account, credit card bills and PayPal purchase lists for 'imp(ulse) trails'. Highlight anything you think might have been an impulse buy, whether it was a coffee or a car. Once you've got a clear picture, you should be able to identify what type of imps you have and learn how to stop impulse buying too.

The treater imp

This imp thinks any occasion *needs* to be celebrated or condoled with your wallet. Put a 24-hour rule on all online purchases. You can add it to a wish list, but not your cart. Then you can come back to it with a cooler head later.

The insecurity imp

If you discover that much of your spending was to cheer yourself up and make you feel better, then you're not alone! Sixty-two per cent of us have used shopping as a way to elevate our mood. This imp needs firm handling. Look it in the eye and tell it daily, 'No material object can make me a better person. I am enough.'

The FOMO imp

This imp is super excitable and is terrified of missing out on a bargain or experience. Make a list of your true priorities and the

Consumerism has become so embedded in our society that we very rarely stop and think about *why* we're buying something, let alone if we really need it. It's like going into Lidl for a pint of milk and coming out with a fence sprayer and a George Foreman grill. It just happens. So much of our buying, our consumption, is completely **un**conscious – it's stuff that's really going to make you happy: more free time; a creative project; experiences with friends; pursuing a passion. Make sure the bulk of both your time and your money is spent on the things that matter.

The guilt imp

Close friend to the FOMO imp, this imp tells you you're a bad friend/father/wife unless you're constantly supplying the people around you with material possessions. Gift these people your time, love and thoughts, not something that will end up stuffed in their cupboard.

The curiosity imp

This imp is excited by anything new; any excuse to change it up or 'freshen' your look or buy something new is going to get this imp tapping on the inside of your head, telling you that it 'neeeeds you to redecorate' or 'neeeeds the latest phone'. Turn the imp's attention to more positive and productive areas of your life. What new thing could you learn about, what new place could you go to? What new people could you meet? What new goal could you aim for?

The faddy imp

This imp is pals with the curiosity imp but is also a massive flake. It gets excited about stuff, gets you to buy all the equipment and then promptly loses interest. The way to subdue this little guy is to give him the benefit of the doubt, but always, always borrow rather than buy the equipment. That way, if you discover a true passion you can always upgrade to your own equipment as a reward.

done with little or no thought about where things are made, what they are made from, who might have made them (and in what conditions) and then ultimately what we're going to do with them once we are done. It's done on autopilot. We no longer seem to value our 'stuff' or, by implication, the people who have made it. Becoming aware of some of the issues that our ever-increasing pace of consumption is causing both people and planet, and of our own buying habits (and very often they are just that, habits) is the first step to addressing them. Giving ourselves the time to take a breath, look around for the best options that work for us, for our families, and for the planet. We need to start to question and push back against the seemingly incessant societal demands that more is better, that new is better, and the constant demand that we upgrade, replace, and buy newer All The Time.

Fashion guru Vivienne Westwood's approach to sustainable fashion is clear when she talks about the need to:

'Buy less, buy better, make it last.'

And in fact that same mantra can be applied in all areas of our lives; from fashion to food, and from tech to toys. Our year buying nothing new forced me to slow down my consumption, purely because the easy, instant, quick fix solution of simply grabbing a brand new item off the shelves, or clicking 'buy' online, wasn't there. Sourcing secondhand things takes more time, and very often that time provided the stopgap I needed to think about whether we actually really needed that thing after all, or whether we might be able to fix it, or use something else we already had.

If we care about the future we're leaving the next generations and if we're going to take action on the climate crisis, we all need to change our ways and consume less. We need to find new ways to get that endorphin hit, to cheer ourselves up, to celebrate, or to spend time with friends. Ways that aren't stripping the planet of resources, filling up landfill sites, and killing people and the planet. I'm not saying that you can't buy stuff and you must deprive yourself, or that you can't have nice stuff, and that all our homes should be minimalist. I am not a minimalist. I wish I were – my lack of any kind of skill or desire to tidy up would be less annoying and my house would be much neater. But it's about time we all curbed our inner toddler and our incessant need for more and more shiny new stuff, and found other ways to make ourselves feel good about our lives instead.

One brilliant approach to help with this is to keep in mind the 'buyerarchy of needs'.

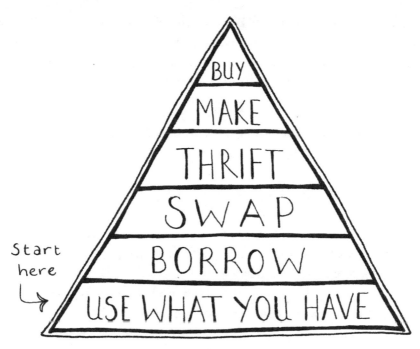

The buyerarchy of needs by Sarah Lazarovic

I wish I could claim this as my own, but I'm neither that clever nor that creative. This beautifully simple picture is the work of Canadian designer Sarah Lazarovic and it sums up so succinctly what we all need to think about when it comes to consumption. The idea is obviously to start at the bottom – use what you have – and only resort to buying new when you've exhausted all the other options. I would even chuck in another layer – repair – but as I said, it's not my genius, so I'm not going to mess with it. It's a fabulous framework to live and buy by. I urge you all to stick it on your fridge or tattoo it on your forehead – whatever you need to do to make sure that it's at the forefront of your mind next time you feel the urge to shop sneaking up on you.

So first up …

Use what you have

Not rocket science. And not hugely exciting either. But just think of the money you could save. And the baby polar bears with no ice to sit on. You can do this. Look around your home – which, if it's anything like mine, consists of bulging drawers, cluttered worktops, and an array of stuff on the stairs that people keep walking past and not actually taking upstairs. Do you actually have most of what you need hiding in there somewhere? Can you get creative with the stuff you already have and 'upcycle' it into something you need (*see* pages 42–43)?

- What do you already have that you've forgotten about? Shop your wardrobe – drag everything out and see what old favourites you discover, what things you could mix and match to make whole new outfits.
- Clear out the clutter drawer – you're guaranteed to find batteries, chargers, earphones and more that will save you buying new.
- Do you really need to upgrade your phone just because Apple says you should? I see not upgrading and not buying the latest whatever as a kind of countercultural thing. I like to think it makes me hip and rebellious. It doesn't, but I will happily take any opportunity to feel slightly less grown-up and middle-aged.
- What could you 'upcycle' into something useful rather than buy something new?

Borrow

Borrowing isn't just for books anymore! There's a whole 'sharing economy' waiting out there for us to borrow what we need rather than buy – from clothes to tools, it's all there for the ~~taking~~ borrowing. And borrowing makes so much sense.

> **DID YOU KNOW?**
> The average drill is only used for around 13 minutes in its entire life.

I have no idea where that statistic originally came from, but it totally feels like it could be true, doesn't it? How many minutes have you used your drill for? Probably not all that many (especially if your DIY skills are anything like mine), yet lots of us feel the need to own one. Just in case there's a shelving emergency and we need immediate access to more holes in the wall. But we don't all need to own a drill. Or a power washer.

Or even a posh frock we only wear once or twice. It makes way more sense to borrow these things, rather than buy them. It saves us money, it saves us space in the garage, or the shed or the wardrobe, and it saves the resources and carbon needed to make thousands of copies of things that are only used a couple of times.

Thankfully, borrowing is becoming easier and easier. In the US and Canada, Tool Libraries are pretty commonplace – as you'd imagine, they work like a library, but lend out tools rather than books. Such a wonderfully simple idea. The Edinburgh Tool Library (www.edinburghtoollibrary.org.uk) is the first one here in the UK and it has proved that the model works and can be financially sustainable – so hopefully pretty soon we should see more and more springing up around the country, making it easier for us all to access tools when we need them, without needing to own our own. You could even set one up yourself in your local community.

Another brilliant idea is 'Share Shops'. The UK's first sharing shop opened in Frome in Somerset in 2015, closely followed by the 'Library of Things' in Crystal Palace, London. And they both do what they say on the tin, working like libraries, for things! You can borrow tools, fancy dress outfits, tents and camping gear, highchairs for visiting babies and pretty much anything else you could imagine. How amazing would it be to see schemes like this one in every town and city, making it easy for us all to borrow rather than buy?

If you're sitting there thinking, 'Well, that all sounds great, but what about me? Do I just have to wait until there is one of these projects near me?' No you don't. Borrow from your neighbours. Borrow from your friends, and your family. Just ask and you may well be surprised what people have lurking in their sheds and cupboards that they're more than happy to lend you. Some communities have set up their own informal sharing networks, where they have clubbed together to buy something like a hedge trimmer, and it just does the rounds. Keep it simple!

Alongside that, in the UK, projects like Streetbank (www.streetbank.com) aim to make it as easy as possible for us to share the stuff we have with our neighbours by providing an online platform where you can list them.

Three things you can easily borrow or rent rather than buy

1 **Posh frocks** I very rarely (never) have any need for a posh frock post-children, but I am reliably informed by those with more glamorous lives than mine that dresses can be rented from both bricks and mortar, and online dress agencies. So you never have to worry about the social faux pas and the world-crushing shame (can you sense the irony in these words) of being seen in the same dress twice. (This may be time for a quick reality check: I challenge you to remember what everyone was wearing at the last event you went to – unless you're Kate or Meghan, no one actually cares. Harsh but true.) Or the even easier option is to simply borrow one from a similar-sized friend. You get to wear a posher dress than you might otherwise buy, and you get to wear it once with a clear conscience. #winwin

2 **Power tools** If you need a sander for rubbing down your floorboards don't buy one, rent it from your local tool hire centre. The added bonus of this is you have a deadline for getting the job done, limiting the amount of procrastination before having to crack on.

3 **Glasses and crockery** If you're planning a big party (again, clearly your social whirl is far more whirly than mine) then glass and crockery hire is easy to come by. Waitrose do an in-store free glass hire, and a quick internet search should reveal vintage crockery hire if you're wanting gorgeous mismatched cups and saucers.

Swap

Swapping isn't just for football stickers and Pokémon cards. Oh no. It can be for stuff that's actually useful too. Clothes swapping, or swishing to give it its fancy name, is probably the most widely known swapping activity and I'll talk about it in more detail later (*see* Chapter 5 on sustainable(ish) fashion). It's a fabulous way to refresh your wardrobe for very little money, keeps clothes out of landfill, and helps to slow down the fast fashion cycle.

- Kids' clothes
- Kids' toys
- Books
- CDs and DVDs (if you still use them – showing my age here)
- Skills – if you're a contender for *Bake Off* and need the hem taking up on your trousers, swap skills with your sewing friend and offer to make a cake for the next birthday that is coming up.

Thrift

This is American for buying secondhand. Whatever you call it, it's my favourite way to shop and I challenge you to not be able to find at least 95 per cent of what you need or want secondhand – you might just need to pop on your patient pants for a minute or two. There is a whole heap of ways you can find what you need 'pre-loved' – some of them don't even involve money changing hands.

CHARITY SHOPS

This is the obvious one that we probably all think of when we think about buying stuff secondhand. I will hold my hands up and say I was not a natural 'thrifter' until we spent our year buying nothing new – I found it all too cluttered, and I could never find anything I liked. I used to want to punch those infuriating people who, when you asked them where they got their dress/top/bag, would say, 'Oh this? I found it in a charity shop for 57p.' Now I AM one of those people – which just goes to show that if I can learn how to get my 'eye in' when I'm in the charity shops, then anyone can.

Call it pre-loved, call it vintage or retro if that makes you feel better, but I promise you, it's what all the really cool kids are doing. I know that I would say that, given that I know some of the staff in my local ones by name, but honestly – who's to know? If you really don't want your friends and acquaintances knowing that you're an awesome human being who is saving the planet *at the same time as* finding fabulous stuff at knockdown prices, don't tell 'em!

THERE ARE MANY REASONS TO LOVE CHARITY SHOPS:

1 You can pick up some absolute bargains.
2 You save stuff from landfill.
3 You get to curate your own look and aren't sucked into wearing the same 'uniform' as everyone else.
4 You're not contributing to the supply and demand for more and more new stuff.
5 If you're shopping locally you don't have to brave the 'big city', the parking nightmares and the crowds.
6 And my favourite thing of all – you can usually park the kids in front of the toys section while you whiz round the rest in relative peace!

Is there still a stigma around charity shops? I asked this question in my Sustainable(ish) Facebook group and got a resounding 'No' – but I will admit that it's a case of preaching to the converted there, as many of them are already hardened sustainable types. I personally don't have any issue with shopping in charity shops, but my parents just couldn't get their heads around it. I don't know if it's a generational thing, or if it's geographical, or if it just comes down in the end to not giving too much of a toss what people think. If you're apprehensive about it, maybe go with a friend who you know is a seasoned 'pro' (of the charity shopping kind, obvs). Or pick a particularly posh-looking one to start with!

Here are some top tips for shopping in charity shops:

TOP TIPS

Get to know your local shops

If you're not used to frequenting charity shops then you might be vaguely aware that there are 'some' in your local town, but you probably don't know all of them. Go for a wander, and really start to look for them. Or if you are new to a town, use the Charity Retail Associations website (www.charityretail.org.uk) to search for ones near you. I live in a small market town, and we have at least eight – I have developed a little route around town that will take in all of them and it's my favourite type of shopping (says someone who pretty much hates shopping).

Not all charity shops are created equal

You will find that the quality and type of goods will vary from shop to shop. Some almost look like 'new' shops now; clothes are sorted by colour, everything is laid out very neatly, the lighting is bright. It all looks very lovely and is probably priced accordingly. There are, however, still 'old-fashioned' ones out there where everything is a bit of a jumble – things tend to be a bit cheaper, and you get to have a good old rummage and see what you can unearth! And you will also find that some shops specialise in just one thing, for example clothes or electrical items. Get to know your local ones, and which one suits your style, budget and shopping list.

Location, location, location

I have never actually tested this out, but there is a theory out there that charity shops in more upmarket places will have better quality stuff, and are more likely to have high-end fashion brands in them. It makes sense, and I keep meaning to check it out! Be aware, though, that charity shops are now pretty clued up as to what brands are worth what, and the prices will reflect that.

Make a list, check it twice

Make a list of the things that you need, and keep this with you (I use the 'notes' facility on my mobile and keep a list of measurements if, for instance, I'm looking for a bedside table or chest of drawers for one of the kids) to consult when you do your charity shop rounds. It will help you to remember what you are on the lookout for and be more targeted when you are browsing.

Don't fall into the trap that I did at the beginning of my year buying nothing new when I got a little bit charity shop happy, buying four dresses in the space of a couple of days along with all kinds of little knick-knacks for the house and toys for the kids that they didn't need. Consumerism is still consumerism, and too much stuff is still too much stuff, whether it's secondhand or not.

Top Tips continues overleaf

Go frequently

Don't just go once! I think this was my issue before – I would go once in a blue moon and have a desultory rummage before grumpily declaring there was nothing I liked and stomping off. Keep popping in regularly as the stock turns over pretty quickly, and if they don't have what you need one week, they might in a week or two's time.

Time your visits

Again, this is an untested theory, but some people recommend going on a Monday or Tuesday, as people will have been clearing out their wardrobes/cupboards over the weekend, so there will be lots of new stock at the beginning of the week.

Have an open mind

I once nearly walked away from a coat because I didn't like the buttons. It took longer than it should have done for me to register that I could actually change the buttons really easily! I bought it, and rummaged in my button collection for some suitable ones, and now I LOVE it, and everyone always comments on it. Furniture can be sanded back and/or painted, and clothes can be adjusted or tarted up.

Think outside the box

Cast your eye over the menswear section for snuggly jumpers and cardis. Duvets and sheets are a great source of quite a lot of fabric for sewing projects, and jeans are super versatile for upcycling in all kinds of imaginative ways. Look at things with your upcycler's specs on: all kinds of things can be repurposed into something you need (*see* pages 42–43).

The sniff test..!

It's true, some shops have a particular smell to them, and this can pervade the clothes. Check the labels to see if things can be chucked in the washing machine, and if they can then this should get rid of most whiffs. Hanging out on the line to air is another great way to get rid of smells. If neither of these work, then bicarb is a great deodoriser (soak items in bicarb and water overnight), and a top tip from a theatre wardrobe mistress I know is that neat vodka sprayed on to smelly areas will remove the smell!

VINTAGE SHOPS/FAIRS

Vintage is cool. In fairness probably too cool for me, but that's not to say that I don't sometimes wander longingly around vintage shops wishing I were cooler, or a little bit braver with my style choices. If you have a vintage fair or shop near you, venture in and see what gems you can unearth.

CAR BOOTS

If you can cope with the early start (or find an afternoon one), car boots are a delight for anyone looking for secondhand stuff – kids' toys and clothes can be found by the bootfull, sometimes for ridiculous prices (because no one wants to cart it all home again, having gone to the effort of sorting it all out). They are also another way to make shopping with kids slightly more bearable – give them a pound each and let them go K-RAZY!

> If you go for this option, you might want to start operating a 'one in, one out' (by out I mean donated to a charity shop/passed on to a friend, not landfill!) system for 'new' toys, otherwise your house will soon become stuffed to the gills.

EBAY

If you are looking to source as much as you can secondhand, the temptation to hit eBay for everything you need might be pretty strong. It's easy, you can find some brilliant bargains, and you don't even have to leave the house! But be aware that you might be missing out on some of the richest and best experiences of buying nothing new – things like discovering the joys of charity shop shopping, or exploring flea markets, or seeing the generosity of your local community on Freegle.

However, if you're looking for something really specific, it can be a godsend, and can save you hours of trawling your local charity shops in the hope that a pair of size 12 black jeans will magically appear. Just remember to tick the 'used' box in the search filter.

FREE STUFF

Sometimes you can find the very thing you need or want without even having to pay for it. Sites like Freecycle (www.freecycle.org) or Freegle (www.ilovefreegle.org) provide the mechanism to connect people with stuff they no longer want with people who do. And it's super simple to use; simply search online for your nearest group (I pretty much guarantee you will have one near you), sign up, and then you will receive daily or weekly emails (your choice) of the things on offer locally. You can use it to get rid of random things you no longer have a use for, like the half bag of food your dog suddenly turned its nose up at, or the tin of paint you opened before realising it was the wrong colour. And you can also add WANTED posts if there's something specific you need – say waterproofs for the kids, or a tent. You will be surprised what people are happy to give away.

Make

This isn't going to be everyone's cup of tea – not all of us have the skills, time or inclination to make our own clothes/furniture/loo roll (yes, that's a thing…) – but I reckon even the most time-stretched, skill-poor among us could still rustle up the odd handmade thing or two. If Dame Judi Dench can create sweary embroidery on the set of the latest Bond film, there must be something we could all turn our hands to.

Making is good for the soul. And the mind. And the planet, if done right. It forces us to slow down and to appreciate, maybe for the first time ever, the resources and skills that go into making the stuff that we consume and discard so quickly. It forces us to learn to love our stuff again – I guarantee you, if you've spent three months at an evening class every Tuesday making a side table, you're not going to chuck that out next time you redecorate. Even if it is a bit shit. Because YOU made it. YOU put the time, the love, the energy into that. And you did something, you made something that maybe you never in a million years thought you could.

> As a child I was crap at anything arty, I still am. But after having
> our eldest I randomly decided I wanted to learn to sew and signed
> up for a three-week 'Learn to Love your Sewing Machine' evening
> class. William was about eight months old at the time, and I can't
> describe the freedom of a couple of hours a week all to myself – it
> felt totally decadent. I had no clue how to make a sewing machine

work, or even what the hell a bobbin was, but I did it. And shortly after that, with a LOT of very close supervision, I made a skirt! Even more impressive, I made a skirt that I could actually wear, AND that survived the washing machine. I've made very few clothes since, but the skills I've learned have been invaluable – I now happily take up hems, have made the obligatory bunting and cushion covers, and even a pair of curtains. And I learned that maybe, just maybe, I am a little bit creative after all.

So go on, enrol in an evening class, or that spoon carving day you've been eyeing up. Skill swap with a mate, or just get on YouTube and have a go. Step off the treadmill of 'busy' for a minute, slow down and see what you can create. It's the perfect antidote to consumerism, especially at times like Christmas. Check out Chapter 11 for ideas for quick and easy presents – it's surprisingly empowering to break the cycle of buying and to create rather than consume.

Buy

And so we reach the top of the buyerarchy – buying new. Although it's a last resort – kind of the cream cakes and chocolate bars of the food pyramid – we can all still indulge. Just not all the time. In the same way that we shouldn't make fast, highly processed food the mainstay of our diet, we shouldn't make cheap, mass-produced stuff the bulk of the things we buy. I am in no way telling you never to buy new again. I'm simply saying to buy better when you do buy new. So instead of three T-shirts for a tenner from the fast fashion brands of the high street that you'll wear for one summer and then discard, buy one good-quality one that you can mix and match and that will last you for years to come. Instead of buying a cheap toaster that will undoubtedly break within about three months, look for one that is made to last (there are still some out there, and yes, they will probably be more expensive as a result). Sustainable(ish) consumption is essentially all about *thoughtful* consumption.

So what should we all be thinking about when we've exhausted the rest of the buyerarchy and are looking to invest in something new?

A few questions to ponder before you buy

What is it made from?

What are the materials? Where have they come from? How have they been produced? For example, is the cotton Fairtrade? Or organic? Is the wood from sustainable sources? Is the paper recycled?

Who made it?

Is there a chance child labour could have been involved? Are the workers being paid a living wage? In most cases you will probably never be able to find out – supply chains are now so complex and convoluted that even the manufacturers might not know, as so much is outsourced and subcontracted.

Buying local, and buying handmade direct from artisans, is one way to try and ensure that you know exactly who made your stuff. Buying clothes from ethical and sustainable brands is another – these brands have supply chains that are monitored and regulated (*see* Chapter 5 for suggestions and resources). In addition, when you buy from local independent retailers and makers, you're not simply boosting the profit margins of some massive corporation, instead you're helping someone to pay their mortgage and put food on the table.

How long will it last?

If you buy something cheap and mass-produced it is unlikely to last. Often products are built to fail (*see* page 49). It's why you can't update your phone once it gets past a certain age, and it's why you can't get inside your toaster to fix it even if you wanted to. The vast majority of stuff is now made to be used for a short period of time and then discarded and upgraded – certainly not fixed. Which is bonkers.

Buy the best quality you can afford, buy with repairability and longevity in mind. And only buy something if you really love it, need it and know you will get lots of use out of it – we're talking pairing up for life here, rather than a one-night stand.

What will happen to it when I no longer want or need it?

Because we are fortunate enough to have proper waste disposal services in the developed world, we all too often throw stuff 'away' and never give it a second thought. We'll discuss this more in Chapter 2, but there is actually no such place as 'away' – all our rubbish has to go somewhere. So give a thought to the 'afterlife' of the stuff you buy – will it still be in good enough nick when you've finished with it to pass on to someone else? Can it be 'upcycled' into something else? Will it decompose naturally? Or will it sit in landfill for hundreds of years to come slowly leaching toxins into the soil and contributing to methane emissions?

All of our stuff, each of our buying choices, has an impact. We get to choose whether that's a positive or a negative one by making more thoughtful choices. Our money has power.

> 'Every time you spend money, you're casting a vote for the kind of world you want.'
> Anna Lappé, author and sustainable food advocate

So if you buy cheap, poorly made electronics that are designed to break, made using metals mined by schoolchildren, and destined for landfill, that's what you're telling the world you want. And who would ever vote for that?

Vote for better. Buy better.

5 QUICK SUSTAINABLE(ISH) WINS FOR CONSCIOUS CONSUMPTION

1 Think before you buy This takes no time at all, but it does take time to embed it as a habit. It's disturbing to realise quite how automatic and unconscious a lot of our consumption has become.

> *When you see something you like or want, make a note of it, and then review that list in a week. Chances are you will have forgotten about it by the next day. If you still really like it or want it in a week, then you can think about buying it! This is especially good for online shopping, when it can be all too easy to just click 'buy' without even having to get off the sofa to find your purse (thank you PayPal).*

2 Check out your local charity shops Next time you're in town, take a minute to make a note of the charity shops, where they are, and what kind of stuff they have. Maybe even have a browse!

3 Join your local Freecycle or Freegle group Keep your eye out on the daily digests, or post a WANTED if there's something specific you're looking for.

4 Ask friends or family before you buy This doesn't have to involve extensive half-hour phone calls with each of your relatives, especially the ones you've been trying to avoid; it can be as simple as posting on your Facebook profile. I did this once when the kids needed yellow T-shirts for sports day and a friend came up trumps!

5 Do a quick eBay search You can narrow down your search terms to really specific items, sizes, colours etc and you just never know when the eBay elves might be looking out for you. Make sure you check the 'used' box in the search terms though!

MORE SUGGESTIONS:

- ☐ Commit to sourcing a percentage of your purchases secondhand
- ☐ Create a list of the things you need/want and see how many you can find secondhand
- ☐ Borrow at least one item instead of buying it in the next month
- ☐ Find a Fairtrade version of a regular purchase
- ☐ Learn a new skill and make something from scratch
- ☐ Next time you're looking for a new phone, consider a Fairphone (www.fairphone.com) – mobiles made to last and be repaired and made from sustainable materials
- ☐ Visit your local library – they are usually happy to order in books if they don't have what you want
- ☐ Check out your local artisan shops or craft market for gifts and homewares
- ☐ Support local independent businesses – whether that's clothes, food or books
- ☐ Rent an outfit rather than buy next time you have a posh 'do' to go to

Over to you (aka now get up and do!)

List three or four ideas below for changes you could make to consume more consciously, slowly and sustainably.

Action	Timeframe
1.	
2.	
3.	
4.	

Resources

- **CHARITY RETAIL ASSOCIATION (WWW.CHARITYRETAIL.ORG.UK)**
  Find out where your nearest charity shops are.

- **FREECYCLE (WWW.FREECYCLE.ORG) AND FREEGLE (WWW.ILOVE FREEGLE.ORG)**
  Find your local group and give away/find free things within your local community.

- **STREETBANK (WWW.STREETBANK.COM)**
  An online resource that facilitates sharing of things and skills between neighbours.

- **EDINBURGH TOOL LIBRARY (WWW.EDINBURGHTOOLLIBRARY. ORG.UK)**
  The first tool library in the UK and a brilliant example of how projects like these can work and work well.

- **THE LIBRARY OF THINGS (WWW.LIBRARYOFTHINGS.CO.UK)**
  Currently London based, but with plans for more locations.

- **BUY ME ONCE (WWW.BUYMEONCE.COM)**
  Website and online shop selling items that are built to last and made to be repaired.

- **THE GOOD SHOPPING GUIDE (WWW.THEGOODSHOPPINGGUIDE.COM)**
  An ethical brand comparison site for everything from energy to homewares and fashion to food and drink.

- **ETHICAL CONSUMER (WWW.ETHICALCONSUMER.ORG)**
  Website and magazine containing in-depth reviews and comparisons of brands and retailers.

2

Zero waste(ish)

In this chapter we're talking rubbish. And how to reduce it.

DID YOU KNOW?

- There are 20,000 sites across the UK that have been used as landfill at some point. Currently there are around 500 active sites.
- It's predicted that by 2024 we will have run out of landfill space in the UK.
- Each year we bury 18 million tonnes of waste.
- The average person in the UK will throw away their own body weight in rubbish every seven weeks.
- We recycle less than 50 per cent of our waste in the UK and lots of reusable items are discarded every day.
- Landfill sites are a major emitter of methane gas, which is approximately 30 times more potent as a heat-trapping gas than carbon dioxide, and contributes significantly to climate change.

For those who've not come across the term before, the 'zero waste' movement does exactly what it says on the tin – encourages people to produce as little waste as possible, with the ultimate goal being zero waste to landfill, and as little recycling as possible. It's really gained momentum and traction over the last few years, and a little light browsing of the

#zerowaste hashtag on Instagram will produce images of beautiful hip millennials in minimalist homes holding jam jars that contain all their landfill waste for the last three years.

It's potentially a pretty intimidating term – it feels extreme and for many (most?) of us, it can feel unachievable. So as with everything sustainable living, for me it's all about the 'ish'. We can work *towards* zero waste, we can make a start, and make positive changes, even if we realistically know that zero waste perfection may well be out of reach.

Now, if you were paying attention in Chapter 1 you will know that I do love a hierarchy – my favourite being Sarah Lazarovic's buyerarchy of needs (*see* page 19). But a very close runner-up is something called the 'waste hierarchy', which I know sounds like something that middle-aged middle managers at waste conferences might discuss, but actually it's brilliant.

It's basically an expansion of the good old 'reduce, reuse, recycle' mantra that has been doing the rounds for years now and it's a fabulous model to keep in mind when you're buying something or thinking about throwing something away. The idea is that you start at the bottom of the

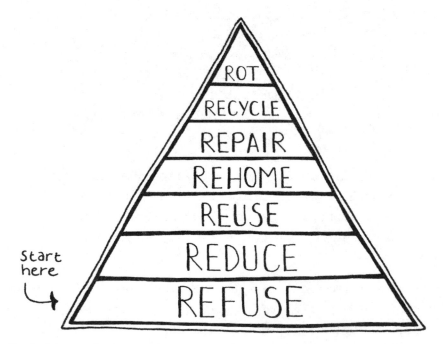

Waste hierarchy

hierarchy with Refuse, and that Recycle and Rot (compost or landfill) are very much the last resorts.

In this chapter we'll look at each section of the waste hierarchy in a bit more detail, and I'll do my best to convert you into a waste hierarchy geek like me.

The mythical land of 'away'

You may have heard the phrase, 'There's no such place as "away".' And it's true. Here in the UK, as much as we might like to moan about the frequency or infrequency of our rubbish collections, we are in the hugely fortunate position of having the infrastructure and facilities in place to collect our rubbish and dispose of it for us. So when we put things in the bin, the story for us ends there. We've thrown it 'away' and very few of us give any thought to what happens to it after the magical rubbish-chomping bin lorry comes and collects it.

But for over 50 per cent of the world's population who don't have access to a regular rubbish collection, it's a different story. They are very much more aware of the fact that there is no 'away' as the rubbish mounts up in their streets, their rivers and in ad-hoc unmanaged landfill sites that often double up as people's homes.

It all has to go somewhere. For us, it's collected and it's taken to properly managed, lined landfill sites. But it's predicted that by the year 2024 we will have run out of landfill space. Meaning that the vast majority of our unrecyclable waste will be incinerated. And while incineration is dressed up as a good option by being called 'energy from waste', it's a controversial matter.

> There is no 'away'. And I think of that phrase every time I toss something into our bin in the kitchen. I picture it sitting in landfill and I feel bloody guilty. It's a great motivator to find alternatives!

Energy from waste

Energy from waste means exactly that – creating energy that can be used to fuel and light homes and businesses, from waste. Sounds pretty awesome, right?

Well... yes and no.

There are two main types of energy from waste – incinerating plastics and 'residual waste' (what's left after it's been sorted for recycling); and anaerobic digestion, where food and agricultural waste are broken down by microbes to create gas. And it's the former that proves most controversial.

Years ago, burning rubbish was plain old incineration and quite rightly had a pretty bad reputation, belching fumes into the atmosphere and contributing to air pollution. In the 1990s, when we started to realise that simply burying our waste in landfill might not be the best idea, landfill diversion targets were introduced and a new generation of incinerators started to spring up that also have the capacity to harvest the heat and energy produced burning the waste rather than simply releasing it into the environment. And here the debate begins.

Supporters claim that these new waste plants are better for the environment than landfill as they create energy, whereas landfill doesn't (although some landfill sites are now starting to 'mine' the methane produced and harvest it to create energy). And there is the added argument that we are rapidly running out of landfill space. Opponents are concerned about air pollution, the safe disposal of the residual ash, and the fact that once these plants are built they need a constant supply of rubbish to burn, potentially disincentivising councils from recycling.

It's a complex debate. The only thing for sure is that both landfill and incineration should be last resorts and that we should be working hard to REFUSE, REDUCE, REUSE first.

Refuse

Refuse the things you don't need – think the free pens, the balloons and goody bags given out at events, the junk mail, the teeny little bottles of shampoo in hotels. These are all things that we take, or have thrust upon us, which we just kind of accept because 'it's free' or because we don't want to seem rude.

> *Confession: I am not immune. A few years ago I was invited to the Observer's Ethical Awards and simply couldn't resist the lure of the goody bag. Yes, it was all ethically produced and there were some temporarily exciting things in there, but I didn't need any of it. In fact, it just gave me extra stuff to carry on my way home and yet another reusable shopping bag to lose in the cupboard under the stairs.*

When we take or accept these things, what we're doing is reinforcing the message that people want them. If no one took the goody bags, or the balloons, or used the 'free' (obviously they aren't actually free – their cost is factored into the cost of your room) toiletries in the hotel bathrooms, then they would cease to be a thing. And I know it's easy to think that as one person we can't impact on these kinds of things, and that our actions are futile, but all any of us can do is take responsibility for our own actions. If I decide to just say no, and you do too, and then your work colleague sees what you're doing and decides to join in, the message spreads, and change will come about.

How to opt out of junk mail

Unfortunately, there's not one simple email you can send that will opt you out of all junk mail, which shows quite how insidious the whole thing has become. Doing one or all of these things should help to stem the flow.

1 Put a 'No Junk Mail' sign on your letter box You can make one yourself or order one from the Stop Junk Mail website (www.stopjunkmail.org).

2 Stop leaflets via Royal Mail Royal Mail get paid to deliver all those leaflets that the postie drops off with your bills, bank statements and occasional bit of more exciting mail. Which might explain why they appear to have made it so difficult and onerous to opt out of receiving unaddressed mail. You have to download, print out and fill out a form that contains all kinds of dire warnings about the fact that you might miss out on important information from local or central government (if it's that important, I'm assuming they will make the effort to address the letter). And once you've done all of that you have to remember to update it after two years, otherwise it will all start again.

3 Register for the Mail Preference Service (MPS)

Register at www.mpsonline.org.uk and it will remove your name and details from the various lists that get sold among list brokers (hurray!). What it means is that you should see a slow reduction in the amount of unsolicited addressed mail you get. However, you will still receive mail from companies you've bought from or charities you have donated to.

4 Contact the sender direct via snail mail or email

This might seem like hard work, but might be the most effective way to tackle any that slip through the net after doing all the things above.

Reduce

There are two parts to reduce: one is reducing what we're buying and bringing into our homes; and the other is reducing what's already there, aka decluttering. Doing the decluttering bit is really helpful when it comes to the buying less bit, because once you've gone to the hassle of decluttering responsibly (*see* below), you become far more selective about what you're bringing into the house that might end up needing decluttering again down the line.

> *Confession: I hate decluttering. And I am very much not a minimalist. Sometimes I wish I were, but I am way too untidy for it to ever work. And I have kids. With lots of toys (see Chapter 6 for my trials and tribulations with toys).*

There are whole books and websites dedicated to the subject of decluttering but here are a few different methods to try:

The Mins Game

This is a technique recommended by the minimalist gurus, the Minimalists. You pick a month and on day 1 you get rid of one thing, and on day 2, two things and so on, until you're getting rid of 30 things on day 30. Meaning that by the end of a 30-day month you will have cleared your home of 465 items. One suggestion is to reverse this and do 30 items on day 1 when you're feeling all motivated and excited and have more stuff to clear out, working down to just one item on day 30, when you may well be regretting your decision to start the whole thing and starting to struggle to find things (depending on how rammed your house is).

Room by room

Don't try to do it all at once. Your head will explode and you will probably give up before you've got more than halfway. Also, you'll have a huge amount of stuff to rehome, which may well sit there for weeks before you can garner the energy to go about redistributing it, and it will sit there making you feel rubbish. Go room by room. Or even cupboard by cupboard, if it's all feeling really overwhelming. Go for the low-hanging fruit first, by which I mean the easiest room to tackle – the bathroom is usually a good one to start with.

Packing party

This is another technique showcased by the Minimalists and is not for the faint-hearted. The idea is that you pretend you're moving and pack up all of your stuff into cardboard boxes, label them so you know what's in each one and then store them in a room in your house. When you need something over the next month, go and get it out, and find a home for it. The theory is that anything left at the end of the month isn't something you use much, and can be eradicated from your home. There are some holes in this theory but I reckon it would be a real eye-opener to see just how much of our stuff is surplus to requirements!

After decluttering comes the hardest part – rehoming all of that stuff (*see* rehoming on page 42). But once you've decluttered you should find that your motivation for not 're-cluttering' and buying loads of new stuff is pretty high, and you can invoke the 'Buy Less, Buy Better' mantra and lots of the other alternatives to buying new stuff detailed in Chapter 1.

Reuse

'Refuse single use' is another great mantra and especially pertinent when it comes to plastic, as discussed in Chapter 3. But reuse has also been given a makeover with the advent of 'upcycling'.

The Oxford English Dictionary definition of upcycling is: *'reuse (discarded objects or material) in such a way as to create a product of higher quality or value than the original.'* With a little bit of thought/creativity and

Top five items for easy upcycling

1 Old furniture Old furniture can be given a new lease of life with a simple lick of paint. And thanks to the wonders of chalk paint you don't even need to go to the effort of sanding it down first! There's a wide range of different brands available. Alternatively, you can buy chalk paint powder to add to regular paint to magically transform it, or even make your own (there are a ton of recipes online). Having said that, please do resist the urge to paint things just because you can. Some old traditional furniture is made of beautiful solid wood and would be much happier sanded down and lovingly rewaxed.

2 Old duvets and sheets If you simply see them as 'fabric' there is a multitude of ways that old clothes can be reused or upcycled. Old duvets and sheets are a great way to get a LOT of fabric for not very much money, and if you're lucky and it's your kind of thing, you might pick up some fab retro prints.

3 Tin cans The simplest upcycle is to cover an old tin can in wrapping paper and use it as a pen holder, or as a plant

Rehome

The easiest thing to do with stuff we no longer want or need would be to chuck it away into landfill. Out of sight, out of your house, and out of some lost hours down the rabbit hole of Pinterest, pretty much anything can be upcycled now. We've upcycled all kinds of things:

- Egg boxes into a Christmas tree (yes, it was as crap as it sounds!)
- A sideboard into a guinea pig cage
- An old dog kennel into a fully insulated tortoise house with heat lamp
- A drawer left over from the sideboard into a bookshelf
- Old maps to cover filing cabinets and give them a funky new look

pot. The mini ones work well for little succulents. If you have any bigger ones, for example tins of formula milk or giant coffee tins, these can be covered and used as storage as they are, or if you collect together a few they can be fixed to the wall and used for alternative shelving.

4 **Wooden pallets** Lots of businesses end up with leftover wooden pallets from deliveries that they have no use for, so you should be able to get your hands on them for free. It can take a bit of elbow grease/brute force to get them apart (there are proper pallet splitters you can get that might be worth investing in if you're going to be using lots) but once you have, the planks can be used to make furniture, or I've even seen them used as a kind of cladding on walls. Hubby and the kids made a Christmas tree out of one last year that looks great!

5 **Old books/maps/sheet music/comics** If you see any of these in charity shops, snap them up and start 'decoupaging'. This is basically a fancy name for covering things in paper. We've done it with old filing cabinets and the sides of a lovely set of drawers we had that looked a bit tired. And they can also be used to make easy-peasy homemade cards with the aid of some cookie cutters to give you some shape guides to cut round.

mind. But we're obviously not going to do that, having established that there's really no such place as 'away'. The next easiest option is to simply dump all the heaving sacks outside your local charity shop for them to sort out – after all, they need stuff to sell, don't they? Well, yes and no.

Charity shops need good quality stuff to sell. Stuff that other people are likely to want to buy. They are very unlikely to be able to sell your old video tapes, or probably even your CD collection. And as for that half-used packet of dividers or the out-of-date bottles of shampoo you unearthed in your rummage through the bathroom cupboard, again, it's going to be a 'no'. All we're doing is assuaging our own consciences, and passing the work of sorting it all out, and the guilt of sending some of it to landfill, on to the good people who work in the charity shop. Our consumer culture has, I guess, been something of a double-edged sword for charity shops; as things have become cheaper and as we have bought and discarded things at an ever increasing pace, they are often the ones left dealing with the stuff we no longer want or need. And while this can be great for them in terms of revenue generation, I can't help but think that many of them may well be drowning under the sheer volume of stuff they receive.

I asked in my Sustainable(ish) Facebook community for volunteers who worked in charity shops to answer a few questions – here are some of the answers:

Q Do you find that some people use charity shops as a dumping ground to make them feel better about not sending stuff to landfill and donate stuff that can't be sold on?
A – Yes, it's a dumping ground. (Caro)
   – Yes, we get all sorts of stuff, much of it unsalvageable. (Caroline)
   – Yes, definitely, our rubbish bin is permanently full. (Claire)

Q Do some donations end up in landfill?
A – We receive more rubbish than donations sadly. (Kama)
   – Yes, there's simply too much rubbish to deal with. (Caroline)

Q What things do people commonly donate that can't be sold on?
A – It's a big range – mainly broken toys, broken furniture, things with bits missing, incomplete sets that can't be sold as individuals, out of date things. (Caroline)
   – A lot of baby items can't be sold. Some places have a special safety checklist for prams and highchairs etc. No car seats or bike helmets

allowed. Lots of secondhand pants that people donate can't be sold on! Any work uniforms with logos can't be sold either. Homemade toys can't be sold – they need a CE mark. (Eleanor)

– We've had soiled bedding, cracked and broken china and glass etc, ripped and dirty clothing, books with no covers or pages torn out, broken toys, puzzles with pieces missing... (Caro)

Q What's the weirdest thing you've ever seen donated?
A – Someone donated a wax jacket and left shotgun cartridges in the pocket. (Eleanor)

– A vibrator (ewwwww!) (Claire)

Golden rules for donating to charity shops

- Only donate items that are clean, undamaged and in good condition – if you wouldn't buy them, the chances are no one else will.
- Not all charity shops will take electrical items as they need PAT testing (portable appliance testing is the term used to describe the examination of electrical appliances and equipment to ensure they are safe to use) before resale. Check with your local shop if you're unsure.
- Most charities will have a list of things they won't accept for selling on, including car seats, bike helmets, medical appliances and safety devices. Again, if in doubt, check.
- For clothing – check if it fastens, if it's stain- and rip-free, if it smells OK. Basically, would you let your family members wear it?
- Never leave donations outside a charity shop if it's closed – donations left overnight are often tampered with and can be stolen.

SPECIALIST CHARITIES

There are some items that general charity shops don't accept, but that specialist charities will:

Bikes

Re-cycle (www.recycle.org) are a charity who refurbish bikes in the UK and then send them to Africa where many children have over a two-hour walk to school, meaning that some children miss out on their education entirely. Having a bike makes it much easier for them to make the commute.

Mobile phones

Many of the major phone manufacturers have their own refurbishment schemes, meaning that phones are kept in use for longer. Have a look online to see if you can send yours off, or alternatively lots of charities have recycling schemes for old mobiles.

Computers

There are several charities that will take computers and laptops, recondition them and then sell them on to raise funds. Edinburgh Remakery (www.edinburghremakery.org.uk) has schemes to resell items, and also works with the council to provide laptops for local refugee families. Also check out Donate a PC (www.donateapc.org.uk), which provides a platform to connect individuals with computer equipment to pass on to good causes who can make use of them. It also provides some useful info on how to wipe your data from your computer.

Glasses

Many opticians will have collection banks for secondhand specs, which are then donated to charity.

OTHER OPTIONS FOR REHOMING

Pass on to friends/family

Possibly the easiest option ever. Especially if they've got younger kids than yours, or are just moving out of home etc. Just make sure you ask before assuming they want ALL your old baby clothes, or the duplicate contents of your kitchen drawers.

Freecycle or Freegle

Visit www.freecycle.org or www.ilovefreegle.org to join your local group and then post OFFERS of your items. This is a great option for passing on things that charity shops won't take, like half-used files of paper, or craft bits the kids have grown bored of.

On your pavement/lawn or drive with a FREE sign

If you live on a road that gets a decent amount of footfall/traffic, you may well be pleasantly surprised how quickly things get snapped up when offered in this way!

Car boot/garage/lawn sale

A great chance to get rid of your stuff and generate a bit of cash at the same time. Just make sure you have a plan in place for the stuff you don't sell.

eBay

Maybe an obvious one but still worth mentioning. If you've got well-known brands of things, these tend to do well. Otherwise, consider bundling things up into job lots – this can work well with things like arts and crafts supplies and saves you having to photograph and list everything separately.

Repair

Up until a few years ago, repair and mending seemed to be a dying art, but in the last couple of years it seems that people are waking up again to the magic and joy of the fix.

Confession: Until we spent our year buying nothing new, I had never even sewn a button back on to a shirt. I was weirdly afraid that I wouldn't be able to do it and that it would just fall off again, and consequently used to have a little mending pile that would get handed over periodically to my mother-in-law. When I started the blog that documented our year buying nothing new, I decided enough was enough and I really should have a try. Imagine my surprise when it wasn't really that hard after all. And even if the button did fall off again, it really wasn't all that much of a big deal, and I simply had another go. I quickly graduated on to patching the many, many pairs of jeans that both we and the kids seemed to go through the knees of, and have even been known to darn the odd sock or two.

The common (mis)conception is that much of our stuff can no longer be repaired. And while planned obsolescence is very definitely a thing (*see the box on planned obsolescence opposite*), it doesn't mean that a fix is out of the question. We have managed to fix our toaster, dishwasher (yes we have one, no it might not be the greenest option depending on which article you read, don't judge me), washing machine and microwave (this one quite frankly terrified me), all with a little light googling and the help of YouTube. And it's not just us; repair is making a comeback. Darning is bang on trend, and there's a whole movement of 'visible menders' who wear their mend with pride as a badge of honour, a thing of beauty and a brilliant conversation starter – take a look at the #visiblemending hashtag on Instagram if you don't believe me!

Just in case you aren't convinced yet, here are some reasons why mending is such a powerful tool in our sustainable(ish) toolkit:

1 It keeps stuff out of landfill, which is one of the main aims of our lovely waste hierarchy.
2 It saves the resources and carbon footprint that would be needed to replace it and make a new one.
3 It values the resources already in that item, and in doing so, values the people who have made the item, and produced the raw goods.
4 It's hugely satisfying, and I think really empowering, to take something that you think is beyond repair, and to have a go. I'm often surprised at the things we manage to fix, and I'm not going to lie, it does generate a feeling inside that could be said to be verging on smug…
5 You get to save your favourite things, or the things that really mean something to you. Whether that's your favourite pair of jeans that fit just right or a family keepsake, when these things rip or break, mending them gives them a second chance, and allows you to hold on to them for longer.
6 You get to learn new skills. As I said earlier, I had never even sewed on a button until we spent our year buying nothing new, but now I'll have a go at most things.
7 Mending can be a form of therapy. Katrina Rodabaugh is an American visible mender who talks about the concept of 'mendfulness', and it's true that the act of mending can allow us to

become engrossed in a very analogue task and to switch off from our worries and be in the moment.

8   It's a form of quiet disruption and protest. A way of saying 'No' to the status quo of cheap, disposable goods and taking a stand.

9   It saves you money. We've saved ourselves a small fortune, both from smaller mends of things like jeans, but also things like the washing machine and dishwasher. Neither needed anything massively complicated, but in times gone by, I think we would have just assumed they couldn't be repaired, and bought a new one.

10 It starts conversations. All of my jeans are patched to a greater or lesser extent, and if anyone comments on them, it's a great way to start a simple conversation about mending, fast fashion, why we do it, and why it matters.

Planned obsolescence

'A policy of producing consumer goods that rapidly become obsolete and so require replacing, achieved by frequent changes in design, termination of the supply of spare parts, and the use of non-durable materials.'

I always used to think this was an urban myth, but sadly it's not. It's a concept that was actively designed into products and came about in the post-war years as a way to boost economies through increased consumer spending. And it's now something that seems to have become very much the norm for the vast majority of manufacturers, whether they're making phones that are constantly upgraded, toasters that can't even be opened up, or clothes that just aren't up to being worn and washed.

COMMUNITY REPAIR EVENTS

If you're not feeling all that confident getting started mending, or you've got a tricky mend that you'd rather not tackle yourself, have a look and see if you have Repair Events local to you. I first stumbled across Repair Cafés (www.repaircafe.org) during our year buying nothing new and was instantly fascinated and enthused by the idea. At that time, about seven years ago, there were just three Repair Cafés listed in the UK. Now, at the time of writing, there are over 1600 worldwide, including nearly 100 in the UK. And that's just the ones officially registered on the Repair Café website – there are other independently run events happening too.

This is the official Repair Café definition of what a Repair Café is: 'Repair Cafés are free meeting places and they're all about repairing things (together). In the place where a Repair Café is located, you'll find tools and materials to help you make any repairs you need. On clothes, furniture, electrical appliances, bicycles, crockery, appliances, toys, etc. You'll also find expert volunteers, with repair skills in all kinds of fields.'

Useful things to have in your mending toolkit

- Needle and thread – useful for all manner of textile repairs. A spot of hand sewing can darn a hole, patch a pair of trousers, and adjust a hem.
- Sewing machine – although this is optional, I usually do most of my repairs on the sewing machine. Partly because I don't trust my hand sewing skills, and partly because I am impatient! You can usually pick one up pretty easily secondhand and I quite often see them on Freegle.
- A variety of basic tools – things like hammers, screwdrivers and pliers – are always handy to have around! You might find that you hit lucky and find some on sites like Freecycle and Freegle, or they are also the sort of thing you often find at car boot sales and can pick up secondhand pretty cheaply.
- A variety of glues and adhesives – sometimes, you can't beat a bit of good old-fashioned glue! We tend to keep some superglue in

Recycle

'Recycling is a great place to start, but a bad place to stop.'

Lindsay Miles,
www.treadingmyownpath.com

There is a very real impact of these events in terms of items saved from landfill. In 2017, the Repair Café estimated that over 300,000 items were repaired worldwide, saving over 300,000kg of CO_2 emissions. That all sounds very impressive, but I have to confess that kgs of CO_2 means nothing to me, so I did a quick google to see if I could find out what this is equivalent to. A saving of 300,000kg of CO_2 is equivalent to driving over 735,000 miles in an average car. If you love the sound of Repair Cafés, take a look on the website to see if there is one near you (or start one up yourself)!

stock, and also something called Q-bond, which is a two-part glue that hubby swears by. Fabric glue is also useful to have on stand-by, and I always forget that Copydex (you know, that glue that smells of fish that you probably used at primary school) actually works well on a variety of substrates. I don't think any of these options are especially eco-friendly, but I weigh up the impact of needing to replace an item versus the impact of a spot of glue, and the glue usually wins.

- Sugru – I discovered sugru (www.sugru.com) right at the start of our year of buying nothing new and we've been big fans ever since. We've used it to mend everything from butter dishes to a wooden railway, and always keep a stash in the fridge. It's a bit like plasticine, in that you can mould it around whatever you are fixing, but then it self-cures and hardens in 24 hours to effect a permanent repair. It's the invention of a British woman, which for me is another great reason to use it, as well as the whole ethos of hacking and fixing, and the community that has been built up around the product. You can buy it online from their website, or in some B&Q stores.

This is a quote from my friend and fellow blogger Lindsay at Treading My Own Path. For a long time (I'm looking at you, 1990s), sustainability was pretty much just about recycling. If you were doing your recycling, you were a bona fide eco-hero. But now the message is slowly filtering down that maybe there is more to living lightly than sorting our rubbish into different bins. As we can see from looking at our wonderful waste hierarchy, recycling is not a cure-all for the sheer excesses of our consumption and is actually almost the last resort after we've worked our way through the other options.

It takes energy (i.e. fossil fuels) to transport, sort and clean our items for recycling. And not wanting to seem like some kind of English language pedant, more often than not items are 'downcycled' rather than 'recycled'. Probably most of us think that recycling a plastic water bottle means that more plastic water bottles can be made from that same plastic. They can't. I'll be totally honest and say that the details of the chemistry lose me a little but basically food grade plastic cannot be easily melted down and used again to make food grade plastic. It is usually shredded up and used in things like park benches, or even fleeces. Which sounds great, and has to be better than using 'virgin plastic' to

How to be a good recycler

- Get super clear on what your local authority will and won't collect. Yes, I know it's a total pain that there is so much discrepancy from one county to the next, and it's a complicated old system that's evolved over time, ripe for restructuring. For now, we have to put up with it and make sure we're utilising it to the best of its abilities. The Recycle Now website (www.recyclenow.com) is a great resource that allows you to type in your postcode and then gives you the lowdown on what can and can't be recycled locally.
- Rinse out plastic bottles, squash them and put the lids back on – this means they take up less space in the bins in the lorry and at the recycling centre.
- Similarly, flatten your cardboard boxes.

Rot

At the very tip of our waste hierarchy, the very last resort is 'Rot'. This is the stuff we put in our black bins that is destined for either landfill or incineration. And ideally if you've been able to implement some of the ideas from this chapter and also Chapter 3 on all things plastic-free(ish), it should be an ever-decreasing amount.

make these things. But then we discovered the whole microfibres issues (*see* page 127).

I'm not saying don't recycle. Please please recycle the things you can recycle. Sort out your rubbish and put your kerbside recycling out. You can even go one step further and save up the recyclables that your local council don't collect at the kerbside and take them down to your local recycling centre next time you visit. And always have recycling at the back of your mind when you're out shopping – pasta in a recyclable cardboard packet is a far better choice than pasta in a non-recyclable plastic bag. BUT instead of seeing recycling as 'job done' and a way of salving our consciences and feeling like we've done our bit to save the planet, I think we should all be looking a little bit deeper than that.

- Envelopes with plastic windows can be added to your recycling – the windows themselves aren't recyclable but the sorting system at the recycling centre can cleverly extract them (don't ask me how).
- Rinse out tins to get rid of any food residues (use your washing-up water). **Food contamination can lead to whole batches of recycling being rejected and ending up in landfill.**
- Even if you really really **want** an item to be recyclable, don't put it in your recycling bin if it's not on the list of things your local council will collect (there's even a term for this – 'wishcycling'). For years my husband kept putting the big yoghurt pots in our recycling bin, even though it clearly said 'plastic bottles only'. I could see his point that they really do look like they **should** be able to be recycled, but by trying to recycle more, you run the risk of less being actually recycled. The wrong types of plastic can contaminate the waste stream, and again can lead to whole massive batches being rejected and ending up in landfill.

There are lots of ideas and suggestions for reducing food waste in Chapter 4 but even the most hardened zero waster will generate some 'unavoidable' food waste – things like eggshells, pineapple skin, tea leaves/bags etc. But the good news is that there are lots of options for this to ensure it doesn't end up in landfill.

Local kerbside collection

Many local authorities now have a kerbside food waste collection, which is totally the easiest option. If you have one, use it!

Regular compost bins

If you have a reasonably sized garden then you may well already have a compost bin for your garden waste. You can add to this your uncooked kitchen waste – things like fruit and veg peelings, apple cores, eggshells etc. But you mustn't add cooked food or meat.

Hot composter

We have a hot composter and I love it! I confess to not really understanding how it works, but we can add garden waste and all of our kitchen waste, including cooked food and meat scraps. Some local councils subsidise them, especially if they don't provide a food waste kerbside service. Ours is called a Green Johanna and we got it from Great Green Systems (www. greatgreensystems.com).

Bokashi bins

Bokashi bins ferment waste rather than break it down in the traditional manner, and you can add all kinds of food waste, including cooked food and meat. The drawback is that you have to have a compost heap or some garden space to dig the fermented waste into.

Wormeries

These are potentially a good option if you live somewhere without the space for a conventional compost heap. You can make your own, or buy a ready to go set-up from somewhere like Wiggly Wigglers (www. wigglywigglers.co.uk). The worms eat your food waste and then poo out nutrient-rich 'castings' that make a great soil additive for houseplants. Apparently, if looked after correctly they shouldn't smell and can be kept indoors, making it the ideal solution for those without access to a garden.

> *Confession: we experimented with a wormery several years ago but managed to kill all the worms – I'm still not sure what we did wrong and feel very guilty for all the needless worm deaths caused...*

THINGS YOU SHOULD NEVER THROW AWAY

- Textiles – synthetic clothing in landfill conditions could potentially take hundreds of years to decompose. Clothes that you no longer want or need can be passed on to friends, 'swished' (*see* page 118) or donated to charity shops. Anything that is beyond wear can be put into textile recycling bins, from where it is shredded and recycled.
- Electronics – there are e-waste bins at most recycling centres for all kinds of electronics, where many of the precious metals and other materials can be rescued for reuse.
- Batteries – they rust and start to leach heavy metals like magnesium and lead, and can also cause landfill fires.
- Plastic bags – these should be reused and then recycled in the collection points at your recycling centre or supermarket. In landfill they degrade and break up into microplastics rather than break down.
- Plastic bottles – these are widely and fairly easily recycled. In landfill they take hundreds of years to start to break down.
- Aluminium cans – again, these are widely recycled and it's a huge waste of valuable resources to simply throw them 'away'.
- Glass – this can be recycled almost infinitely, so keep it out of landfill!
- Smartphones – these are rich in valuable metals, the mining of which is fraught with human rights abuses and conflict and is a very destructive process. It takes a tonne of gold ore to produce a gram of gold. That same gram of gold could be harvested from just 40 iPhones (*see* page 57 for what to do with them).

I often get asked what I do about bin liners, and the answer is that we've stopped using them. Because we're composting all of our food waste, it's only dry stuff that goes in the bin, so once it's full we simply tip it out into our black bin, and give it a wipe around.

These top tips come from zero waster extraordinaire Rachelle Strauss, founder of Zero Waste Week (www.zerowasteweek. co.uk) – an annual online grassroots campaign raising awareness of the environmental impact of waste and empowering participants to reduce waste. Rachelle started the campaign in 2008 and in 2018 the #zerowasteweek hashtag reached 42 million accounts.

Don't be put off by the term zero waste

Zero waste is just a goal; a lofty idea, but taking small steps to put new habits in place can add up to significant impact and I promise it isn't as daunting as it sounds.

Get clear on your big WHY

Why do you want to reduce waste? Is it to save money (I save around £1500 per year by not wasting things!), preserve resources, to be part of the solution for your children and grandchildren, to protect wildlife or for moral reasons? Getting clear on this will help you retain focus when the lure of that shiny plastic object calls you!

Once you know your motivation, it's time to do an audit

Yep, that means putting on a pair of rubber gloves and delving into your bin! Write down everything you are throwing away. After all, if you can't see and measure it, you can't track your progress. Grab the list of everything you are throwing 'away' then choose ONE item you could either swap for a more sustainable option, are prepared to go without or can divert into a compost bin or recycling container.

Here's how the start of our zero waste journey looked for us:

The first thing we did was to swap disposable carrier bags for reusable ones. The next month we made full use of our kerbside collections. The third month we looked at what we could take to a local recycling centre when on errands. In month four we swapped out plastic bottles for reusable ones and in month five we started taking our own reusable containers to the butcher, deli and bakery. Rinse. Repeat.

When you break it down like that and take small, incremental steps, you'll achieve your zero waste goal easily and effortlessly.

5 QUICK SUSTAINABLE(ISH) WINS FOR WASTE

1 **Do a waste audit** How much rubbish are you currently sending to landfill? One wheelie bin a fortnight? More? Less? What makes up most of your bin? Plastic waste? Food waste? Recyclables? Set yourself a challenge to reduce your landfill waste – do you want to cut it by a quarter? Or halve it? When by? What's the easiest thing you could change first?

2 **Check the Recycle Now website** Visit www.recyclenow. com to make sure you're recycling everything you can.

3 **Dig out your old mobiles and send them off for recycling** You can put them in the 'small electricals' bin at your local recycling centre, or alternatively lots of charities have recycling schemes.

4 **Join your local Freecycle or Freegle group** See what you can pass on and save from landfill.

5 **Learn to sew on a button** Visit www.loveyourclothes.org. uk/videos/fast-fix-how-sew-button

MORE SUGGESTIONS:

- ☐ Allocate some space for recycling bins
- ☐ Put a 'no junk mail' sign on your letter box
- ☐ Swap one disposable item for a reusable one
- ☐ Refuse freebies like balloons and pens – just say no!
- ☐ Find your local Repair Café and take along the next item that breaks
- ☐ Get a compost bin/bokashi bin or hot composter for your food waste (*see* page 54)
- ☐ Before you replace something, stop and think – could you repair it or reuse something you already have?
- ☐ Swap your rubbish bin for your recycling bin in the kitchen – make it easier to recycle than it is to simply chuck everything into the landfill bin
- ☐ Next time you have a clear-out, challenge yourself to send nothing to landfill
- ☐ Mend your broken mobile and laptop chargers with sugru (www.sugru.com/tech-gadget/how-to-repair-a-usb-charger-cable)

Over to you (aka now get up and do!)

List three or four ideas below for changes you could make to reduce the amount of rubbish you send to landfill.

Action	Timeframe
1.	
2.	
3.	
4.	

Resources

- LOVE YOUR CLOTHES (WWW.LOVEYOURCLOTHES.ORG)
  Lots of great tutorials for mending clothes.

- IFIXIT (WWW.IFIXIT.COM)
  This site is fabulous for all kinds of repairs. There are repair guides, as well as videos of 'teardowns' (where someone strips a product down and puts it back together again), and toolkits for all kinds of fixes.

- YOUTUBE (WWW.YOUTUBE.COM)
  We've had some success with searching YouTube for help with various fixes. Hubby found the information he needed to take my phone apart, and also to fix the washing machine, so it's definitely worth having a search.

- THE RESTART WIKI PAGE (WWW.THERESTARTPROJECT.ORG/WIKI/MAIN_PAGE)
  Lots of information from the fabulous team at the Restart Project, including a great page 'Scared to Repair', as well as a useful list of tools.

- SUGRU (WWW.SUGRU.COM)
  Sugru is one of the products I recommended to include in a mending toolkit, and the sugru site has lots of step-by-step guides to show you how. Check out how to fix broken headphones, and how to fix a phone charger cable.

- REPAIR CAFÉ (WWW.REPAIRCAFE.ORG)
  See if you have a local Repair Café near you.

- RECYCLE NOW (WWW.RECYCLENOW.COM)
  Pop in your postcode and find what can and can't be recycled near you.

- **THE URBAN WORM (WWW.THEURBANWORM.CO.UK)**
  A gold mine of information on easy worm farming for householders, along with worm farm kits, and tutorials for making your own.

- **ZERO WASTE WEEK (WWW.ZEROWASTEWEEK.CO.UK)**
  The first week in September each year sees an annual focus on 'zero waste' aimed at getting individuals, families and businesses taking action to reduce their waste.

CHAPTER

3

Plastic free(ish)

Just a couple of generations ago, plastic wasn't even really a 'thing'. It's only in the last 70 years or so that plastic has entered our everyday lives, and due to its cheapness and versatility it's now hard to imagine a life without it.

DID YOU KNOW?

- Over the last 10 years we have produced more plastic than during the whole of the 20th century.
- Almost half of all the plastic produced is used just once and then thrown away.
- Unless it's been incinerated, every piece of plastic ever made is still in existence.
- Around 300 million tons of plastic is produced each year, and of that only about 10 per cent is recycled.
- Seven million tons of plastic ends up in the oceans each year.
- One in three fish caught contain plastic.
- Research by the Ellen MacArthur Foundation has estimated that by 2050 there could be more plastic in the ocean than fish.
- Plastic microfibres have been found in human poo – which means most of us have unwittingly eaten plastic at some point (excluding that piece of Lego you inadvertently swallowed when you were three).

One of the reasons that plastic has seen such a stratospheric rise in use is that it is strong, flexible and durable. Which means it is really useful stuff. But because it's strong, flexible and durable, it never ever really breaks down. Yes, it will slowly degrade, but all that happens is that it breaks 'up' into smaller and smaller pieces, eventually ending up in the oceans as a kind of microplastic 'soup', which is how it then enters the food chain. We casually toss our plastic bags, our coffee cups and our water bottles 'away' when we are done with them, but as we now know from Chapter 2, there is no 'away' – it all has to go somewhere.

SO IS ALL PLASTIC BAD PLASTIC?

No. Plastic is actually a brilliant material. In the right place. We couldn't now run our hospitals without it, it's a big component of computers and phones and TVs, and it can help to keep our food fresh to reduce food waste. It's also lightweight, reducing the emissions needed to transport plastic bottles, for example, compared with glass bottles.

When we start to talk about 'plastic-free' living, we might imagine that we need to eradicate all plastic from our lives, which some diehard plastic-free gurus might advocate. But to me it seems crazy to ditch all our perfectly usable existing plastic Tupperware, for example, to replace it with aesthetically pleasing hipster-style glass jars. That's why this chapter is referred to as 'plastic-free(ish)'. The real problem comes from *single-use* plastic, and how we dispose of it.

IS RECYCLING IT THE ANSWER?

Recycling your single-use plastic – things like milk bottles, water bottles and plastic bags – is infinitely better than sending it to landfill. But sadly, recycling isn't a silver bullet solution. Recycling plastic uses roughly double the energy, labour and machinery necessary to put it into landfill. We generate over 2 million tons of plastic packaging waste in the UK every year. Nearly 65 per cent of that goes to landfill, and of the remainder, until recently around 23 per cent was exported for recycling to China. In 2018 China placed a ban on plastic recycling imports, forcing the UK to find other avenues for our plastic – in the first six months following China's ban, imports of plastic waste increased by 56 per cent in Indonesia and by 1370 per cent in Thailand – poorer countries than ours, with arguably far less infrastructure in place to deal with this plastic. Why we imagine that these countries have the technology, resources or capacity to deal with our rubbish when we don't is beyond me. And indeed we are now seeing that coming back to bite us, with Malaysia returning thousands of tonnes of imported plastic waste back to the countries it came from in 2019.

Globally, only about 14 per cent of the plastic waste we produce each year is recycled. And plastic is often 'downcycled' – so plastic water bottles tend to be made into things like fleece jackets, rather than turned back into more plastic bottles. Which in turn creates issues with microfibres (*see* page 127).

WHAT ABOUT BIODEGRADABLE PLASTICS?

These sound great, don't they? And I know lots of people and brands have excitedly jumped on the bandwagon of biodegradable plastics. It holds the promise of a magic solution – all the convenience of plastic, with none of the pollution, right? Wrong.

'Biodegradable' or 'compostable' plastic is a great example of greenwashing (*see* page 13). Take 'compostable' plastic cups, for example – these are marketed as the environmentally friendly option for everything from the Pimms tent at the village fair through to large scale festivals. No washing-up, no broken glasses, no guilt. So what's the problem? When we hear the word 'compostable', our assumption is that they will break down in our home compost heap. Or at the very least break down into nice natural substances if they end up in landfill. And sadly they don't. The vast majority of compostable plastics are only compostable under a very specific set of industrial composting conditions. In landfill they will act in exactly the same way as regular plastics, and if they enter the plastic recycling stream they cock it up (technical term) as they tend to be made of lower quality plastics and this can lead to whole batches of plastic recycling needing to be jettisoned.

The same applies to 'biodegradable nappies' and things like 'biodegradable dog poo bags' – in landfill they will behave in the same way as ordinary plastic, so although they might salve our consciences, they do very little else of benefit.

Ultimately, as George Monbiot pointed out in one of his *Guardian* pieces, a different kind of disposable coffee cup won't save the world.

What we need is to rethink our attitudes to all things single use and consider how we've arrived at a place where convenience is king and trumps our desire for anything else – even, it seems, leaving a habitable planet for future generations.

SO WHAT IS THE ANSWER?

Plastic pollution is a huge and complex issue. Action needs to be taken on all levels; we need legislation from the world's governments, we need to rethink design so that plastics can be reused or recycled more easily, and we need manufacturers and retailers to reduce their reliance on single-use packaging. All of which is important, but as individuals and families, it doesn't feel like there is a huge amount we can do to meaningfully impact on whether these things happen.

But remember I said that action needs to be taken on ALL levels, and we as individuals and as families are one of those levels. So the big question is, what can *we* do? The answer, as with pretty much everything when it comes to sustainable living, is to consume less. In simple terms, if less single-use plastic is being used, less single-use plastic will be produced, and there will be less to try and deal with. And as ever, it's all about baby steps. Picking one thing to work on, finding a **reusable** alternative to ONE type of single-use plastic. And then moving on to the next.

Making a start – the 'Big Four'

These are some of the most commonly used single-use plastics and are a brilliant place to start when it comes to your plastic-free(ish) journey. Remember with all of these, though, that reusables are only a better option if you actually reuse them! As they are more robust, they usually contain more resources and probably have a higher initial carbon footprint than their disposable counterparts. Getting into the habit of taking your reusables with you is key – rather than buying them and leaving them languishing at home.

PLASTIC BOTTLES

Of the bottles bought in 2016, less than half were collected for recycling. And of those, only 7 per cent were turned into new bottles. I'm sure you don't need me to tell you that reusable bottles are the answer.

HERE ARE THREE OF THE BEST:

1 Klean Kanteen (www.kleankanteen.com) – stainless steel, BPA free and in a range of different sizes and types. They have insulated bottles as well, and you can buy caps and tops separately just in case your little darlings have a habit of losing/chewing (I know! Why?!!) them.

2 Jerry Bottle (www.jerrybottle.com) – stainless steel and BPA free, with the option of steel or bamboo lids. All profits from their sale go to making clean water projects in India and Tanzania.

3 Chilly Bottles (www.chillysbottles.com) – eye-catching bottles in bright colours, they keep drinks cold for 24 hours and hot for 12 hours.

PLASTIC BAGS

Before the 5p levy was introduced on plastic bags here in the UK, the major supermarkets gave out 7.4 billion plastic bags each year. The good news is that the 5p levy has seen that number reduce by nearly 85 per cent, and we are all now very au fait with the idea that we need to take our reusable bags with us when we do the shopping. Here are some top tips for reducing the use of plastic bags even more:

Reuse the bags you already have

If you have a stash of plastic bags rammed into a drawer, use these before going out and buying a reusable replacement. Cotton shopping bags need to be used hundreds of times before their carbon footprint is lower than a single-use plastic bag (bonkers and confusing I know, but true).

Use reusable bags for loose fruit and veg

Hopefully you're already in a routine of taking your reusable bags when you go and do your weekly shop, but what about the plastic bags for fruit and veg? You'll be pleased to learn that there are reusable options for these too! First of all, though, keep and reuse any of the ones you might still have from your last shop as many times as you can. You can make your own from something lightweight like old net curtains (give them a good wash first...) or if you're short on time or skills for DIY-ing, then you can now easily find reusable bags in lots of places, including Lakeland, and at the time of writing Sainsbury's have started stocking them in their fruit and veg aisles.

Keep a bag on you at all times!

I'm pretty good at remembering my bags for my weekly shop, but I used to find myself getting caught out when I just popped in for milk or something. My solution is to keep a bag in my handbag, one in the car, and one in my backpack, minimising the chance I'll get 'caught short'! A friend of mine clips a fold-up reusable bag to her house keys, which is quite frankly genius. Another great idea is to put your shopping bags straight back into the car again when you've unloaded the shopping!

COFFEE CUPS

Here in the UK 7 million disposable coffee cups are used every single day, equating to 7.5 billion over the course of a year. And because of the plastic lining, coffee cups are pretty hard to recycle. If you can't resist the lure of posh coffee, or you need a cuppa to keep you going on a day out with the kids, there are so many different options and there really is no excuse!

TOP TIPS

Make and take your own

I've recently started taking a thermos of tea with me if we go out for the day. I totally feel like a Nana, but it not only negates the need for a disposable cup, it saves the price of a couple of cups of tea each time too #winwin.

Find the cup that works for you

Find a cup that you love – that suits your style and your lifestyle. You're way more likely to want to use it.

- Insulated cups are a great idea – that way, you have the added option of making your coffee or tea at home and simply taking it with you, knowing it will still be hot on arrival. I have a thermal mug from Klean Kanteen (www.kleankanteen.co.uk) which I love!
- Collapsible cups – one of the things that sometimes puts me off taking a reusable cup with me is the thought of having to lug it round all day once it's empty. This obviously bugs other people too, as there are now a few different options of collapsible cups that squash down when empty to easily fit into your bag. Have a look at the stojo (www.stojo.co).
- Made from coffee cups – this cup from rcups (www.rcup.co.uk) makes me smile. It promises to keep your drink hot for up to 1.5 hours, is leakproof, AND is made from recycled disposable coffee cups!

STRAWS

Some people would argue that if you're over the age of four, then you really shouldn't need a straw, but we all know that kids of all ages love a straw. And actually there can be some really valid reasons for people needing to use straws – the elderly and infirm, and disabled people might all be unable to drink independently without them.

DID YOU KNOW?

Americans use enough straws every single day to wrap around the Earth 2.5 times.

#2MINUTEBEACHCLEAN (www.beachclean.net)

Martin Dorey is a writer, surfer and activist, who wanted to take action to help to clean up the beaches near him in Cornwall. In 2013 he took a picture of the litter he had collected and shared it on social media with the #2minutebeachclean hashtag, thinking that if just one person joined in, that would double his beach-cleaning efforts.

Since then, at the time of writing, over 79,000 posts have been shared on IG using the hashtag, and the latest estimate is that at least 130 tonnes of plastic have been picked. #2minutebeachclean is now so much more than a hashtag, it's an international movement for change – next time you go to the beach, look out for one of the #2minutebeachclean boards, which have litter pickers and plastic bags to help you to do your very own #2minutebeachclean.

And it doesn't have to be confined to the beach either – do a two-minute litter pick when you walk the dog, go for a jog (the technical term for picking up litter when jogging is plogging, FYI),

If you really can't do without a straw then paper straws are making a comeback. Or even better is a reusable option like bamboo or stainless steel (these come with very cute teeny-tiny pipe cleaners to help you clean them!).

We have a set of stainless-steel ones that I bought for the kids – the main problem I have is remembering to take them out with us on the rare occasion we venture for a meal out, and also saying 'no straw please' when ordering. (There was also the memorable occasion when I remembered to take them out, we remembered to use them, took the obligatory pic to show off on social media, and then I left them behind in the café…).

or take the kids to the park. Every piece of litter picked up and properly disposed of won't be harming local wildlife or ending up in our waterways. I interviewed Martin for my Sustainable(ish) podcast and perhaps unsurprisingly he's a total inspiration:

'Everybody should be personally responsible for their own space. I don't want to be the one who walks past a piece of rope that ends up round a seal's neck. If I pick up a bottle it won't become a thousand pieces of microplastic. It's no longer enough to 'leave no footprints', we need to be leaving places nicer than they were when we got there. Plastic pollution is a dreadful, drastic, horrendous problem. We all have a part in it, and we all have a part to play in making it better. It's a human problem and as humans we are responsible. You have to believe that by changing habits in this country, choosing loose fruit and veg, or taking your own tubs to the deli counter, those decisions that you make every day will have some influence at some point. If we do nothing, nothing happens. If we do something, things change. We have to free ourselves from the tyranny of convenience and think about where things will go when we're finished with them. Maybe we can't all be plastic free, but we can be plastic conscious, or plastic clever.'

Martin Dorey, founder of #2minutebeachclean

Next steps

Once you've conquered the Big Four, you've made the first and some of the most impactful steps you can to reduce your own personal plastic footprint. But once your awareness of the plastic problem is raised, you're probably now noticing it everywhere. So what next...?

I want you to keep hold of your plastic rubbish. Just for a week, so that you can start to get a better handle on exactly what you are regularly throwing 'away' and can then start thinking about potential alternatives. And it's really pretty easy.

Do a plastic audit

1. Find a week when you know you're not on holiday, and it's not a crazy time of year like Christmas.

2. Tell the rest of the family what you're doing and get them on board. If they need motivating, show them the horrible pictures of the dead birds with stomachs full of plastic. Or that awful video of the turtle having a straw pulled out of its nose. On second thoughts, don't show these to tiny ones, you will give them nightmares...

3. Set yourself a start and an end date – if you can manage a full week I would really recommend it.

4. Assign a bag/box/jar for plastic waste and put your rubbish in there – it's as simple as that! And make sure you don't cheat! So that means bringing back any plastic rubbish you might otherwise put in the bin at work, or school, or when you're out and about, back home with you to put in too.

5. At the end of the week, don your rubber gloves and go all rubbish detective.

What are the most common things in there?

Is it crisp packets? Or yoghurt pots? Have the odd water bottle or coffee cup snuck in there? Maybe it's empty bottles and tubes of toiletries? Do a little audit – make a list of the types of rubbish in there. For example, ours might look like this:

- milk bottles
- crisp packets
- yoghurt pots
- cereal packet liners
- pasta packets
- ear buds
- toothpaste tubes
- deodorant cans.

Then pick one thing to tackle and give yourself a deadline to have it sorted by. If after a little research it feels unresolvable, that's not a problem. Go back to your list and pick the next thing. Once you've de-plasticked (technical term) that thing, pick one more, and one more, and one more. The key to tackling it without overwhelm is the step by step, item by item approach.

PLASTIC-FREE SWAPS FOR THE KITCHEN

Once you've done your plastic audit, you should have a pretty good idea of the plastic packaging you are throwing away on a regular basis. Here are some of the common ones:

Cereal packet bags

Unless you want to ban cereal altogether, there aren't really easy plastic-free alternatives. Buy the biggest box you can store, and avoid the mini multipacks.

> *Confession: We let the kids have these when we go on holiday. One way to ease your conscience a little is to reuse the little bags as wrappers for individual snack portions and to use the big ones for sandwich wrappings, or as freezer bags.*

Crisps

As hard as I've tried to work on the rest of the family, they really aren't ready to give up on crisps yet. My compromise currently is to buy the large share bags and then decant them into smaller plastic bags (which we reuse until they fall apart) for lunch boxes.

Things are looking up for crisp lovers, though – in late 2018, Walkers teamed up with recycling company Terracycle to create a free recycling programme for any brand of crisp packet and local collection points are now available all over the country. And after three years of development, a small Herefordshire-based crisp company Two Farmers (www.twofarmers.co.uk) have produced a 100 per cent home compostable crisp bag, proving that the technology is out there and hopefully acting as a massive incentive for the big brands to follow suit.

Pasta and rice

These are staples in our house, and pasta is my go-to quick meal for busy after-school nights.

- Barilla pasta – this is quite widely available on mainland Europe and comes in cardboard packaging.
- See if you have a 'bulk' or 'zero waste' store near you – in the US, bulk aisles are commonplace in many supermarkets, but this isn't the case in the UK. The good news is that 'zero waste' or 'plastic free' shops are on the rise, with nearly 60 around the country at the beginning of 2019. From bricks and mortar shops or pop-up stalls and mobile vans, you take your own container along and can fill up with pasta and other staples without the plastic packaging.
- In June 2019 Waitrose trialled an 'Unpacked' section in their Oxford store, and after an 'overwhelmingly positive response' have introduced parts of it to three more stores. Fingers crossed it will be rolled out in all their stores (and that other supermarkets follow suit).
- If you don't have easy access to a local zero waste store, then Plastic Free Pantry (www.plasticfreepantry.co.uk) is a great online option – most things are packaged in paper bags, and the 'plastic bags' that are used are Natureflex, made from plant-based material, and will compost in your home compost bin.

- Make your own pasta – admittedly this detracts a *little* from the 'quick and easy' option, but I am reliably informed that it's actually pretty easy to do...

Milk

With more and more people aware of the issues around plastic pollution and actively seeking out plastic-free alternatives, it is becoming easier to find milk in glass bottles.

- Take a step back in time, and see if you have a local milkman who could deliver. Make sure to check that they do glass bottles, though, as some deliver in plastic. Find your local milkman at www.findmeamilkman.net.
- Do you have a milk 'vending machine' near you? These are pretty common in Europe and we are just starting to see them popping up here in the UK. It's a genius idea – you take your own glass bottle with you, and get fresh milk straight from the farm dispensed into it. We have one near us and I am ridiculously overexcited each time I use it!

*Milk in glass bottles **is** more expensive – the supermarkets use milk as a loss leader and sell it at ridiculously low prices. What you pay for milk in glass bottles is probably a fairer reflection of the 'true cost' of producing it. But if the jump is too much to stomach, could you have milk delivered just once a week? Or only at the weekends? It doesn't have to be all or nothing – every little bottle helps!*

Plastic vs glass vs tetrapacks

As with most things, nothing is ever black and white, or should that be green and white. Here's my summary of the key points for each of these packaging types:

- Plastic milk bottles are made from HDPE (high density polyethylene), which is one of the most commonly and easily recycled of the different types of plastic. Some sources state that up to 75 per cent of HDPE bottles are in fact recycled (compared with 44 per cent of other types of plastic bottle). And currently 'new' plastic milk bottles can contain up to 30 per cent recycled plastic milk bottles.

- Glass milk bottles are more energy intensive to create in the first place, but their carbon footprint decreases dramatically with reuse, dropping to less than that of a plastic milk bottle after five uses. The average glass milk bottle is reused about 15 times, and can be reused up to 50 times. Although milk in glass bottles is heavier to transport, most is coming relatively short distances from local dairies, and if we could see the re-emergence of the good old-fashioned electric milk floats, this would further decrease transport impacts.
- Tetrapacks are traditionally difficult to recycle, being a composite of paper, plastic and aluminium, although they are now more widely recycled both by some local councils at kerbside and via schemes like Terracycle. Both glass and plastic are more easily recycled.

Yoghurt

As with the crisps, the compromise we have arrived at for now is to buy large tubs and decant it out into small Tupperware pots for lunch boxes. It's still single-use plastic, but one 500ml pot and lid instead of four small ones each time. Alternatively, you may be able to find yoghurt in glass jars – some farm shops and health food stores stock it, although there are issues with the increased transport costs of heavier packaging (it's never black and white, is it?!).

The 'gold standard' is probably to make your own – I've tried and failed on several occasions, but you might have more luck than me!

Cheese and meat

If you take your own Tupperware with you to the deli section of your local supermarket, your local butchers, or your local farmers' market, you can ask them to dispense whatever you need straight into your Tupperware, bypassing the plastic wrapping.

Morrisons introduced this as a policy in 2018, and I'm keeping fingers crossed that the other big chains will follow suit.

Fruit and veg

The ideal solution is to buy your fruit and veg loose and use reusable produce bags (*see* page 66). Frustratingly, organic produce is difficult to find loose in supermarkets as it is usually packaged to protect it from contamination with pesticides from the non-organic stuff.

Farmers' markets and fruit and veg box delivery schemes are a great solution, and if all else fails any 'stretchy plastic' bags can go in the carrier bag recycling bins that are outside many supermarkets.

Chocolate and sweets

The stronger-willed among you might just choose to simply forgo, but in our house this is never going to happen.

- Look out for cardboard/paper and foil-wrapped bars of chocolate.
- Some independent chocolate makers will sell glass jars of giant buttons, which make a nice indulgence, although I haven't seen anywhere you can refill them.
- If you have an old-fashioned sweet shop anywhere nearby, then take the opportunity to stock up on your favourite treats in paper bags.
- For the school disco, we visited our local wholesalers and bought the giant plastic jars of sweets, which we then dispensed into paper bags for the kids – the plastic jars were then passed on via Freecycle to someone who wanted them for storage.

Clingfilm

We've been clingfilm-free for a couple of years now. Here are four easy reusable alternatives:

1 Tupperware (yes, still plastic, but not single use!) – any leftovers get squirrelled away in the fridge in a trusty Tupperware pot (only after spending several minutes rooting through the drawer to find a matching pot and lid).
2 Use a plate to cover bowls of food in the fridge or microwave (I totally remember my Nana doing this).
3 Use beeswax wraps or reusable sandwich wrappers (for example, www.ecosnackwrap.co.uk) for sandwiches in lunch boxes. You can

buy beeswax wraps online (www.beeswaxwraps.co.uk) or if you're the hardcore type you can make your own.

4 Reusable clingfilm (for example, www.agreena.world) – use it like clingfilm, then simply wash and reuse.

> *Foil as an alternative to clingfilm is a great first step, but it's still essentially a single-use product. We still use some, but I tend to wipe it off and reuse it until it starts to fall apart.*

Baking parchment at first glance looks like it should be compostable, but it is usually coated with a very fine layer of silicone to give it non-stick properties so probably won't break down completely in a home compost heap (If You Care make home-compostable baking paper and cake cases, and is available online and in many health food and zero waste stores). And again, it's a single-use product – remember the waste hierarchy from Chapter 2 (how could you forget?!) – reuse is always a better option than recycling or rotting.

The five easiest plastic-free(ish) swaps for the kitchen

1 Milk bottles – find your nearest milkman (www.findmeamilkman.net).
2 Tick the 'no plastic bags' on your online shop.
3 Choose the loose fruit and veg and use reusable bags.
4 Swap out clingfilm for a reusable version.
5 Refill your washing-up liquid – lots of health food stores offer this service or Ecover have refill stores around the UK (www.ecover.com/store-locator/). Alternatively, if you've got space, buy a massive bottle and refill yourself – we get ours from here: www.biodegradable.biz.

PLASTIC-FREE SWAPS FOR THE BATHROOM

After the kitchen, the bathroom is probably the most densely plastic-populated room in our homes. Think about it – bottles of shampoo, conditioner and shower gel; plastic roll-ons of deodorant; tubes of toothpaste; even toothbrushes themselves – it's everywhere! Here are some simple swaps:

Liquid handwash

- **BAR SOAP**

  This is such a simple swap – it's quite easy now to find good-quality soap, packaged in paper or cardboard. You will need a soap dish to prolong the life of your soap, and your kids might need a little light instruction in the lost art of using a bar of soap, but other than that it's a super simple swap (NB See my confession overleaf).

- **SPLOSH (WWW.SPLOSH.COM)**

  Splosh make dissolvable sachets that you simply pop into your empty bottle of handwash, top up with water and shake!

- **BUY IN BULK, OR REFILL YOUR BOTTLES**

  Some health food shops and zero waste shops have large bottles of handwash that you can use to refill your smaller bottles. Failing that, you should be able to find 5L bottles of handwash online that are a great option to use to refill your bottles if you have the space to store them.

  If you do use liquid soap, get a foaming dispenser – it uses way less soap as it aerates the soap on its way out, meaning that you use less soap with each pump.

Shampoo

- **BUY IN BULK**

  As with the handwash, if you have space to store the large 5L bottles, you can order these online and then simply refill the smaller bottle that you keep in the shower. Yes, still plastic, and still technically single use, but it's significantly less plastic than lots of smaller bottles, and you may well find someone who will take the 5L empties off your hands to reuse on sites like Freecycle (www.freecycle.org).

- **SOLID SHAMPOO BARS**

  Lush sell solid shampoo bars that work brilliantly; however, they do contain SLS (sodium lauryl sulphate – a commonly used foaming agent in cleaning products and cosmetics), which is controversial as it can be irritant for some people, and can be derived using palm oil. There is now quite a wide range of shampoo bars available from independent makers online, so have a search – it might take a little bit of trial and error to find one that suits you and your hair, but if you can find one that works for you it's worth it! NB You may find that your hair initially feels quite different after using shampoo bars due to the pH of the soap – you can reduce this by rinsing your hair after washing with apple cider vinegar.

- **'NO POO'**

  Some hardcore zero waste gurus advocate the 'no poo' (no shampoo) method and swear that once your hair has 'transitioned' you will have clean, glossy, healthy hair without the need for shampoo at all. I think this works better for some types of hair than others – curly hair seems to do very well. I did try but only got about two weeks in before being driven back to shampoo by my grease-laden, stinking mop!

Shower gel

You're hopefully getting into the swing of this now – soap or buying in bulk are a couple of simple options.

> *Confession: We tried soap for handwashing, in the shower, and for hair for about two years, but I was eventually forced to concede that everyone else in the family hated it, and that my hair felt crap. Our plastic-free(ish) solution currently is 5L bulk bottles of shower gel (which doubles as handwash AND bubble bath) and shampoo online from Faith in Nature (www.faithinnature.co.uk) – my hair feels better and the kids do actually wash...*

Deodorant

I have to confess to being incredibly sceptical that more natural deodorants would actually work, but I'm happy to report that they do!

- **BUY IT**

  Try something like Fit Pit Deodorant (available online) – it comes in a glass jar with an aluminium lid, and is a kind of paste that you apply with your finger. It gets absorbed quickly and easily and smells pretty great too! For additional brownie points, you can return the glass jars to one of their stockists or via the post to be cleaned and reused.

If you prefer the idea of a roll-on type deodorant, then try this Natural Deodorant Stick from Earth Conscious (www. earthconscious.co.uk). Hubby couldn't cope with rubbing deodorant on to his armpits with his own finger for some reason, but gets on fine with this one!

● MAKE IT

Before you dismiss me as a crazy smelly hippy, let me reassure you that this actually does work! And the bonus is it's super easy to make.

Homemade deodorant (that works!)

This is what you need:

- 6–8 tbsps of coconut oil in its solid state – this is widely available in most supermarkets – look out for one that is Fairtrade.
- ¼–½ cup of bicarbonate of soda
- ¼ cup of cornflour
- essential oils of your choice (I went with lemon and tea-tree oil – about 5 drops of lemon, and 3 of tea-tree)

NB Bicarb can be quite astringent, but it is this that provides the deodorising qualities – start off with ¼ cup and see how you go – if you're still a little whiffy, add some extra bicarb. If your armpits start to get a little red and sore, add some extra cornflour and when you make your next batch, dial back the bicarb a little.

This is what you do:

- Place all the ingredients into a largish bowl and simply mush it all with a fork until it comes together into a paste. If you're feeling lazy, you can also do this in a free-standing food mixer.
- Decant into a lidded container (an old body cream tub will work well).
- To use, simply take a small pea-sized amount on your index finger and smear it on to your 'pits. The coconut oil will melt with your body heat and it disappears like magic!

Toothpaste

Having been convinced I would never find a plastic-free option for toothpaste, I'm happy to report there are a growing number of different products to try.

- **TRUTHPASTE (WWW.TRUTHPASTE.CO.UK)**
  This comes in glass jars and is made in the UK by a fabulous social enterprise. Hubby and I have been trying it out, and I have to say I love it! We've gone with the fennel flavour, but there is a mint version too. It takes a little bit of getting used to as it's a very different texture, and it doesn't foam like 'normal' toothpaste. I'm not convinced I could get the kids used to it, and it doesn't contain any fluoride, but it's certainly one for the grown-ups to try.

- **DENTTABS (AVAILABLE ONLINE FROM WWW.ANYTHINGBUT PLASTIC.CO.UK)**
  These are little tablets that you chew and then brush your teeth with as normal. I was excited to try them as I thought they might be THE answer – they are mint flavoured, contain fluoride and allege to foam. And… they're OK. The kids don't like them, hubby is ambivalent, and I'm ploughing through them as I feel guilty about the packaging using normal toothpaste.

- **GEORGANICS (WWW.GEORGANICS.CO.UK)**
  They do a variety of different flavoured natural fluoride-free toothpastes (they don't do a version with fluoride), which I have yet to try.

Toothbrushes

Bamboo toothbrushes have sky-rocketed in popularity in recent years, but they aren't the only option. If you go down the bamboo route and want to be 100 per cent plastic free, make sure to find out what the bristles are made of – most are nylon that won't degrade. A 100 per cent plastic-free option is available from Life Without Plastic (www.lifewithoutplastic. com) where the bristles are made from pig hair (yes, really – you pays your money, you takes your choice…).

If you still prefer a plastic option, a great choice might be one with a replaceable head – you simply press a button to pop off the old head when it's worn out and replace it, saving the handle from landfill. You can find some on Big Green Smile (www.biggreensmile.com).

Electric toothbrushes are surprisingly not a horrendous option, as long as you buy a good-quality base that will last, as it is just the heads that need replacing each time.

Whatever you do, steer clear of those electric kids' toothbrushes where you can't get inside to replace the batteries – kids inevitably love them as they are usually heavily branded, but the whole kit and caboodle has to hit the bin when they run out.

Confession: I couldn't convert the rest of the family to bamboo toothbrushes – the kids didn't like the feel and still use regular plastic ones, and hubby and I use an electric one.

SANITARY PRODUCTS

DID YOU KNOW?

- Over 1.5–2 billion sanitary products are flushed away each year in the UK.
- During beach cleans, an average of nine plastic tampon applicators were found for every km of beach in the UK.
- A packet of conventional sanitary pads can contain the equivalent of about four plastic bags.
- Ninety per cent of a sanitary pad is plastic; 6 per cent of a tampon is plastic.

Thankfully, there are now widely available plastic-free alternatives.

Non-applicator tampons

Lil-Lets launched a campaign in 2018 to 'give plastic the finger', citing that their tampons contain up to 97 per cent less plastic than other brands. Non-applicator tampons make sense, but if you really struggle without an applicator, help is at hand with an innovative reusable applicator from

Dame (www.wearedame.co). Use organic cotton tampons if possible, as organic cotton uses less water and pesticides when it's grown. And tampons and pads should never be flushed down the loo – pop them in your landfill waste, otherwise they block pipes and sewers and can ultimately end up getting washed into waterways and washing up on our beaches.

Menstrual cups

I've had a mooncup (www.mooncup.co.uk) for about the last 10 years and I totally love it. It takes a bit of getting used to, and you need to be able to cope with the slight ick factor of emptying and washing it, but it really is super simple. If you're out and about and need to empty it, you can get away with a quick wipe with some loo roll or rinsing with water from your (reusable) water bottle and give it a good wash when you get home. There are lots of different brands – check out the quiz on putacupinit.com to get advice on the best one for you.

Reusable sanitary towels

There are oodles of places online making and selling cloth sanitary towels (I saw them referred to as 'fluffy vagina blankets' in an article in the *Telegraph*). You use them as you would a normal sanitary towel, and then wash them on a cool wash. Try to avoid ones made using microfibre fabric, though, as these contribute to the problem of microplastics when washed (*see* page 127).

Period pants

I had no idea these were even a thing, but they are, and quite a big thing as it turns out (as in quite popular, not massive granny pants!). They have a specially absorbent gusset and come in a range of absorbencies so you simply pull on your 'special pants' and off you go. They even got the thumbs up from *Cosmo* mag.

Remember again that it's not all or nothing. Pick what you think will work for you, ease yourself in gently and don't beat yourself up if you resort to disposables every now and then (although once you've made the switch, I'm reasonably convinced it will stick!).

The five easiest plastic-free(ish) swaps for the bathroom

1 Bulk-buy shower gel if you have the space – it doubles up as handwash and also bubble bath.
2 Dental floss – swap out your plastic tub of plastic floss for a cute refillable glass pot and silk floss (www.georganics.co.uk) (there's also a non-silk version for vegans).
3 Deodorant – there are so many different plastic-free versions available now. Try out a couple of different ones and find one that works for you.
4 Switch to an old-fashioned safety razor for a plastic-free shave (of face/legs/whatever takes your fancy). Try Edwin Jagger (www.edwinjagger.co.uk). Honestly, they aren't as scary as you might think!
5 Swap make-up remover wipes for reusable versions – there are tons of different types available online, or just use a flannel.

HIDDEN PLASTICS

Not all plastics are visible – there are some that are so teeny you don't see them, or maybe they just don't look like plastic. Sadly, it doesn't stop them causing problems for the planet.

Microbeads

As the name implies, these are teeny-tiny beads of plastic and until the start of 2018 (when a ban came into force), they were found in lots of our cosmetics and personal care products, largely as exfoliators. The problem with them is that they are so small they slip through the filters at the water treatment plants, straight into our waterways and on out into the ocean, where they can be ingested by microorganisms and then enter the food chain.

Check your bathroom cupboards for any products you might have bought before January 2018 and if you're not sure whether or not it contains microbeads, you can check on the Beat the Microbead website (www.beatthemicrobead.org/product-lists/).

Glitter

Bad news for festival goers and/or those of us with young children but most glitter is made of plastic, and when we attempt to tidy up from a crafting session or our kiddiewinks wash their hands, these tiny particles of plastic are being washed into our water system and then act in the same way as microbeads. For those that simply can't go without their glitter fix, the good news is that you can now get biodegradable glitter made from plants that is designed to break down in our sewerage systems. Try Eco Glitter Fun (www.ecoglitterfun.com).

Chewing gum

Chewing gum is actually made from plastic, which is pretty grim when you stop and think about it. So what are your options for keeping your breath minty fresh without the plastic? Iceland supermarket became the first UK supermarket to stock plastic-free chewing gum (Simply Gum) in August 2018, and UK-made plastic-free gum 'Chewsy' is available online (www.chewsygum.co.uk) .

Microfibres (*see* page 127)

Teabags

Did you know that most teabags contain plastic? Total shocker I know, especially for a nation of tea-drinkers. The most obvious solution is to choose loose tea, but finding that without plastic packaging is harder than you might think.

I am reliably informed that Whittard will allow you to fill your own containers with loose tea, which is a perfect zero waste option if you have one near you. For those who aren't quite ready to give up on the bag, Co-op is the best bet – plastic-free teabags in a cardboard box – sometimes the simplest things are the best!

Coffee pods

Coffee drinkers don't escape scot-free, especially if you are among the 30 per cent of the UK population with a coffee pod machine. The pods are often a complicated mix of plastic and aluminium, making them difficult to recycle, and more often than not they end up in landfill. There is a recycling scheme run by Terracycle and you may be able to find a collection point online (www.terracycle.co.uk) or you can order home-compostable pods online from the Eden Project (www.eden project.com/shop/coffee/colombian-coffee-capsules). Or better yet, dig out the cafetière from the cupboard and go 'old school'.

Wine

I know! Is there nothing sacred any more? First the tea and the coffee, and now the wine. Many wine corks are no longer corks, but are in fact made of plastic, and that's before we even start on the screw tops. If you can, try and find (and then stick to) a brand that uses corks (this might take some trial and error, as it can be hard to see what's under the foil cover – it's a tough job…).

5 QUICK SUSTAINABLE(ISH) PLASTIC-FREE(ISH) WINS

1 Make sure everyone in the family has a reusable water bottle (and remembers to take it with them!)

2 Find yourself a reusable coffee cup and pledge to forgo your coffee if you forget it…

3 Get some extra reusable bags if you need to, so that you can keep one in your bag, and one in the car to reduce the chances you'll get caught short without one!

4 If your kids love straws, talk to them about the alternatives and make a decision together about which one to trial.

5 Next time you buy cotton buds, look out for ones with cardboard tubes and 'switch the stick'.

MORE SUGGESTIONS:

- [ ] Visit zero waste stores if you have one near you, or take a look at the Plastic Free Pantry for online plastic-free dried goods
- [ ] Take your Tupperware shopping with you for unpackaged meat and cheese
- [ ] Make or buy some beeswax wraps to use instead of clingfilm
- [ ] Ask for a cone instead of a tub next time you have an ice cream
- [ ] Consider investing in a secondhand SodaStream if you get through a lot of plastic bottles of fizzy drinks
- [ ] Check out Who Gives a Crap (uk.whogivesacrap.org) for plastic-free loo roll (wrapped in paper and delivered in cardboard). As a bonus, the company donate a proportion of their profits to help build toilets in the developing world
- [ ] Swap your plastic bottles of tonic for cans or bottles for a plastic-free gin and tonic
- [ ] Try out swapping liquid soap for bar soap
- [ ] Find a plastic-free deodorant that works for you (*see* page 78)
- [ ] Could you have a plastic-free period? *See* page 81 for options

Over to you (aka now get up and do!)

List three or four ideas below for changes you could make to go plastic-free(ish).

Action	Timeframe
1.	
2.	
3.	
4.	

Resources

- MARINE CONSERVATION SOCIETY (WWW.MCSUK.ORG)
  The UK's leading charity for the protection of seas, shores and wildlife. The MCS has been one of the leading voices in calling for action on plastic pollution and hosts an annual Great British Beach Clean weekend every September.

- SURFERS AGAINST SEWAGE (WWW.SAS.ORG.UK)
  UK charity working to protect the marine environment. They run a brilliant programme to help people get 'plastic-free status' for their local communities and towns.

- #2MINUTEBEACHCLEAN (WWW.BEACHCLEAN.NET)
  Join the #2minutebeachclean community, download the app, or bag your beach a #2minutebeachclean board.

- *NO. MORE. PLASTIC.: WHAT YOU CAN DO TO MAKE A DIFFERENCE - THE #2MINUTESOLUTION* BY MARTIN DOREY (PENGUIN, 2018)
  Written by the founder of the #2minutebeachclean movement, this book is brilliant. Packed with easily actionable ideas, and a checklist at the end to tick things off as you do them.

- *HOW TO GIVE UP PLASTIC: A GUIDE TO CHANGING THE WORLD, ONE PLASTIC BOTTLE AT A TIME* BY WILL MCCALLUM (PENGUIN, 2018)
  Will McCallum is Head of Oceans at Greenpeace UK so I think it's fair to say he knows his stuff when it comes to single-use plastic and the impact it's having on our waterways. This book is split into different areas of our homes/lives with practical ideas and inspiration for each one.

- *HOW TO LIVE PLASTIC FREE: A DAY IN THE LIFE OF A PLASTIC DETOX* BY MARINE CONSERVATION SOCIETY (HEADLINE, 2018)
  This book walks us through the different options available to us from the moment we wake up, to the moment we go to bed.

- *TURNING THE TIDE ON PLASTIC: HOW HUMANITY (AND YOU) CAN MAKE OUR GLOBE CLEAN AGAIN* BY LUCY SIEGLE (TRAPEZE, 2018)
  Starting with an introduction to all things plastic and setting the scene for how we ended up in a world of plastic, Lucy then goes on to help us work out our own plastic pain points, and encourages us to think about how we can reduce, replace, refuse, refill, rethink and recycle!

- A PLASTIC OCEAN (WWW.PLASTICOCEANS.ORG)
  An eye-opening and often harrowing documentary exploring the extent and impact of plastic pollution on the world's oceans and wildlife.

- PLASTIC FREE PANTRY (WWW.PLASTICFREEPANTRY.CO.UK)
  Online store selling pantry staples (pasta, rice, dried fruit etc) in plastic-free packaging.

- ANYTHING BUT PLASTIC (WWW.ANYTHINGBUTPLASTIC.CO.UK)
  Online store selling reusable and plastic-free alternatives such as water bottles, toothpaste and sun cream.

- FAITH IN NATURE (WWW.FAITHINNATURE.CO.UK)
  Natural beauty products and natural shampoo – available in 5L bottles.

4

Sustainable(ish) food

Food is a big issue. We all have to eat, and everything we eat has an impact on the planet. It all has to be grown or reared, and processed, and transported, before it even makes it on to our supermarket shelves, and all of these processes use energy (carbon), water and resources. Our food has a carbon (and water) footprint, and this varies depending on what we eat, where it's grown, how processed it is, what it's packaged in and so on.

DID YOU KNOW?

- Food production is responsible for a quarter of all global greenhouse gas emissions.
- More than half of food emissions come from animal products.
- Approximately 30 per cent of the food that is produced never even reaches the table.

Eating sustainably will mean different things to different people, and it's such a complex and sometimes emotive topic that it can often feel hard to even know where to start. In early 2019, a group of over 30 world-leading scientists from around the globe got together to create a consensus to define a healthy and sustainable diet. One that is capable of not only feeding 10 billion people (expected global population by 2050) but that would also minimise greenhouse gas emissions, prevent any species going extinct, have no expansion of farmland, and preserve water. Oh, and it had to be healthy for us humans, as well as the planet. The headlines are:

- Just 100g red meat and 200g of chicken a week.
- 250ml (a small glass) of milk a day.
- 200g fish a week.
- 1 egg a week.
- The majority of our protein should come from pulses and beans – 500g a week.

But just radically shifting our diets won't be enough   they also concluded that we need to halve food waste (*see* page 99) and make efficiencies in farming so that more food is produced on existing farmland.

As a family we're a long way from that recommended ideal, and I feel a little overwhelmed thinking about the changes that we should be aiming for. But as with everything, baby steps are the key. We might not all be able to switch to this 'ideal diet' overnight, or even at all. But we can all take steps in the right direction.

Here are 11 easy things we can all do to eat more sustainably.

1. Meal plan

This is something I resisted for a very long time – it felt far too sensible and grown-up, and there was something in me that rebelled against it. But honestly, it's one of the most useful things I do, both in terms of helping me feel more in control of life in general (I know, who knew a meal plan could do that?!) and also in terms of reducing food waste.

We get a veg box, so I generally wait until that has been delivered and I know what I have to work with, as the contents can vary week to week, and then create a meal plan and shopping list from there. Having a meal plan makes it easier to generate a shopping list, and to know that I will use up what I buy. It also means I can cut down on the amount of cooking I need to do by making double batches of, say, mashed potato, and then having something like potato gnocchi as one of our meals a couple of days later.

Potato gnocchi

This is mind-blowingly easy to make – mix 500g cold mashed potato with 150g plain flour and keep mixing/kneading until it all comes together. Divide your mix into 4 or 5 pieces and then roll each one out into a long snake about 3cm diameter, like you're making play-dough snakes. Chop each snake into gnocchi-sized (about 5cm long) pieces. Bring a pan of water to the boil and then drop them in. Once they float to the top, they're done. Scoop them out and serve with pesto or a tomato sauce and cheese.

TOP TIPS FOR MEAL PLANNING

- Look at your diary and the schedules of others in the household to work out how many people you will need to feed each day.
- Meal planning doesn't have to include crazily adventurous meals – beans on toast has as much place on a meal plan as a full Sunday roast.
- Batch cook at the weekend to stash 'ready meals' in the freezer for days when you have no time to cook.
- Plan 5 days' worth of meals, and leave yourself some white space to use up any leftovers or to allow for unexpected meals out.
- Develop an arsenal of easy to prepare meals that you can vary – we invariably have pasta at least weekly with a variety of quick sauces.

2. Meat-free Monday

Or Tuesday, or Friday. It doesn't really matter which day of the week it is, the idea is just to have at least one meat-free day a week. Livestock farming accounts for 14 per cent of global carbon emissions, so simply reducing the amount of meat we are eating is a really simple way to cut our 'food footprint'.

Check out the Meat Free Monday website (www.meatfreemondays.com) for loads of ideas for veggie meals, including breakfast as well as puddings and snacks.

- Switch to plant-based milk, but remember that soya and almond milk have a bigger environmental impact than other types of plant milk. Soya production is leading to the destruction of vast areas of Amazon rainforest, for example, while almonds are often grown in California and require huge quantities of water to produce, in an area that already suffers from long-term water shortages. It's best to look for brands such as Alpro soya milk, which sources most of its soya in the EU, or Oatly oat milk. Making your own oat milk at home is cheap, easy and eco-friendly, especially if you use British-grown oats (there's a recipe here at Ecojam – www.ecojam.org/news/plastic-free-zero-waste-recipes-homemade-oat-milk).
- Grains – it's easy to get into a grain rut and just eat pasta and rice on a loop, but there are so many interesting grains that add texture, flavour and nutrients to your diet. Try quinoa (a complete source of protein), teff, millet, barley, freekeh and buckwheat, and again always look for UK or European-grown varieties where possible.
- When cooking without meat, many people find they miss the 'umami' savoury flavour that meat brings to a dish – but your store cupboard can offer plenty of options to add this depth of flavour back into your cooking. Try experimenting with ingredients such as miso paste, dried porcini mushrooms, smoked paprika, soya sauce, pomegranate molasses, nutritional yeast flakes, chipotle/chilli pastes, harissa, toasted nuts, garlic, herbs, spices and even a squeeze of lemon to help to bring veggie dishes to life.
- Many cuisines around the world focus heavily on meat-free cooking, so look to these for inspiration. Mexico, India and the Middle East all pack loads of flavour into their veggie dishes using their distinctive spices and ingredients, so look for recipes from these countries.

3. Eat seasonally

Many of us have lost touch with the seasons and what they mean for the food that should normally be available at particular times of the year. We have become so used to being able to get whatever we want, whenever we want, that we forget that if we buy tomatoes in the middle of winter, they will have been grown somewhere halfway around the world and then shipped or flown in to our local supermarket.

Eating seasonally requires quite a shift in the way we think about food, but after the initial research, it can easily be incorporated into weekly meal plans. Knowing that you can only have British strawberries for a relatively short window in the summer makes them so much more of a treat, and something to really look forward to! More details about seasonal fruit and veg can be found here: www.lovebritishfood.co.uk/british-food-and-drink/fruit-and-vegetables.

> *Get a veg box – see below – and then you get to eat seasonally without really having to think about it.*

4. Get a veg box

We get our fruit and veg from Riverford, delivered to our door every week, and I have to say I love it. It ticks so many of my 'sustainable eating' boxes – it's organic, the fruit and veg is seasonal, most of it is local (and the stuff that isn't is never air-freighted), and it cuts down hugely on the amount of plastic packaging coming in to the house. For me, it takes some of the hassle out of trying to eat seasonally – if something is in season it will be in my veg box, and if it's not, it won't. Simple!

5. Cook from scratch

Yes, cooking from scratch might take you a bit more time than relying on ready meals, but it's cheaper and healthier, you'll massively reduce your plastic footprint, and there are lots of hacks to reduce the time you need. And remember, as with everything, it doesn't have to be all or nothing. Could you commit to cooking from scratch just a couple of days a week to start with?

I started cooking more from scratch when we first had kids and started weaning – it felt really important to me to know that the food I was giving my precious baby was as natural and chemical free as possible. And I've just kind of carried on (not with the natural and chemical-free precious-baby thing, the kids get their fair share of cake and sweets!).

Here are some ideas to help to streamline the whole process:

- Embrace the slow cooker – a few minutes' work in the morning before work will pay dividends when you walk through the door to the smell of a delicious meal that can be on the table in minutes (and you will feel very smug indeed).
- Batch cook – when you do have time to cook, cook double (it takes the same amount of time) and then freeze some for another day.
- Love your freezer. I freeze anything and everything – leftover tomato sauce for pizza or pasta, even biscuits and cakes (unless they get scoffed first).

Easy tomato sauce recipe

(This is based on my favourite sauce recipe, from *The Five O' Clock Apron* by Claire Thomson)

1 Heat 2 tbsp olive oil in a saucepan on a medium-low heat. Add a finely diced onion, and cook for about 10 minutes until soft. Add 3 cloves of finely chopped garlic and continue to cook for another 2-3 minutes. Keep it moving in the pan and don't let the garlic colour or go brown.

2 Add 400g tinned plum tomatoes, followed by a pinch of sugar and a small splash of red wine vinegar. Season with salt and pepper. Bring to a simmer, turn down the heat to low and leave to simmer for about 45 minutes, stirring from time to time.

3 Take the sauce off the heat and add a final tbsp of olive oil. Freeze any leftovers for a quick meal another day.

6. Reduce consumption of red meat

As well as having a meat-free day at least once a week, cutting down on the amount of red meat we eat is another really simple way to quite dramatically cut the carbon footprint of our diet. Lamb and (especially) beef are the biggest culprits in terms of greenhouse gas emissions – beef production emits five times more greenhouse gases, compared with the production of chicken and pork.

Buy less, buy better — for meat

There is no doubt that we all need to consume less meat but if you can't quite face the thought of going cold turkey (forgive the pun), here are some ways to lessen the impact:

- USE EVERY SCRAP

  When you do eat meat, make sure none of it goes to waste. Use up any leftovers cold in sandwiches the next day, make a risotto, or freeze any leftover meat to make more meals at another time. Lastly, you can use the bones to make stock really easily by chucking them in the slow cooker with some water, some seasoning and maybe some herbs and leaving to simmer overnight. Freeze this to make gravy next time you have a roast, or to make soup next time you find some sorry-looking limp veg at the bottom of the fridge.

- BUY BRITISH

  If you're buying milk, meat and cheese, buy British. Not only will the food miles be less but our farm welfare standards

7. Go organic

The organic system is not perfect – there are issues around certification, land use and productivity, and preventative medicine, among others – but I do believe that in general terms it is much kinder to the planet and more sustainable. More and more organic products are becoming

We do eat meat in our house, and we do love a roast lamb, or a chilli con carne, but we eat it sparingly. If I do a roast, I make sure that my meal plan for that week incorporates at least one meal that will ensure any leftovers are used up. Another way to sneakily reduce the amount of red meat in things like casseroles and spag bol is to substitute up to half of it with something like lentils, kidney beans or some grated carrot or courgette – this really bulks up the dish, and most of the time no one even notices.

are generally higher than they might be in other parts of the world.

- GO FREE RANGE

   This applies for eggs, but also for meat. Outdoor reared meat is generally farmed much less intensively, reducing carbon emissions and generally meaning the animals have a more pleasant life. Yes, it's more expensive, so buying meat might become more of a conscious act, a treat, or something to be eked out/avoiding waste.

- AVOID PROCESSED MEAT PRODUCTS AND FAST FOOD

   If you're buying ready meals and burgers from fast food chains, unless you really scrutinise the labels or the company's website, you are unlikely to know where the meat they're using has come from. In order to keep costs down and profits up, it could well be that they are using 'mass-produced', intensively farmed beef and meat from areas that have been deforested to make way for cattle ranches.

available and the price has really dropped in recent years. I imagine it will always be more expensive than conventional products, but the same issues apply to 'fast food' as they do to 'fast fashion' and we have lost sight of how much food really should cost. Organic food is produced less intensively, and with less potential for exploitation of either the land or the producers, and for me, that's a price worth paying.

Best foods to eat organic, aka 'The Dirty Dozen' – the 12 foods that contain the highest levels of pesticide residue:

- Strawberries
- Spinach
- Nectarines
- Apples
- Grapes
- Peaches
- Cherries
- Pears
- Tomatoes
- Celery
- Potatoes
- Peppers

8. Shop local

In an ideal world, we would all shop from our independent butchers, greengrocers and fishmongers, but this is becoming increasingly difficult as these small local businesses get squeezed out by the supermarkets. Shopping locally is a great way to incorporate sustainability into your diet – money spent in the local economy is far more likely to stay within the local economy, rather than go towards lining the pockets of shareholders and CEOs.

Keep your eye out for your local farmers' market, or seek out an independent butcher. Going supermarket free would be a big step for many of us, but could you commit a certain proportion of your weekly spend to local shops? If you are in the supermarket, then look out for British meat and veg, which will have lower food miles (as I said earlier, British farms usually have higher welfare standards too).

9. Choose Fairtrade

Fairtrade is really taking off and the range of products available is expanding every day – from coffee to bananas, and chocolate to peanut butter, there are so many more options available now. Buying products with a Fairtrade certification means that the producers have been paid a fair price for their goods – enabling them to send their kids to school instead of out to work; pay off any loans associated with their businesses; and put food on their own tables. Again, I feel like the slightly increased costs of Fairtrade goods is simply a truer reflection of how much things really cost to produce. The peace of mind that comes with knowing that other people aren't being exploited or suffering as a result of my choices makes it a premium I am happy to pay.

10. Grow your own

I am the least green-fingered person that there is, meaning I am in no way qualified to talk about growing your own. Having said that, even I manage an unruly strawberry bed, and a few raspberry canes that save us both money and plastic punnets during the summer months.

It's a brilliant way to reduce plastic packaging, ensure that you eat seasonally, and slash food miles! You don't need an allotment or a huge garden – lots of things can be grown in pots on patios, or even in hanging baskets and window boxes.

According to Sara Venn from Incredible Edible Bristol, the top things for beginners to start growing are:

- Cherry tomatoes
- Berries – strawberries, raspberries etc
- Mangetout, French beans and peas
- Mini cucumbers (great for lunch boxes)
- Microgreens – basically normal greens like peas etc but picked at the 'shoot' stage – they work really well sprinkled on salads and can be grown on a windowsill all year round.

11. Love your leftovers

Reducing food waste is one of the most impactful things we can ALL do to make our diets more sustainable. Getting canny with leftovers and those slightly limp veg left at the bottom of the fridge or the over-ripe bananas in the fruit bowl is a brilliant way to not only eat more sustainably, but to save money too. And the good news is that these uninspiring leftovers can be turned into delicious meals and snacks with relatively little effort. The Love Food Hate Waste (www.lovefoodhate waste.com) site is a great place to look for inspiration.

Which leads us neatly on to food waste. This book wasn't just thrown together, you know!

The three most commonly wasted foods in households:

1 POTATOES

5.8 million potatoes hit the bin every day in the UK. Keep your potatoes in a cool, dark place, and simply cut off the 'eyes' if they start to sprout. Potatoes that are getting a bit soft can either be added to soups or boiled up and mashed and then frozen.

Potentially life-changing fact alert Chip shop chips can be frozen. Oh yes. So next time your eyes are bigger than your belly and you ask for a large chips from the chippy, freeze what you can't eat and then reheat in the oven (or refry in a frying pan with a little oil) for a chip shop treat later on in the week.

2 BREAD

Over 24 million slices of bread are chucked away daily. If you find that your loaf keeps going mouldy before you get through it, keep it in the freezer and simply take out slices as you need them. Whiz up stale bread in the food processor to make breadcrumbs and then store them in the freezer ready to top pasta bakes.

3 MILK

Every day, 5.8 million glasses of milk are poured down the drain by UK households. If you're going away on holiday, freeze any remaining milk rather than tip it down the drain.

FOOD ITEMS YOU MIGHT NOT KNOW YOU CAN FREEZE

- MILK

  OK, so you probably did know this one, but it's worth reminding you. Make sure there's a bit of space in the bottle for the milk to expand as it freezes.

- CHEESE

  Cheese tends to keep really well but if for any reason you're worried about its shelf life, grate and freeze in a Tupperware pot.

- BUTTER

  Just whack it in the freezer in its packet. Simple.

- EGGS

  You can freeze eggs, just not in their shells. Crack them into (reusable) muffin cases in a muffin tin, give them a little whisk with a fork and then freeze. Once frozen, pop them out of the cases and into a Tupperware pot and then simply defrost as many as you need – great for scrambled eggs or baking.

- AVOCADOS

  Millennials rejoice! Avocados can be frozen and then used in dips or smooshed up on toast.

- HUMMUS

  Yummy mummies rejoice! Hummus (shop bought or homemade) can be frozen – either freeze all of it in one batch, or portion up into something like an ice cube tray if you need small portions each day for the kiddos' lunches.

- OPEN BAGS OF CRISPS

  This has blown my mind. Apparently there is no need for me to selflessly finish off large bags of open crisps in order to prevent food waste. Curses.

A quick note on best-before and use-by dates

I ignore best-before dates. You are very very unlikely to come to any harm eating anything that is past its best-before date.

Use-by dates I tend to see as helpful guidance rather than a strict rule. Use your senses, including your common sense. For things like yoghurt and milk, if it looks OK, smells OK, and when you tentatively try a teeny bit it tastes OK, it's probably OK.

But be sensible. If you're in any doubt, certainly don't give it to young kids, elderly people, pregnant people or anyone who might be immuno-compromised. I'm also a bit more careful about fresh meat and fish.

VEGETABLE PEELINGS AND LEAVES

On page 53 I talk about the options for 'unavoidable' food waste to prevent it ending up in landfill. If you're pushed for time, composting your veg peelings and leaves is infinitely better than sending it to landfill (where it contributes to methane emissions due to the conditions that exist in landfill sites). However, if you want gold star status for your food waste efforts, then here are a couple of ideas:

- SLOW COOKER VEG STOCK

  Save all your veg peelings (make sure you scrub your veg first, otherwise you will end up with very 'earthy' stock) in a large Tupperware pot in the freezer and when it's full, bung the whole lot in the slow cooker with a couple of pints of water, a few bay leaves, peppercorns and a sprinkle of salt and cook on low overnight. Strain in the morning (compost the solids) and then freeze your homemade veg stock in 500ml portions.

Make sure you have a good mix of different veg peelings – go steady on the cabbage/cauliflower leaves, otherwise your stock will just taste like watery cabbage soup.

• HOMEMADE POTATO 'CRISPS'

Tip your (clean) potato peelings on to a baking tray, drizzle over some olive oil, sprinkle with salt and bake at 180°C for 10–20 minutes (depending on how crispy you like your crisps). Eat immediately.

Sustainable(ish) supermarket shopping

In an ideal world we would all waft around our local farmers' market, independent butchers and zero waste stores with our wicker basket and our glass mason jars at the ready to be refilled. It sounds idyllic, but the reality for me is a mad dash around the supermarket (usually having left my carefully prepared list on the kitchen table) with the kids whingeing at me for a magazine and sneaking packets of sweets into the trolley.

Supermarket shopping is the reality for most of us, so how can we make it more sustainable?

- Go for the loose fruit and veg wherever you can and take your own reusable bags (*see* page 66). If all else fails, use the plastic bags they have at the supermarket, but reuse them again and again until they fall apart.
- Buy British. Look out for the RSPCA freedom food logo or the Soil Association symbol for higher welfare meat.
- Use the deli counter and the butcher's counter. You can ask for exactly how much you want/need, and it will probably come with less packaging. If you're feeling brave you can take your own Tupperware and ask them to put meat/cheese in there (*see* page 74).
- Use the bakery. If your local supermarket has an in-store bakery, use it! Take reusable bags (old pillowcases work well) and use them for bread, rolls, pastries etc.

- Go for butter. Ditch the plastic tubs of margarine and go back to butter. If you can find butter in foil packs, with some brands you should be able to peel the foil and the greaseproof paper apart and recycle both separately. Simply chuck your empty butter wrapper into the washing-up bowl after doing it and leave it to soak until the two layers magically float apart.
- Look for paper. Look for the things that you can find easily in paper – you might be surprised just how many there are – flour, sugar (caster sugar, granulated sugar and icing sugar) and porridge oats can all be found relatively painlessly in paper bags.
- Look for cardboard. Sometimes we're so 'in the zone' when we're shopping, and we just grab the same old brands week in and week out. Take a look and see if there are any alternatives to your usual items that are packaged in cardboard instead. Lots of washing powders are now available in cardboard boxes – how about trying one of them instead of your usual liquid? Several of the major supermarkets also do dishwashing powder in a box, so it's worth looking.
- Pasta is a BIG staple in our house. Barilla pasta is available in a cardboard box with just a small plastic window and you should be able to find it in some of the larger supermarkets. Waitrose do a gluten-free pasta that is available in a box made from food waste – more of this please, supermarkets! Rice is another one that can sometimes be found in cardboard boxes – just be sure to do the squidge test (*see* below).
- Sometimes you can buy a product in paper or cardboard, full of excitement and the very best of intentions, only to get home and find there is a sneaky plastic bag inside. To try and avoid this, do the squidge test – simply hold said product up to your ear and give it a gentle squidge, listening out for the tell-tale crackle of plastic inside (ignore any strange looks you might get from fellow shoppers – Superman didn't care about wearing his pants outside his trousers, so we can't let getting a few strange looks stop us on our mission...).
- Go large. If you can't find a plastic-free solution that suits you and the family, buy the largest size that you can. We get the big share packs of crisps and then ~~scoff the lot~~ portion them

out into plastic bags that we reuse for lunch boxes. And do the same for yoghurts too – get the 500ml pots and scoop it into little Tupperware pots for the kids to have at school. Totally not a perfectly plastic-free solution, but plastic free(ish) and it keeps the kids vaguely happy, so it's a win in my book.

ALTERNATIVES TO SUPERMARKETS

Not all supermarkets are created equal when it comes to all things sustainable(ish). Some seem to be genuinely trying to do the right thing, while some cynics might suggest that others are employing an element of 'greenwashing' – trying to be seen to be doing the right thing while all the time protecting the profits of their shareholders by turning the screw ever tighter on producers and suppliers. The vast majority of us will do our food shopping at the supermarket because it's convenient, and we're all pushed for time. And that's OK. But in the spirit of all things sustainable(ish), I want to share with you some alternatives. No one is saying you have to go supermarket free, but if there are occasions when you've got a bit more time, or just fancy going the extra mile every now and then, here are some alternatives you might like to check out.

1 FARMERS' MARKETS

You should be able to find your local farmers' market easily with a little light internet searching. Most towns of any size will have one happening at least once a month. You will find inside a collection of amazing fresh produce direct from the producers in your local area, everything from bread to beef, and veg to local honey. The money goes straight to the producers, there is no middle man taking a cut, and you get to support farmers directly.

2 FARM SHOPS

Local farm shops can be a brilliant way to source your weekly shop from local producers and seasonal produce. Some of them have policies of only sourcing things from within a set distance away to limit food miles, and others will grow a lot of the produce right there on the farm. You probably already know where your nearest and best ones are, but just in case you don't you can search at www.farmshop.uk.com.

3 VEG BOX SCHEMES

There are some national veg box schemes such as Riverford and Abel and Cole, where you can not only get fresh, seasonal, organic veg delivered to your door, but also organic meat and dairy products too. But if you do a little bit of research, you will undoubtedly uncover a local version, run by local growers and producers. You can search for organic veg box schemes on the Soil Association website (www.soilassociation.org/organic-living/buy-organic/find-an-organic-box-scheme/).

4 LOCAL SHOPS

Take a walk down your local high street and see how much of your weekly shop you might be able to source from local independent retailers. Do you still have an independent butcher, or a greengrocer, or a baker? If you do, then support them! They are a font of knowledge about their own products, and will often be comparable to the supermarkets. And your money stays in the local economy, and helps a local business put food on their family's table.

5 GROW YOUR OWN

Most of us won't have the space or time to be entirely self-sufficient, but we can all devote a couple of pots on the patio to some herbs, or a tray on the windowsill for some cut and come again lettuce. I am not green fingered at all, but along with the satisfaction of eating something you have grown yourself, I love the feeling that what I am doing is like a gentle form of activism.

6 COMMUNITY FRIDGES

The first of these in the UK opened in Frome in Somerset a few years ago and since then a whole network of Community Fridges has grown (www.hubbub.org.uk/the-community-fridge). They are a brilliantly simple idea – if people have food in their fridge that they know they aren't going to eat because they are going away on holiday, or have just misjudged their shopping, they can simply pop it into the community fridge and anyone who wants it can take it. Local businesses also use it to get rid of any leftover fresh goods at the end of the day, and it seems to work really well.

Three great food apps to help you eat more sustainably

1 **Olio (www.olioex.com)** Olio is a food waste app, where you can sign up and post pictures of any food you have that you need to get rid of, as well as keep your eye out for things that your neighbours might be offering up. It is still getting off the ground in many areas of the country, but it's worth signing up for to see if you have any local connections and to get the ball started where you live.

2 **Giki (www.gikibadges.com)** Simply download the Giki app and then next time you're out food shopping, scan the barcode and see which of the 13 badges your particular food choice gets awarded – it gives you instant information about things like whether the packaging is recycled, whether the product was responsibly sourced, or what the animal welfare standards are.

3 **Too good to go (www.toogoodtogo.co.uk)** This is such a beautifully simple idea – restaurants and takeaways can list any unsold meals at the end of service, and you can claim it via the app for a much reduced price, helping to tackle food waste within the industry.

PALM OIL

This is another tricky subject that people tend to view in a pretty black or white way. Iceland's banned Christmas TV ad of 2018 with the adorable cartoon Orangutan certainly did a good job of raising awareness around the damage that the food and cosmetics industries' love affair with the stuff is causing when it went viral. Many people loudly proclaimed their disgust on social media and vowed to boycott any products with palm oil. But as with most things, it's complicated, and I personally can't see any clear-cut 'right things' to do at the moment.

You see, palm oil is a hugely productive crop – it produces 4–10 times more oil per unit of land than comparable crops like soy and rapeseed, and it's used in everything from food to cosmetics to biodiesel.

As demand for it grows, 270,000 hectares of rainforest are cleared annually. But it's not the only product implicated in deforestation – cattle ranching is by far the biggest contributor, alongside soy and timber production.

Boycotting palm oil and pressuring companies to find alternatives could arguably leave us in a worse position with respect to the rainforests, with more land needed to generate the same volume of oil. There are certifications in place (RSPO being one) that are supposed to ensure palm oil is produced in a sustainable way, not contributing to deforestation, but there is little confidence in the current schemes.

So what, as consumers, can we do?

- Let manufacturers and retailers know that you want them to source sustainable palm oil with robust sustainability certifications.
- Avoid the worst offenders who make no effort to source palm oil sustainably (Ethical Consumer has a list of the good, the bad and the ugly for palm oil). Greenpeace lists Kit-Kat, Colgate toothpaste, Johnson's baby lotion, Dove's soap, Doritos, Kellogg's Pop Tarts, Ritz crackers, M&M's and Head & Shoulders shampoo as some to avoid that are sourcing their palm oil from 'the dirtiest palm oil producer in the world'.
- Consume less – the rise in the popularity of palm oil has come about in some part in response to the demand for processed foods. Cooking from scratch and reducing consumption of highly processed foods is one of the key ways we can avoid inadvertently consuming palm oil. And again, it doesn't have to be all or nothing – no one's saying you have to become a 'clean eating' fiend, but every little really does help.

5 QUICK SUSTAINABLE(ISH) WINS FOR FOOD

1 **Shop your cupboards** Spend a week (or longer if you can) shopping only for fresh fruit and veg and things like milk. For everything else, use up what is already in your cupboards and freezer. Not only will this save you some cash, it means that there's no danger of things getting lost at the back of the cupboards and creating food waste.

2 **Eat less beef** Sub in lentils/beans for half of the beef in stews or mince dishes, or swap for chicken for your roast.

3 **Visit the Love Food Hate Waste website (www. lovefoodhatewaste.com)** They have a recipes section where you can add in what leftover ingredients you've got and it will generate some ideas for you.

4 **Have at least one meat-free day a week** Or more if you can!

5 **Challenge yourself to throw away no edible food for as long as you can** Rustle up some banana bread from manky bananas (or freeze them until you have time), whiz up a smoothie from the tired-looking fruit in the fruit bowl, or make soup from the limp veg left in the fridge at the end of the week.

MORE SUGGESTIONS:

☐ Do a meal plan – try it once a week for a month

☐ Have a look at your usual fruit and veg purchases and identify those that aren't in season and think about what substitutes you could make

☐ Cook from scratch at least once a week

- ☐ Shop local – what percentage of your shop could you buy from local shops?

- ☐ Swap one of your usual items for a Fairtrade alternative

- ☐ Buy loose fruit and veg in reusable bags

- ☐ Download the Olio app and see who you can start sharing any unneeded food with locally

- ☐ Research the feasibility of a veg box delivery

- ☐ Do a food waste audit – keep your food waste in a separate bin for a week, and then don your rubber gloves to identify your worst offenders. Pick ONE to work on

- ☐ Find out where and when your local farmers' market is and check it out

Over to you (aka now get up and do!)

List three or four ideas below for changes you could make to eat and drink more sustainably.

Action	Timeframe
1.	
2.	
3.	
4.	

Resources

- LOVE FOOD HATE WASTE (WWW.LOVEFOODHATEWASTE.COM)
  Lots of great ideas and recipes to help you use up leftover food, including a search bar to allow you to look for recipes for the ingredients you have.

- OLIO (WWW.OLIOEX.COM)
  App and movement that allows you to share food that would otherwise go to waste with your local community.

- ETHICAL CONSUMER (WWW.ETHICALCONSUMER.ORG)
  Provides ethical rankings for all the major UK supermarkets and manufacturers.

- *RIVER COTTAGE: LOVE YOUR LEFTOVERS* BY HUGH FEARNLEY-WHITTINGSTALL (BLOOMSBURY, 2015)
  Creative ideas to transform leftovers into delicious meals.

- THE ZERO WASTE CHEF (WWW.ZEROWASTECHEF.COM)
  Blog by American Anne Marie Bonneau with some great ideas and recipes for cooking from scratch and cooking without waste.

- HUBBUB (WWW.HUBBUB.ORG.UK/THE-COMMUNITY-FRIDGE)
  To find community fridges near you and for information on how to set one up yourself.

- VEGETARIAN LIVING MAGAZINE (WWW.VEGETARIANLIVING.CO.UK)
  For a plethora of veggie recipes and inspiration.

- MEAT FREE MONDAY (WWW.MEATFREEMONDAYS.COM)
  Set up by Paul, Mary and Stella McCartney, this website is packed with meat-free recipes and you can search by ingredient or by meal type, making it super easy to find recipes to suit.

- **THE SOIL ASSOCIATION (WWW.SOILASSOCIATION.ORG)**
  For information about sustainable and organic farming.

- **PALM OIL FREE LIST (WWW.ETHICALCONSUMER.ORG/PALM-OIL-FREE-LIST)**
  A list of UK products that are palm oil free or use sustainably produced palm oil, from Ethical Consumer.

CHAPTER

5

Sustainable(ish) fashion

Clothes – **whether** you're a clothes horse or love nothing better than slobbing out in your PJs, we all need to wear them. There's a widely repeated statistic in ethical circles that the fashion industry is the second most polluting industry on the planet, second only to petrochemicals (fossil fuel). I've done some digging and I'm not sure where it comes from, or even if it stands up to scrutiny, but the fact that so many people believe it *could* be true is perhaps telling of how destructive the industry is.

What is fast fashion?

Fast fashion: inexpensive clothing produced rapidly by mass-market retailers in response to the latest trends.

The rise in fast fashion over the last 20 or 30 years has had catastrophic effects for both the garment workers in the industry and the planet.

Fast fashion is a relatively new phenomenon – not so very long ago there were between two and four seasons for the fashion year when new collections were produced, and now it's up to 52 – one per week. It's just in the last 20 years that it's really become a 'thing'. I have to remind myself that 20 years ago was the late 1990s and not the 1970s – I get that *I've* changed since the late '90s (there's no more late-night partying and a whole lot more adult-ing), but it's worth reminding ourselves that it wasn't always this way.

- Clothing production doubled between 2002 and 2015.
- Globally we consume 80 billion pieces of clothing every year.
- It's estimated that more than half of fast fashion produced is disposed of in under a year.
- It takes 2720L of water to make one T-shirt, (to grow the cotton, dye it and process it into fabric). That's the same amount of water as you would drink in three years.
- Garment workers typically earn between 1 and 3 per cent of the retail price of an item of clothing. So if a T-shirt costs £8, the person who made it receives 24p at most.
- Beading and sequins can be an indication of child labour.
- Globally, one bin lorry of clothing is landfilled or burned every second.
- As little as 10–30 per cent of all the clothing donated to charity shops is sold on in the shops themselves – the rest goes to landfill or is sold to developing countries, where it can flood the market and kill local industry.
- According to fashion activist Orsola de Castro in the documentary film *RiverBlue*:

'There is a joke in China that you can predict the "it" colour of the season by looking at the colour of the rivers.'

While the fact that we all wear clothes makes us part of the problem, the good news is that it also gives us the chance to be part of the solution.

In Chapter 1, I shared with you what I think is one of my all-time favourite quotes – by Anna Lappé (if I were brave enough to get a tattoo, it might have to be this):

'Every time you spend money, you are casting a vote for the kind of world you want.'

It's time for a little bit of tough love. Brace yourselves. Every time you buy fast fashion, you're casting a vote for: child labour; sweatshops; women (around 80 per cent of garment workers are women) working in unsafe, unhygienic conditions for 12+ hours a day and not being paid a living wage (across Asia in 2015 the national minimum wage was anywhere between 18 and 66 per cent of the living wage – the amount required to cover a worker's basic needs and the needs of her family); pollution of waterways on a vast scale; desertification of whole areas; and cotton farmer suicide (in the past 15 years there have been 250,000 cotton farmer suicides in India because they simply can't make ends meet).

That probably isn't what you're thinking about when you pop into town and get lured into buying just a couple of cheap things that won't make much of a dent in your bank balance. But this is what it means. By this small action you're saying that this is OK. That the health and well-being of other people, sometimes other children, across the globe is less important to you than a T-shirt you might only wear a couple of times.

I'm pretty sure none of us want that. But I think many of us just assume that the fashion industry is looking after its workers, if we think about it at all. That yes, clothing is cheaper than it's ever been, but that's because it's now all produced by machine. Before I started researching this area I never really gave much thought to how my clothes were made, but if I did stop to think, I just assumed that it was all done by machine. It would never have occurred to me that some poor woman was sitting at a sewing machine sewing the same seam on the same T-shirts for 12 hours or more a day, six or seven days a week. But it IS happening. And it's happening on our watch, to fuel **our** demand for ever cheaper, disposable clothes. So what can we do about it? Quite a lot, as it happens… Remember the brilliant buyerarchy of needs from Chapter 1? It applies to clothes as much as it does to everything else.

Use what you have

Aka shop your wardrobe, drawers and cupboards to unearth clothes you may well have forgotten about.

- Set aside an afternoon and go through your wardrobe. Empty out your wardrobe, your drawers, the box under the bed etc and dump it all in a pile on the bed. You may well be shocked by how much there actually is. I always thought I had a pretty minimal wardrobe, but this little exercise proved me wrong!
- Go through it piece by piece and create some piles, for example:
  - Keepers – it fits, I love it and I wear it all the time.
  - Maybes – this could be the stuff that you're waiting to fit into again (be honest, are you ever going to be size 8/10/12 again? If not, ditch it) or the stuff you love on the hanger but you're not sure actually suits you.
    Confession: I have a few of these.
  - Mending pile – anything that you want to keep but that needs a little TLC.
  - No. Just no. The stuff that is never going to fit again, that you're not sure what kind of life you were imagining you lead when you bought them (I'm thinking white trousers – my life is not a white trousers kind of life), the stuff that is saggy and worn, anything that doesn't make you feel good when you wear it.
- Pop the keepers back in the wardrobe and drawers. Hang as much up as you can/have space for – if you can see it easily, you're more likely to wear it! Also, hanging stuff together might give you some more ideas for how to mix and match different things to create different outfits. This doesn't have to be any kind of fashionista

capsule wardrobe, it can be as simple as realising you can wear a jumper over your dress...

- Separate the noes into stuff that can go to the charity shop, and stuff that will have to be consigned to the textile recycling bin – as discussed on page 44, please please don't donate anything to a charity shop that you wouldn't be happy to buy yourself.
- Create a mending pile. If you've got the skills, set aside some time to tackle it yourself. Alternatively, pass it on to someone who does have the time and skills – whether that's your mum, or the mending lady at the sewing machine shop in town (there are more and more of these wonderful beings around, so do have a look). If you're not prepared to pay for it to be mended, you probably didn't really love it enough for it to earn a space in your wardrobe anyway.
- For the maybes, pop them away under your bed or in a drawer for a month or two and see if you miss them. If you don't, donate them.

Borrow

This probably wouldn't work that well for your whole wardrobe, but if you've got a wedding or a Christmas party to go to, why not borrow rather than buy?

- Ask similar sized friends if you can have a rummage through their wardrobe.
- Have a look and see if there are any dress agencies near you where you can rent a dress for an evening. Look online – you can even rent the bags and shoes to match as well. You can also rent more day-to-day work outfits.
- Check out Wear the Walk (www.wearthewalk.co.uk) – you can rent one-off dresses, or take out a monthly subscription to rent from four to unlimited items for a month and then simply return them.
- Another fabulous initiative is Mud Jeans (www.mudjeans.eu) – a sustainable Dutch fashion brand who produce 'circular jeans'. Their jeans are made using a mix of virgin organic cotton, blended with the fibres from recycled jeans. You can lease a pair of jeans for a year, and then decide to either keep them or return them to be recycled while you pick another pair. The idea is that the company retain ownership of the raw materials so that they can be used again and ensure they never go to waste. Genius!

Swap

Swapping, or 'swishing', is a brilliant way to extend the life of clothes you no longer wear. And it's catching on. Swishes can be anything from you and your mates getting together with the contents of your respective wardrobes that you are now bored of and a bottle of wine for a Friday night catch-up and swap, through to a full-on 'charge on the door' event, with wine and canapés, that only accepts designer gear. And everything in between.

Here's a few reasons why swishing is ace:

1   It keeps clothes out of landfill and in use for longer (*see* the Did you Know? stat above).
2   It prevents us swamping the already bulging charity shops with our unwanted clothes.
3   You get to refresh your wardrobe for free or for very little.
4   It's a brilliant way to start conversations around fast fashion without being 'that person who is always banging on about the planet'.

Check out www.swishing.com to see if there are any events near you. And if there aren't, you could consider running your own (don't roll your eyes, I promise you it is SUPER simple!).

Thrift

Shopping secondhand is far and away my favourite way to shop. It's less overwhelming (does anyone else get paralysed with ALL the choice when they shop on the high street? No? Just me then…). It's invariably cheaper. And it's less guilt-inducing, both on the financial and eco side. Do be aware, though, that shopping secondhand doesn't give you carte blanche to start buying stuff willy-nilly and ramming it into your wardrobe.

> *Confession: I got a little secondhand-happy at the start of our year buying nothing new and having never owned a 'casual' dress in my life, I soon found myself the proud owner of four. Only one of which I still have.*

I guess if you're going to be a part of the fast fashion cycle, then buying and re-donating back to charity shops is way better than buying new and then discarding, but ultimately what we all need to be aiming for is to buy LESS and buy BETTER. So be selective. Just because something is cheap and in your size doesn't mean you have to buy it.

Things to ask yourself:

* Does it fit? And be honest.

> *Confession: I was looking for some black jeans and found some in a charity shop, but they were a size 8 (I'm a 10). I persuaded myself they fitted and bought them, but now I don't wear them as they make me feel fat and give me tummy ache when I sit down...*

* Will it go with the other stuff in my wardrobe?
* Does it need dry cleaning or handwashing? If you're more careful about your sorting and washing than I am, this might not be an issue for you, but in my house if it can't survive a 30ºC eco wash, it will never be cleaned.
* Will I wear it? This might sound like a stupid question, but there's no point buying the most beautiful party dress if you never go to parties.
* Do I need it? If you don't, be honest with yourself about why you're buying it (or even shopping in the first place). If you're fed up/bored/feeling like you deserve a treat, is there another way you can self-medicate?

Could you go on a fast fashion fast?

Jo is a member of my Sustainable(ish) Facebook community and hasn't bought any new clothes for the last 12 months. I asked her some questions about the experience.

Q What made you want to reduce your purchases of/reliance on fast fashion?

A I started to reduce the amount of plastic we were purchasing and that in turn made me look at the waste we produced, so it's not just fast fashion I have reduced. Watching *The True Cost* (*see* page 135) should be compulsory!

Q Did you set yourself any 'rules' about where you can buy clothes or what brands you could buy?

A I wasn't too hard on myself but if I saw something I thought I liked/needed, I made a decision to leave it 24 hours and if I still wanted it I would get it. I never did. Secondhand is now first choice.

Q What's the hardest thing about avoiding fast fashion?

A The lack of ethical high street shops doesn't make it easy.

Q What's the best thing about avoiding fast fashion?

A Not having so much 'stuff'! I feel a lot happier as my house is getting decluttered.

Q What tip would you give to anyone thinking about a 'fast fashion fast'?

A Have a 24-hour cooling off period and do an audit of what you already have.

Five places to find secondhand clothes online

1 **eBay (www.ebay.co.uk)** This is an obvious one, but it's popular for a reason – most people know of it and lots of us use it. Search by brand and size to narrow down your search. And make sure you check the 'used' box in the search criteria, otherwise you'll be trawling through all the new stuff too.

2 **Facebook groups** If you're looking for a particular brand, you might well hit lucky with a Facebook search for selling groups for specific makes. I found a Boden and Joules Pre-loved Adults Clothing group with a 60-second search.

3 **Oxfam online (www.oxfam.org.uk/shop)** There's a huge range of secondhand clothes in the Oxfam online store, from the kind of stuff you might find on eBay through to real vintage gems. There aren't the same amusing dodgy selfie shots that you get on eBay, meaning that it's easier to see what you're buying, and it's easy to search by size etc. The items are priced realistically – they aren't necessarily the prices you might expect to see in charity shops, but you're getting all the thrill and the warm glow of shopping in a charity shop, from the comfort of your sofa. Which some argue is a price worth paying.

4 **Depop (www.depop.com)** I confess I had no idea of the existence of this site until it came up in an online search. I tweeted to ask if anyone cooler than me could explain it to me and got this reply:

> 'It's the Etsy for Gen Z with a UI that resembles Instagram. Mostly vintage, sometimes there is handmade artsy stuff, with some new stuff when people resell China junk.'

I was delighted to understand at least some of the words used. UI I think stands for User Interface (feel free to laugh at me and correct me if I'm wrong). Gen Z I have no idea. I've just about got my head around millennials and feeling left out at missing out on being cool by a couple of years. It all looks very pretty though, and does indeed resemble Instagram – all the pictures are square boxes, mostly with achingly hip people pouting and showing off their clothes. But on Depop the clothes are for sale.

5 Vinted (www.vinted.com) Another new one on me but I like this on their 'About' page:

> 'We want to show you just how brilliant secondhand can be. Sell the clothes that have more to give. Shop for items you won't find on the high street. Vinted is open to everyone who believes that good clothes should live long.'

You can customise your feed to your personalised settings, saving you having to scroll through pages of stuff you're not interested in, and you can also swap stuff too!

Make

You may well think I'm bonkers for even including this on the list, but there's a growing community of sewers and crafters out there making their own wonderful creations. Making your own clothes is no longer the realm of scratchy Nana jumpers and 1970s' Simplicity patterns and Clothkits (although Clothkits – www.clothkits.co.uk – are now cool again; they have a range of fabulous patterns, and even some gorgeous organic fabric). There is a whole host of independent microbusinesses run by creative (mostly) women producing gorgeous patterns with (and this bit is important) easy-to-understand instructions. You can also join in with online knit-a-longs (KALs), and crochet-a-longs (CALs), and it's a life-affirming community to be a part of.

There are lots of other advantages too:

- You get to customise the fit and the style to you – so if you've got a big bum, or short legs, or no waist, it doesn't matter!
- You choose the fabric, the colour and the look – no more turning up at a party wearing the same dress as someone else.
- You develop a huge appreciation of the time, energy and skill that goes into making clothes.
- Having invested time and effort making something, you are almost duty bound to love it, to look after it and to wear it for ever.
- Having made the garment in the first place, if it needs adjusting or mending, you can do it far more easily as you have a better understanding of how all the pieces fitted together.

Making your own clothes is the very antithesis of fast fashion. It literally forces you to slow down – there is nothing fast about creating your own clothes. Which in our crazy busy fast-paced world might seem like a ridiculous thing to do, but it's actually hugely empowering. If you're thinking maybe you'd love to have a go, see if there are any classes near you – most sewing and yarn shops now run lessons, as do some adult education centres. You can either join a group or get 1:1 tuition, and learn a skill for life. Alternatively, if you're a bit more confident, take a look on YouTube for some great video tutorials.

Here's a couple of fab online making communities you might like to check out:

- **RAVELRY (WWW.RAVELRY.COM)**
  Ravelry is an online platform for all things yarn – knitting, crochet, weaving, spinning, dyeing. There are free patterns, and independent designers selling their patterns, alongside forums and groups to meet other 'yarny' types, get help and advice and make new friends.

- **THE FOLDLINE (WWW.THEFOLDLINE.COM)**
  The Foldline is a 'sewing community for makers and designers'. There's a whole host of videos and tutorials to help you get started and to inspire your next make, and they support indie pattern designers, providing a platform for them to showcase and sell their patterns.

My only caveat to diving into all things 'make' for sustainable(ish) fashion is to think about the resources that you're using. Making your own clothes obviously means you're side-stepping the whole sweatshop issues (please ensure you have regular loo breaks and a pretty much constant supply of tea and biscuits), but that doesn't mean you're avoiding lots of the other eco-issues around producing fabric or the raw materials needed for your make.

Sustainable fabric

Fabric production is resource and labour intensive – from growing the plants, to harvesting them, processing them and weaving them – all stages involve human labour (and therefore the potential for workers to be exploited) and sometimes heavily industrialised processes.

And that's just for the natural fabrics; synthetic fabrics are by and large made from oil, are plastic based (therefore not biodegradable) and shed plastic microfibres when they're washed (*see* page 127 for more on microfibres).

Conventional cotton production is a water- and pesticide-intense process. Organic cotton is a much kinder fabric for the planet and the dyes used are usually more eco-friendly too.

Bamboo is a very popular eco-fabric – it grows super fast and needs much less water and pesticides than cotton. But bamboo canes are hard, and turning them into silky smooth fabric takes a vast amount of water, and sometimes toxic chemicals. There are some great manufacturers who contain these chemicals in a 'close-loop' system, meaning they are recycled and used again and again, reducing the carbon and water footprint of these textiles. But less reputable manufacturers will most likely wash the toxic chemical straight back into the environment. Lyocell (made from wood pulp) and TENCEL® (made from sustainably sourced eucalyptus pulp) are two other fabrics that both use non-toxic chemicals in a closed loop system and are worth looking out for.

Linen gets a thumbs up (as does hemp) – it's made from the fibres of the flax plant and doesn't take vast amounts of chemicals or water to grow. In its undyed state it is biodegradable so the fabric will break down when garments are no longer wearable.

Check out Offset Warehouse (www.offsetwarehouse.com) for a brilliant range of ethical and sustainable fabrics.

Secondhand fabric

Buying fabric secondhand can be a good option. Charity shops often have sheets and duvet covers for only a couple of pounds, providing you with a lot of fabric for not a lot of money.

You can also buy fabric online on places like eBay and can find some lovely vintage and retro prints.

Bear in mind, though, that you might not be able to ascertain what the fabric is made from, meaning you might end up with synthetic fabrics and the resultant concerns about microfibre pollution (*see* page 127). However, if you're making cushions or bunting or things that won't be washed, this really isn't so much of an issue.

Sustainable yarn

Acrylic yarn is made from oil and therefore doesn't really come very high up the sustainability stakes. Pure wool is miles better (although be aware that 'washable wool' has often been coated in plastic in order to make it washable) and there are loads of small independent yarn makers and dyers online that can show you the sheep that the yarn was spun from (and probably know their names).

Buy

Buying new clothes is the way the majority of us shop, but for sustainable(ish) fashion, it should be the cherry on the cake. I'm not suggesting for a moment that you never buy new clothes ever again, but as a result of what I've learned about the fast fashion industry, I have avoided the high street brands ever since. Instead I've chosen to spend my money casting my vote for a fairer, cleaner, more transparent fashion industry by seeking out ethical and sustainable brands.

Here are five of my favourites:

- People Tree
- Thought
- Finisterre
- Howies
- Monkee genes/Huitt

One of the main things that I think stops many people buying more sustainably and ethically when it comes to fashion (and probably most things) is the price difference. It can come as a shock to see the cost of some ethically made items, especially if we're used to fast fashion prices.

But it's important to remember that the price of ethically made clothes is a truer reflection of what it cost to make them. The 'true cost' of cheap fast fashion is paid by the garment workers, the cotton farmers, and the environment. We don't see, or pay, the true cost.

So if you're looking to buy ethical, but struggling to reconcile the cost, remember this:

- To quote Vivienne Westwood, 'Buy less, buy better, make it last.' Buy fewer, well-made, carefully chosen pieces that you absolutely adore and will cherish and love for years to come.
- Only buy something if you think you will wear it 30 times – the 30 wears campaign was started by Livia Firth (sustainable fashion campaigner and wife of a certain actor) and is a great rule of thumb to use when you're tempted to buy something new.
- 'Buying less costs less.' I totally love this mantra from Elizabeth L. Cline's book *Overdressed*.
- It's not all or nothing – mix and match a few key sustainable new pieces that you will keep for years with some charity shop bits and maybe a couple of vintage finds.

Love your clothes

I've talked a bit already about only buying clothes if you really love them. If they make you feel a million dollars rather than just 'meh' or even downright crappy.

Confession: not even 50 per cent of my wardrobe makes me feel a million dollars – it's a work in progress.

We need to learn to love our clothes (in fact, all of our things) again, and only give wardrobe or house space to the things that earn their place in our affections. And once we've found those things, we need to look after them – honouring the resources and the labour that has gone into making them, and keeping them in use for as long as possible.

'Care for your clothes like the good friends they are.'

Joan Crawford

- Wash less – if it's not dirty, don't wash it! Sometimes all things need is an airing either on the line outside or hanging up in your bedroom before putting away.
- My jeans often go a good couple of weeks in between washes and I will quite often just sponge the mud off the kids' school trousers and put them out for them to wear again (but that might be more down to my dislike of housework than a burning desire for their school trousers to last).
- When you do wash, look at the care labels and ideally wash at 30°C.
- Treat stains as soon as you see them:
  - Fairy washing-up liquid is the absolute best thing for getting grease stains out – squeeze a blob on, rub it in gently and then wash as normal.
  - Soak blood stains in cold water before washing – soaking in warm or hot water sets the stain in place.
- Mend stuff as soon as you spot it – *see* Chapter 2 for more info on clothes repairs.
- Hang your clothes up when you're not wearing them.

This is a case of do as I say, not as I do – I have the world's largest 'chair-drobe' in the corner of our bedroom.

- Wear an apron. I'm not trying to drag you back to the 1950s and wearing a housecoat, I promise, but if you're as messy a cook as me, donning a pinny to make the tea can save your clothes from a myriad of grease stains and splashes.

MICROFIBRES

Every time we wash synthetic clothes (nylon, polyester, polyester blends, acrylic), tiny fibres are shed into the water. And as these clothes are made from synthetic materials, these fibres are actually teeny-tiny plastic particles. They're so small they pass through the filters at water processing plants, heading out into our waterways and ending up in the ocean.

And then what happens to the microplastics in the ocean is that they enter the food chain, starting off with tiny zooplankton, until eventually they reach us, and other top chain predators, and we start to accumulate teeny-tiny plastic particles in our own bodies.

DID YOU KNOW?

Up to 700,000 microplastic fibres are released from a single clothes wash.

That's a staggering number.

There needs to be a LOT more research done into this, and manufacturers are already working on producing filters for washing machines to capture microfibres, but while we're waiting for policy and technology to catch up, what can *we* do about the problem in our own homes?

At the moment there isn't an easy answer, but here are some ideas to help reduce the amount of microfibres coming from your home and wardrobe:

- Wash less – the less you wash, the fewer chances your clothes have to shed microfibres (*see* tips on page 127 for washing less).
- Wash at 30ºC and on an eco cycle – the more water there is in the washing cycle, the more likely clothes are to shed fibres.
- Wash full loads only – when the machine is full, there is less room for the clothes to move around against each other, less friction between them, and therefore fewer microfibres are shed.
- Ditch the tumble dryer, or only use when you absolutely have to. Using a tumble dryer can cause the fibres in our clothes to become more brittle and therefore more likely to break off.
- Choose natural fibres when buying new clothes, so cotton, wool or linen.

- Wash fleeces as infrequently as possible – many fleeces are now made from recycled plastic bottles, which we've always thought was a great thing. But now it turns out that we might just be swapping the macroplastic problem into a microplastic one as these are one of the worst culprits for shedding microfibres when washed.

- Avoid microfibre cleaning cloths – again, another thing we were sold as being the green option. When they first came out, they were heralded as the ultimate in eco-friendly cleaning as using them meant you needed no, or at least fewer, cleaning chemicals. Unfortunately, as the name suggests, microfibre cloths are made of microfibres, and are therefore contributing to microplastic pollution each time we use or wash them. Look out for cleaning cloths made from natural fibres (for example, organic cotton) or cut up old clothes to use for cleaning rags.

- Consider investing in a Guppyfriend bag (www.guppyfriend. com). This is a bag that you put your synthetic clothes into and then place in the washing machine. In tests it prevented 99 per cent of microfibres making their way into the water. Any fibres collected in the bag should be binned – apparently, modern landfill sites are lined to prevent chemicals leaching into the environment, meaning that microfibres in landfill aren't simply washed into the waterways each time it rains (this was one of my concerns). We bought a Guppyfriend bag a couple of months ago and I'm ridiculously excited every time I see a little collection of microfibres forming inside.

WHAT TO DO WITH CLOTHES YOU NO LONGER WANT OR NEED

There will always be clothes in our wardrobes that no longer fit, that we no longer love, or that are simply beyond repair. But whatever you do, **don't put them in the bin**. A lorry full of clothes is tipped into landfill every single minute where it sits and rots, contributing to greenhouse emissions, as well as being a massive waste of resources.

Here are five things you can do with your old clothes so they never reach the bin:

1　If they're in good condition and simply no longer fit or you've fallen out of love with them, swap them with friends, or go to a swish (*see* page 118) or simply pass them on to friends (especially kids' clothes).

2　If they just need a simple repair, have a go! YouTube is your friend when it comes to videos for simple repairs like sewing on a button or patching a hole.

3　Upcycle them. Get creative and think of old clothes purely as fabric. Old jeans are brilliant for upcycling – the simplest being chopping off the legs to create denim shorts. Or stuffing a leg with other old

Fast fashion and charity shops

I think most of us assume that when we donate clothes to our local charity shop, they are sold on in our local charity shop to people in our community. What could be simpler? Well, just as the fashion industry for new clothes is complex, so are the markets for secondhand clothes, as I discovered when I read Andrew Brooks' book *Clothing Poverty*. He cites that the rise in fast fashion in the global North has led to a decrease in the market for secondhand clothes in places like the UK and the US, and the rise in fast fashion means that billions of secondhand garments are traded globally every year. In fact, Brooks estimates that of the clothing donated to UK charities, only 10–30 per cent is actually sold in the UK. Which has led to charity shops and textile recyclers looking for new markets and the emergence of a secondhand clothing trade that was valued at more than $4.3 billion in 2013, with the UK being the second largest exporter in the world.

Shoes

Shoes don't escape the sustainable(ish) ethos and just as clothes consumption has increased, our buying of shoes has done the same. According to Po-Zu (a fabulous ethical shoe company), we each send an fabric, sewing up the end and creating a draught excluder! Have a look on Pinterest for ideas for jeans upcycling and never throw out a pair of jeans again.

4 Reuse them. Old T-shirts (and even pants!) can get a second life as cleaning cloths and face flannels.

5 Recycle them. Lots of local authorities will collect fabric and textiles as part of their kerbside collections, but if not, there will be a textile bin at your local recycling centre. Clothes that are recycled are made into things like packing blankets or sold as packs of rags for the motor trade, for example.

Is this a bad thing? It's hard to tell and there are two schools of thought explored in the book. One is that the secondhand clothing market is killing off local economies in places like Mozambique, Nigeria and Pakistan. The counter argument is that there are benefits to be gained by the creation of local jobs sorting and selling on the West's unwanted clothes.

Unsurprisingly, it's complicated. With a trade worth billions of dollars each year that criss-crosses the globe, there is a lack of transparency and research into the impacts, and unfortunately opportunities for abuse. I'm not saying don't donate your clothes to charity shops. What I am saying is **charity shops shouldn't be the panacea for our overconsumption**. The fact that the clothes can be passed on to someone else (either locally or on the other side of the world) doesn't give us the green light to continue to consume fashion at the rate that we are. Regardless of where the clothes end up, their production is damaging the planet that we all need to live on, and is exploiting people in the developing world.

Think before you buy. Ask yourself #whomademyclothes (*see* page 269) and also where will this end up?

average of three pairs of shoes to landfill each year, and traditional shoe-making has made way for mass production, seeing the same exploitation of workers as in the garment industry.

But ethical shoes are harder to track down than ethical clothes. Here are a few suggestions:

Po-Zu (www.po-zu.com)

Po-Zu was the first ethical shoe brand that I came across and I am a total fan. They create 'sustainable and ethically sourced shoes, made from carefully selected natural and sustainable materials that are healthy for your feet, kind to the environment and safe for all our workers throughout the supply chain'.

They have both men's and ladies' shoes, as well as some kids' shoes, and even a range of *Star Wars* shoes (check out the Chewbacca boots…).

Green Shoes (www.greenshoes.co.uk)

Green Shoes is a collective and collaborative workplace run by women, and the shoes are all handmade in Devon in the UK from either sustainably sourced leather or vegan materials. All the shoes are fully repairable and can be resoled (in fact, the kids' shoes can be resoled up a size, making them better value for money), meaning a pair of shoes should genuinely last you a lifetime.

I loved this paragraph from their 'about us' page.

'Wearing Green Shoes is more than a fashion statement. It is a refusal to endorse the global system of brand name mass-produced shoe-manufacture. We are shoemakers with attitude, and make no apology.'

It's a shoe-based revolution!

Vivobarefoot (www.vivobarefoot.com)

The main USP of these shoes is their 'barefooted-ness' but they seem to be a pretty ethical bunch. All of their leather is sourced sustainably and they only work with factories who follow their code of conduct on human rights. It's also the only place I've been able to find anything that vaguely resembles a school shoe for the kids.

Veja (www.veja-store.com)

Veja are an ethical trainer brand who aim to 'create a supply chain that protects both humans and the environment'.

Dr Martens (www.drmartens.com)

Turns out good old DMs are pretty ethical – who knew? They have some pretty robust environmental and ethical policies on their website, and they are generally well known for being hard-wearing and made to last.

5 QUICK SUSTAINABLE(ISH) FASHION WINS

1 **Shop your wardrobe** I guarantee you have more clothes than you think, and with a little bit of thought they can probably be combined into all kinds of new combos, giving you the illusion (and satisfaction) of a new wardrobe without the expense to your bank balance or the planet.

2 **Never, ever, ever throw clothes in the landfill bin** *See* page 129 for the alternatives.

3 **Wash less** Best quick win ever! Only wash your clothes when they really need it – it helps clothes to last longer and reduces the environmental impact of all that washing and drying.

4 **Unsubscribe!** Unsubscribe from all the tempting emails that drop into your inbox with details of the newest range, or the latest sale. Make it easier for yourself by removing the temptation, meaning that when you do visit clothing sites you're doing it on your terms, when you want or need something, rather than because they told you to.

5 **A challenge if you choose to accept it...** Could you go a month without buying any clothes? Or three months buying only secondhand clothes? Obviously, during our year of buying

nothing new I bought no brand new clothes for that whole year, and I then went a step further a while later and spent a year buying no clothes at all. If you're a bit of a fashion addict, and find that you shop on your lunch break, or on your phone when you're watching telly, or when you're bored or sad or pretty much any other emotion, this kind of 'cold turkey' therapy can be a really effective intro to a slower way of shopping.

MORE SUGGESTIONS:

- ☐ Commit to buying a percentage of your clothes secondhand – it could be 50 per cent or 90 per cent – whatever feels doable for you

- ☐ Wash your clothes at 30ºC

- ☐ Look for natural fibres such as cotton (ideally organic), linen and wool

- ☐ Share clothes with your friends!

- ☐ Shop vintage

- ☐ Check out www.swishing.com to see if there's a swish happening near you

- ☐ Get yourself a Guppyfriend (www.guppyfriend.com) to help tackle microfibre pollution when you wash

- ☐ Look for your favourite brands secondhand on eBay

- ☐ Join in with Fashion Revolution Week in April and ask manufacturers #whomademyclothes?

- ☐ Do a wardrobe audit (*see* page 116)

- ☐ If you're a maker, or an aspiring maker, source your raw materials secondhand or sustainably – swap acrylic yarn for real wool, and look out for organic cotton

Over to you (aka now get up and do!)

List three or four ideas below for changes you could make to your wardrobe and the clothes you buy.

Action	Timeframe
1.	
2.	
3.	
4.	

Resources

- THE TRUE COST MOVIE (WWW.TRUECOSTMOVIE.COM)
  This is a groundbreaking documentary film that pulls back the curtain on the untold story and asks us to consider who really pays the price for our clothing?

- RIVERBLUE (WWW.RIVERBLUETHEMOVIE.ECO)
  This film travels the globe to investigate the impact of the fashion industry on the world's rivers, and on humanity, and looks at solutions that inspire hope for a more sustainable future.

- *TO DIE FOR: IS FASHION WEARING OUT THE WORLD?* BY LUCY SIEGLE (FOURTH ESTATE, 2011)
  An in-depth exploration into the fashion industry by ethical journalist and presenter Lucy Siegle.

- *OVERDRESSED: THE SHOCKINGLY HIGH COST OF CHEAP FASHION BY ELIZABETH L. CLINE (PORTFOLIO, 2013)*

  Published in 2013 this book explores the fast fashion industry: why we have ended up with so many clothes that cost so little, and the implications that this has for people and the planet.

- *SLAVE TO FASHION BY SAFIA MINNEY (NEW INTERNATIONALIST, 2017)*

  Founder of People Tree, the sustainable fashion brand, Safia brings her expertise and experiences of the fashion industry to life in this book with interviews with those caught up in slavery and working in the fashion industry. Coupled with practical solutions and ideas we can all do, this is a powerful book.

- LOVE YOUR CLOTHES (WWW.LOVEYOURCLOTHES.ORG)

  The Love Your Clothes campaign aims to help change the way UK consumers buy, use and dispose of their clothing. It's packed with resources and tutorials to help you keep your clothes in use for longer, from how to wash them well through to tutorials for mending.

- FASHION REVOLUTION (WWW.FASHIONREVOLUTION.ORG)

  A global movement that runs all year long, questioning current standards within the fashion industry and encouraging those who are on a journey to create a more ethical and sustainable future for fashion.

6

Sustainable(ish) family

In this chapter we're exploring the sustainable(ish) changes we can make as a family, and we're looking at family in the widest sense – whether you're married with 2.4 kids, or live on your own with your cat, or you see your friends as your family – there are things we can do to limit the impact of our family life. Families are complicated beasts even at the best of times, and making changes as a family can sometimes be the most challenging. It's one thing to change our own behaviours, it's quite another to try and influence others around to change at the same time.

Getting the family on board

Making sustainable(ish) changes can feel lonely sometimes, as if you're the only one trying to do things a bit differently (please, please know that you aren't), and if your family aren't in the same place as you it has the potential to cause a *teeny* bit of friction. I asked my Sustainable(ish) Facebook community for some suggestions to help us all have 'those conversations' and the top one was to do a beach clean together or litter pick when you're out for a walk (*see* page 68 for #2minutebeachclean).

Here are some other ideas:

- **DO A PLASTIC AUDIT TOGETHER (SEE PAGE 70)**
  For family members who live with you, including kids, do a plastic audit together. Tell them you're really keen to try and reduce the amount of single-use plastic you're getting through and ask for

their help collecting all the plastic rubbish for the week. If you have kids this can be a brilliant way to get them on board, although you may end up regretting it when they turn into officious plastic monitors and start picking out the chocolate wrapper you tried to smuggle into the bin. When the week is over, go through the plastic rubbish together and brainstorm suggestions and alternatives – you're far more likely to get buy-in that way than if you try imposing changes in a dictatorial fashion.

- **WATCH A MOVIE TOGETHER**
  (*See* the box on page 140 for suggestions).

- **SHOW DON'T TELL**
  Make the changes you want to make, and be seen doing them. Sustainable changes need to become the 'norm' and it needs to become totally normal to see people making different choices. Not so long ago you might have felt a little bit awkward about presenting your reusable cup at the coffee shop, now no one bats an eyelid. Being one of the first people to be seen to be doing these things can sometimes feel a little bit scary, but you will be surprised by the conversations it starts with other people (the people in the queue behind you, for example). By doing these things, you're almost giving other people permission to do them too – to feel OK about 'coming out' and being seen to be making different choices.

- **BE OPEN TO CONVERSATIONS, BUT DON'T SHOVE THEM DOWN PEOPLE'S THROATS**
  If you have a friend who is bemoaning the fact that their black bin is full to overflowing each fortnight, commiserate and share the story of how you used to be the same, and how pleasantly surprised you've been at the difference a couple of really easy changes have made.

- **EMBRACE THE 'ISH'!**
  Accept that there will always be a degree of compromise. If I lived on my own I would no doubt be pretty hardcore. I'm fairly all

or nothing in my approach to lots of things, so I think I would have a tendency to be pretty militant and never let a bag of crisps into the house. But I don't live on my own. I have a husband, and two kids. All of whom add to my life immeasurably but annoyingly have their own opinions and focuses. Which a lot of the time don't match mine. But that's part of being a family – annoying the hell out of each other and rubbing along anyway. Finding your way through and trying to work out something that works for everyone (this very rarely happens). You may have to compromise, and chip away at them bit by bit, but that's OK. Just keep taking those steps and doing your best to bring them along for the ride.

- **DON'T JUDGE**
  Sometimes friends and family might feel like we're judging them if we pass comment on the things that they're doing (and let's face it, we kind of are). Starting conversations with things like, 'OMG, I saw this programme/FB post/tweet the other day and it said… I was really shocked and I've decided to try giving up x, or starting to do y. Did you see it? What do you reckon?' is better than accusing them of being planet wreckers when you see them wearing a Primark top.

- **DON'T ASSUME**
  Remember that, especially with friends, we often don't know the whole story. We don't know what additional difficulties or challenges people might be facing, or the very valid reasons they might have for continuing to do things the way they are.

- **FIND MULTIPLE REASONS TO SWITCH**
  Some family members might be more motivated by money than saving the planet, so lead with this if that's the case!

Movies to watch together

All of these films cover big issues that are potentially overwhelming for us as adults. If you are thinking about watching them with your kids, watch on your own first, and then use your own judgement about whether it's something you want to watch with them, depending on their age and sensitivity.

- **THE TRUE COST MOVIE (WWW.TRUECOSTMOVIE.COM)**
  The True Cost is a groundbreaking documentary film released in 2015 that 'pulls back the curtain on the untold story and asks us to consider, who really pays the price for our clothing?' It travels the globe and highlights the stark contrasts between the fashion shows and runways, and the dark cramped factories where our clothes are made, as well as featuring interviews with the likes of Stella McCartney and Livia Firth.

- **BLUE PLANET II**
  This BBC documentary series narrated by national treasure Sir David Attenborough is widely credited with kick-starting the huge public reaction to all things plastic pollution (coined the 'Blue Planet II effect'). The last episode has a short segment on plastic pollution and shows the extent of plastic pollution as experienced by the crew during filming in some of the most remote stretches of water on the planet.

- **A PLASTIC OCEAN (WWW.PLASTICOCEANS.ORG)**
  This film is a tough watch, and has the potential to leave you with more questions than answers, but if you're ready to see the

full impact of our rampant plastic use on the planet, this is the one to watch.

- **OUR PLANET (WWW.OURPLANET.COM)**
The 2019 Netflix documentary series narrated by David Attenborough, exploring the natural wonders of our world and highlighting the damage that we're causing.

- **BEFORE THE FLOOD (WWW.BEFORETHEFLOOD.COM)**
This 2016 film is presented by Leonardo DiCaprio and pulls no punches as he travels around the globe (apparently the carbon emissions from the film were offset!) documenting some of the causes and effects of climate change. It's a sobering watch, but there is some hope towards the end!

- **MY STUFF (WWW.MYSTUFFMOVIE.COM)**
I watched this film at a screening in London where I was part of the Q&A panel alongside the movie's star (I know, get me!) and I really must watch it again. Petri (the main character) has something of an early midlife crisis and decides that the way through it is to put all his stuff into storage (and I mean everything, even his pants…) and then allow himself to take one item out a day for a year. It's really quite funny and an easy watch, but it also raises lots of questions around our relationship with 'stuff' and can be a great one to get those cogs whirring.

- **STORY OF STUFF (WWW.STORYOFSTUFF.ORG)**
The original *Story of Stuff* movie was released in 2007. It's just 20 minutes long, really accessible, and powerful without being too heavy and worthy. There's a selection of other movies on the *Story of Stuff* site, including the *Story of Electronics*, the *Story of Microfibers*, and the *Story of Cosmetics*.

Sustainable(ish) kids

Babies and toddlers

The temptation when expecting a new baby (at least with the first, anyway) is to rush out and buy ALL the things. And to buy them new. And I get that when you're thinking about a precious new human being you want everything to be clean and untouched by human hand, but new babies actually need surprisingly little, and they need very little of it new.

Here's some ideas for how to find the things you need for a fraction of the price and planetary impact.

- **HAND-ME-DOWNS**

  If friends or family offer you outgrown baby clothes, their old pram or a Moses basket (*see* page 143 for more info on mattresses), say yes!

- **EBAY**

  Look out for bundles of baby clothes in appropriate sizes/genders, and larger items like buggies. Restricting your search to your local area and collection only can help to reduce postage costs.

- **CHARITY SHOPS**

  If you've got the time and energy for a mooch round the local charity shops once your maternity leave starts, you may well pick up some bits and pieces there. Alternatively, this is a good strategy to use to divert overly attentive grandparents-to-be from Mamas and Papas – give them a list and ask them to scout out the local charity shops for you.

- **NEARLY NEW BABY SALES (NOT SELLING BABIES, OBVS)**

  The National Childbirth Trust (NCT) has local groups all around the country that often hold regular 'nearly new' sales. These are not for the faint-hearted and the ones I've been to have been akin to a rugby scrum, but you can pick up not only clothes, but also buggies, highchairs, play mats, toys. The list goes on. There are other nearly new sales too, in addition to NCT ones, so do ask around on local parenting FB groups etc.

- FACEBOOK BUY/SELL/SWAP GROUPS
  Pretty much every town will have at least one local buy/sell/swap group on Facebook – have a look on here to see what people are getting rid of that you might be able to make use of.

- FREECYCLE/FREEGLE
  Join your local Freecycle (www.freecycle.org) or Freegle (www.ilovefreegle.org) group and keep your eye out for any baby-related items. Alternatively, post a 'WANTED' for specific items and you might be pleasantly surprised.

Things you should never get secondhand for babies

- MATTRESSES
  'There is some research that found an increased chance of SIDS when using a secondhand mattress brought in from outside of the family home, although the link is not yet proven. To help reduce this risk, if you are using a secondhand mattress make sure the mattress you choose was previously completely protected by a waterproof cover, with no rips or tears and is in good condition. The mattress should also still be firm and flat to keep your baby sleeping safely.'

  The Lullaby Trust, a charity that works to raise awareness of Sudden Infant Death Syndrome (SIDS – previously called Cot Death)

  Personally, we didn't want to take the risk and bought new mattresses for both children, although we happily used the Moses basket donated to us by friends.

- CAR SEATS
  The advice from the Royal Society for the Prevention of Accidents is not to buy a secondhand car seat.

  'You cannot be certain of its history. It may have been involved in an accident and the damage may not be visible. Very often the instructions are missing from secondhand seats, which makes it more difficult to be sure that you are fitting and using it correctly. Secondhand seats are also likely to be older, to have suffered more wear and tear and may not be designed to current safety standards. If you must use a secondhand seat, only accept one from a family member or friend (don't buy one from a secondhand shop, through the classified ads or online). Only accept one from a family member or friend if you are absolutely certain that you know its history, it comes with the original instructions and it is not too old.'

We bought new car seats for child number one, but then used the same car seats for number two. The one time we did have an accident (we were all OK!), we replaced the car seats, and I think this was covered by the insurance company.

• There are a couple of car seat recycling schemes out there (the only ones I could find were in the States) but as yet they aren't widespread. Here's hoping it is something that catches on as there are potentially a lot of resources contained in all those seats that could be put to good use.

BORROW DON'T BUY

If you've got friends or family visiting with a young baby, and they haven't got space in the car for all the paraphernalia that seems to accompany a very small person, see if you can borrow some bits from friends or neighbours. OR take a look at sites like Baby Loft (www.thebabyloft. com) where you can rent everything from buggies to highchairs to car seats for anywhere from three days to a month (renting car seats is OK, as their history should be known, therefore eliminating any concerns that they might have been involved in accidents).

If you're thinking about going 'hands-free' and using a sling – super useful for second (or first!) babies, babies that won't sleep, or if you live in London and need to use the Underground – but feel bewildered by the array of different types, have a look to see if you have a Sling Library, or any sling meet-ups near you. You should be able to try out some different ones, and even borrow one to take home and see how you get on with it.

SUBSCRIPTION SERVICES

I think this idea originated in Denmark, and there are now a few UK-based businesses offering this service – take a look at Bundlee (www.

bundlee.co.uk). You pay a monthly fee and each month get a new (to you) bundle of baby clothes of the appropriate age and gender. All the clothes are professionally cleaned and quality controlled before being packaged up again. Apparently, the average family in the UK will spend around £1000 on clothes and shoes in the first year for their little person, and that's without even buying higher end brands. Using one of these subscription services can make good financial sense and drastically cuts down on your baby's clothing footprint.

NAPPIES

There's no avoiding the issue of nappies with babies, although I am told some people do – look up elimination communication (there's even an app for it: www.happynonappy.com) – but what's the best thing to do for the planet (and your baby's bum)?

There is sometimes debate over which is better for the planet – reusable nappies or disposables – when you factor in things like the water and energy needed to wash and dry reusables etc. If you wash at 60°C and tumble-dry your nappies, then any carbon savings might be eaten away at, so make sure you wash at 30°C and line dry whenever possible. I am, however, of the opinion that the reusable option for anything is better than a single-use option in 99.9 per cent of cases (I confess to not being able to think what the 0.1 per cent might be, but I'm leaving myself some wriggle room for emails correcting me on my sweeping generalisation).

But as with all things sustainable(ish), it doesn't have to be all or nothing. We used disposables at night for both of ours, and it turns out that going on holiday with disposables and doing a couple of loads less washing for the week feels a lot more like a holiday, so there were occasions when we did that too. Remember, **every single-use nappy you don't use is one less going to landfill**. Don't beat yourself up if you choose disposables when you're out and about, or if you or the baby are poorly, or you have to send them to childcare in disposables. It's about working out what works for you – parenthood is already crammed full of guilt and perceived failings, the very last thing I want to do is to give you one more thing to feel bad about.

Having said that, making the decision to move to reusables (at least some of the time) can be quite liberating. When William was born, I wanted to use reusables but for the first two months, like most new parents, we were like rabbits in the headlights struggling to adjust to our new lives of little or no sleep and pretty much constant anxiety. But every time I put a nappy in the bin I felt guilty. So when I did actually make the switch at around the eight-week mark it actually felt great! I felt like I was actually in control of a decision, and it was a decision that made me feel good about my parenting choices (these can come along very infrequently in my experience…).

Here are some things to know about reusable nappies:

- There are lots of different names for reusable nappies: cloth nappies, reusables, real nappies – they all mean the same thing.
- You can try before you buy – many local authorities will have a Nappy Library. Ours was run by our local Wildlife Trust and we had a lovely man (possibly the only 'Nappy Man' in the country) called Gary come and visit, show me all the options, talk to me

about washing, and leave me with a variety to try. We also got a voucher for money off our first purchase of reusable nappies.

- Reusable nappies aren't the terry towelling monstrosities your mum or Nan might remember. You can get 'all-in-ones' that you put on in pretty much the same way as disposables, and there is a potentially bewildering array of different reusable nappy types and systems.
- You can buy secondhand reusable nappies. This might sound a bit grim, but it's really not. Sometimes people will try a brand and not get on with it, so sell it on when it's barely been used.
- You don't need a tumble dryer to make it doable. We've never had a tumble dryer and at one point we had both kids in cloth nappies at the same time – luckily it was over the summer, so it was much easier to get things washed and dried.
- Dealing with mucky nappies really isn't as grim as you might think. Once you've had a baby you're pretty much constantly dealing with 'emissions' from either end anyway. You flush the poo down the loo and then dump the soiled nappy in your nappy bin to wait to be washed.
- Beware microfibres. Lots of nappy liners and inserts are made of microfibre, because it's absorbent and quick drying. However, since the discovery of microplastic pollution and its impact, if you can find cotton or other alternatives, go with them.

Real nappy sites

- The Nappy Site (www.thenappysite.co.uk)
- The Nappy Lady (www.thenappylady.co.uk)
- Parenting forums like Mumsnet and Netmums usually have dedicated forum threads or sections for real nappy chats.

Biodegradable/eco-friendly disposables

I have to say that I think there is a degree of greenwashing (*see* page 13) going on here. Companies have cottoned on to the fact that some of us are feeling guilty about all the nappies we're sending to landfill, so they've made a few tweaks, and branded some nappies as 'green' and 'eco-friendly'. Even without the sleep deprivation and lack of time to have so much as a shower in peace, let alone research the ins and outs of biodegradable plastics, most of us make the pretty reasonable assumption that 'biodegradable' nappies will break down in landfill and therefore feel happier with the compromise – disposable nappies, but ones that are good for the planet.

I'm sorry to be the bearer of bad tidings here, but as far as I'm aware there is no such thing as a genuinely biodegradable and plastic-free disposable nappy. According to sustainable packaging and plastics expert Sarah Greenwood, the term 'biodegradable' is pretty meaningless – when they're in landfill, these nappies will act in much the same way as regular nappies. They might break down a little quicker (no one has yet lived long enough to know how long it actually takes for a nappy to break down in landfill – estimates are around 500 years, so a little quicker may still be hundreds of years) but they will still release methane when doing so, which is one of the most potent greenhouse gases.

On the plus side they are often made with less plastic, and generally fewer resources and chemicals, but they aren't the nice convenient guilt-free solution some would have us believe (and pay more for as well!).

WIPES

Go back a generation or two and baby wipes didn't even exist, which feels pretty bonkers now when they seem to be seen as an essential part of parenthood. We use them not just for nappy changes, but for cleaning up dirty hands and faces, wiping down chairs and tables and mopping up spills. But baby wipes are bad news for the planet. Most contain non-biodegradable plastics, and despite some being labelled flushable, they make up 93 per cent of the material that causes sewer blockages (aka fatbergs). And they're packaged in plastic and single use. Which as we know now is something to be avoided wherever possible.

During our Make Do and Mend Year we took the plunge and went cold turkey on baby wipes, and do you know what? It was way easier than I feared it would be. We were already using washable wipes for nappy changes, but there was a pack of wipes in the changing bag, on the side in the kitchen, and in pretty much every room of the house to wipe sticky fingers and clear up messes. I cut up some old towels to make flannels, and when we went out I'd take a damp one out with us in a freezer bag (that I reused!).

Companies like Cheeky Wipes (www.cheekywipes.com) make it as easy as it can be to make the switch to washable wipes, with wipes kits to use both at home and when out and about.

A compromise for when you're out and about, or a stepping stone to making the switch to reusables full-time, is Natracare's 'Safe to Flush' wipes – these are paper based (not plastic), will break down harmlessly in your home compost and are the first wipes in the UK to pass the water companies' tests and be certified as flushable.

Kids

TOYS

As soon as you have kids, your house will take on the look of the toy department in John Lewis. Even before they are old enough to hold the weight of their own heads, you will have rattles and cuddly toys and about three different play mats/baby gyms cluttering up your once pristine lounge. And variations on that theme will dominate the look of your house for the next decade or so at least.

To attempt to constrain the toy mountain:

- Buy a couple of key things that will grow with them and can be added to. Our boys got years of use out of a good old wooden railway, and the grandparents seemed quite happy to add to it for birthdays and Christmas, which helped a little to stem the flood of a whole host of other plastic tat. With two boys, Lego is a mainstay in our house and I suspect I will be finding pieces of it under furniture and down the side of the sofa for a good many years after they have left home. Yes it's plastic, but it's not single use. We've even unearthed some of hubby's 'vintage' Lego from his mum's loft (although if you've got complete sets of old Lego they can go for good money on eBay!). Both the Lego and the wooden railway can not only be sourced secondhand but can also be sold or passed on once our kids no longer play with them.

- See if you have a Toy Library near you. These work like a regular library, but for toys. Lots of local councils and Sure Start Centres used to have them, but budget cuts saw many of them run out of funding; however, you might still hit lucky and have one near you.
- Toy swap with friends. This is best done when the kids aren't there, otherwise they all inevitably take their own toys back home with them when they remember that it was their favourite ever toy despite not having played with it for the last six months. Sort out a box of toys your kids haven't played with for a while, and get together with a couple of friends to do a swap.

Online toy swap/subscription sites

- WHIRLI (WWW.WHIRLI.COM)
  Choose from three different monthly subscription packages that give you access to the whole range of toys suitable for pre-schoolers up to age seven. Pick the toys you want, return them once the novelty wears off, and find some more. All the toys are triple checked and sterilised on their return.

CLOTHES

Kids have a habit of growing. And trashing their clothes (or is that just mine?).

Following the same principles for bigger kids as outlined for babies, hit the charity shops! But there will be some occasions when you either need or want to buy new, and the good news is that there is a growing number of sustainable and ethical alternatives.

There are some gorgeous ethical kids' brands, big and small, that you can support safe in the knowledge that the clothes have been

- If you're buying new, buy with longevity in mind. Buy Me Once (www.buymeonce.com) has a great selection of toys all selected because they fit the site's ethos of being built to last.
- Operate a 'one in, one out' policy. It can be all too easy for the toy collection to slowly expand while no one is looking. I found the worst thing was going to the charity shops with the kids and giving in to their demands for yet another toy car 'because it's only 50p'. It might only be 50p but it's still got to find somewhere to live! Now when the kids pester I ask them what they will get rid of, and if they can't think of anything they are willing to sacrifice for the shiny new (to them) excitement, it's a no from me.

- **TOY BOX CLUB (WWW.TOYBOXCLUB.CO.UK)**
  For a monthly fee you receive a box of toys, books and puzzles suitable for pre-school children delivered to your door each month. Each toy is cleaned and checked before being sent out again to a different family.

- **BUILD UR BRICKS (WWW.BUILDURBRICKS.CO.UK)**
  After having to physically clear a path across the floor through the carpet of Lego to say goodnight to my eldest recently, I had the 'amazing idea' of a Lego rental service. Where you can rent Lego sets, and then return them once you've done the fun bit of building them. Thankfully I am spared the need to create this service (and count all those Lego bits) because it already exists!

produced with people and planet in mind. They are almost inevitably more expensive than you might be used to paying on the high street, but as we discussed in Chapter 5, this is a reflection of how far detached we have become from the 'true cost' of our clothes. In my experience, these clothes tend to be of far higher quality and will easily last to be passed down to siblings and cousins etc. Keep your eye out for sales too when you can often pick up a bargain, or when relatives ask what your kids need/want for birthdays and at Christmas, point them to these sites!

- **FRUGI (WWW.WELOVEFRUGI.COM)**
  I love Frugi stuff. All of the bits I have bought my kids have
  been incredibly sturdy and well thought out and have lasted
  through two rough and tumble boys. They go from baby
  and toddler up to 10 years old, and also have maternity stuff
  and bedding.

- **TUTTI FRUTTI CLOTHING (WWW.TUTTIFRUTTICLOTHING.COM)**
  Ali at Tutti Frutti Clothing handmakes all of the beautiful clothes
  in the range herself, using organic bright and colourful fabrics in
  really practical unisex garments.

- **WHERE DOES IT COME FROM? (WWW.WHEREDOESITCOME
  FROM.CO.UK)**
  All the clothes from Where does it come from? come with a code
  on the label that you can enter into their website to find out the
  whole journey and supply chain of your garment. It is the ultimate
  in traceability and a great way to start to talk about some of the
  issues associated with fast fashion with your kids.

- **PATAGONIA (WWW.PATAGONIA.COM)**
  Patagonia are a great example of a big company making every
  effort to reduce its own impact and the impact of its clothes. They
  have a great range not just of coats and outdoor gear but everyday
  wear too.

- **JAKE AND MAYA (WWW.JAKEANDMAYA.COM)**
  Another small independent brand doing great stuff! The
  clothes are designed to be gender neutral, and easily adjustable
  and repairable so they will grow with your kids and last for
  longer. They also have the cutest iron-on plaster patches to aid
  your repairs!

- **NEWBIE (WWW.NEWBIESTORE.COM)**
  One hundred per cent organic clothing made in Sweden. Beautiful
  clothes made in Europe, and reasonably priced too.

SHOES

Ethical options for kids' shoes seem to be few and far between, especially when it comes to school shoes. Shoes for the kids were one of our exceptions for our buying nothing new year – the kids were still really little and I wanted to know that their shoes fitted them properly, and that my crazy idea for a 'fun project' (that turned into so much more!) wasn't going to result in them having deformed feet.

New kids' shoes are expensive enough, especially when you know they will probably grow out of them within months (weeks if you're super unlucky and mistime your buying for just before a growth spurt). Even so, buy the best quality you can afford, especially when it comes to school shoes – they wear these pretty much constantly and on a pay per wear basis they certainly get their money's worth.

In addition to the ethical shoe brands highlighted in Chapter 5, it's worth noting that website Buy Me Once (www.buymeonce.com), which curates its stock based on longevity and quality, includes Start-Rite shoes in its kids' shoe section – pointing to them being a brand that are made to stand up to the rigours of daily wear and tear. If you can't find a 'properly' sustainable option, then buying to last is the next best.

Are secondhand shoes ok?

Was I right to be worried about the effect of secondhand shoes on my kids' feet during our year buying nothing new? I spoke to podiatrist Tracy Byrne to find out:

Q Are secondhand shoes a no-no for children's growing feet?
A Absolutely not, as long as the shoes are not visibly torn or worn down, and let's face it, kids don't wear shoes long enough for that to happen.

Q Is it better to try and find good-quality secondhand shoes, or cheap new ones?
A Good-quality secondhand!

Q What things should we look out for when buying secondhand shoes or accepting hand-me-downs?

A The same as we'd look for in any shoe, natural materials, flexibility, wide toe box, NOT tapered, lightweight.

Q How can we check that they fit properly?

A They should have no slippage when the child is walking at the back and sides, and there should be around 12mm extra room at the end of the shoe to allow for growth, and flex.

Q What potential problems should we keep our eyes out for?

A Tears, holes, very worn down spots on the sole.

SCHOOL UNIFORM

Our eldest started school just a few days after the official end of our buy nothing new year. I had resigned myself to having to purchase it all new in a last-minute panic as the start of school drew nearer and nearer, but must have posted something about it on my FB page and before I knew it there was a bag full of pre-loved uniform sitting beside our back door when we arrived home. I very nearly cried – it was such a lovely gesture and totally unexpected.

We're super lucky in that our PTA runs a secondhand uniform service. People donate their outgrown uniform – everything from regular run-of-the-mill grey trousers and checked summer dresses, through to the branded jumpers and PE shirts, and then it's all sold for £1 an item with proceeds going back into the school. It's a total win-win and I love it! If your school doesn't have a service like this, you could suggest it to the PTA (be aware, though, that it's very likely you will be commandeered to run it yourself!).

Non-branded stuff (without your school's name/logo) like trousers, skirts and pinafores can be picked up pretty easily in charity shops or on eBay, but if you want to buy new have a look at Eco Outfitters (www. ecooutfitters.co.uk/shop) who stock organic cotton uniform basics.

Teens

Teens are tricky and from what I'm told (and what I remember) need handling with kid gloves at the best of times. I guess our natural expectation is that they will rebel against us and our sustainable(ish) efforts and become rabid consumers of all things fast, including fashion and food.

My main goal when I was a teenager was to be accepted. Ideally, I wanted to be one of the cool kids, but that was never going to happen, so the best I could hope for was to blend in and not become too much of an object of ridicule. Having said that, I was hugely passionate about lots of things, as many teenagers and young adults are. I had a strong sense of right and wrong, and wouldn't use anything tested on animals and gave up eating meat for several years. But none of that was at my parents' instigation (in fact, I think they just thought I was a massive pain in the arse and my mum got fed up having to cook two meals and read all the labels on shampoo in the supermarket).

As my kids get older, I do ponder periodically how long it's OK for me to continue to expect them to live under my 'rules' and to live by my values. At what point do we let them go out into the world and make their own choices about what's right and what's wrong? I guess that's all a part of growing up in general – allowing them to develop their own moral code and trusting they will know right from wrong, but I have to confess I'm already feeling twitchy about the choices mine might make when they reach the teenage years.

Do we have to accept that there will be times when their need for social acceptance and to fit in with their friends will trump any of our values and concerns? Yes, I think we do. I would love it if my kids were 'one of those kids' who was confident in their own skin, even as a teenager, and who was quite comfortable shopping in charity shops, and didn't really care what brand of trainer anyone wore. But chances are they won't be. I certainly wasn't. I guess we have to let them make their own choices, not judge or preach, and keep those all-important lines of communication open. And hope that once they're through the worst of the teen angst, and they grow more confident in their own choices and the values they want to live by, that they'll come back to all things sustainable(ish) – because we all know that this is the only 'right' way to live ;).

If you're lucky and your teen is on board with all things sustainable(ish), that teenage passion, that black-and-white thinking and that 'I can conquer the world' attitude can be harnessed to very powerful effects. Here are some inspiring teens doing amazing things:

- **GRETA THUNBERG (@GRETATHUNBERG)**
  In 2018 this Swedish teenager went on 'school strike' and instead sat outside the Swedish parliament buildings handing out leaflets that stated: 'I am doing this because you adults are shitting on my future.' After the Swedish General Election she returned to school but only for four days a week and she continues to strike every Friday, has been interviewed in the national and international press, and addressed a crowd of over 10,000 people at Finland's climate march in Helsinki in 2018. In 2019 she addressed the UK parliament and has pretty much become the figurehead of the climate action movement, appearing on the front of *Time* magazine and regularly hitting the headlines with her impassioned and powerful speeches.

- **KIDS AGAINST PLASTIC (WWW.KIDSAGAINSTPLASTIC.CO.UK)**
  Amy and Ella Meek are two teenagers from the UK who decided to take action on plastic pollution when they learned about the UN's Global Development Goals. Since that point they've picked up over 60,000 pieces of single-use plastic litter and developed an app to log it, done a TEDx talk, created a whole range of learning resources for schools and other kids wanting to learn more about how to tackle the issues around single-use plastic, and more!

- **BOYAN SLAT**
  No longer a teenager, but as a 16-year-old Boyan found out about plastic pollution while diving in Greece (and seeing more plastic than fish in the water) and proceeded to embark on a high school project investigating ocean plastic and possible solutions. At the age of 18 he dropped out of university to found the Ocean Cleanup (www.theoceancleanup.com) and has raised over $31.5 million to develop and test equipment that could help to rid the oceans of plastic.

Sustainable(ish) pets

How sustainable or otherwise is it to have a pet?

The immediate assumption would be that it's not – after all, dogs and cats eat meat, the production of which is a contributor to greenhouse gas emissions and climate change. But it's not clear cut. Two recent studies of pet ownership and its impact on climate change seem to contradict each other. What was, however, clear from both of them was that the smaller the pet, and the less meat it eats, the smaller its carbon pawprint.

Pet food

We've all got to eat, and pets are no different. While at first glance it might appear impossible to find food that isn't encased in plastic, it's easier than it might seem:

- **BUY TINS NOT POUCHES**

  The pouches of food are great in terms of 'food waste' but they are nigh on impossible to recycle and destined for landfill (although there is now a Terra Cycle scheme for pouches, www.terracycle. com/en-GB/brigades/petfood). Tins are a great plastic-free alternative – some brands do half-sized tins if you need smaller portions, and get yourself one of those reusable tin cap things to keep it fresh in the fridge. The little individual aluminium trays are another good option if you have a very pampered pet!

- **AVOID THE PLASTIC SACKS OF DRY FOOD**

  Once upon a time dry pet food came in paper sacks, or in cardboard boxes, but now they all seem to come in overly robust thick plastic bags (I'm sure this has something to do with customers' perception of value rather than an actual need). Some brands do still sell their food in paper bags, so keep your eyes peeled, and the good news is that pet food companies are cottoning on to the demand for plastic-free alternatives – Lily's Kitchen (www.lilyskitchen.co.uk) and Beco (www.becopets.com) both now have entirely home-compostable packaging on their dry food, which will happily degrade on your compost heap.

• BUY LOOSE

Some pet shops (especially the good old-fashioned independent ones) will still have loose food that you can buy in your own bags – everything from dog biscuits to bird food to rabbit pellets.

The world's most sustainable pet food?

- -

In January 2019 a new pet food, Yora (www.yorapetfoods.com), was launched in the UK that claims to be the 'world's most sustainable pet food'. Pets are estimated to consume around 20 per cent of the world's meat and fish, and with a growing trend for 'boutique' pet foods that use human-grade meat, this statistic could even increase. Pet product developer Tom Neish set about looking for alternative protein sources that could be used in pet food and after much research he eventually settled on a larva called *Hermetia illucens*. These are dried, powdered, combined with potatoes, oats and beetroot and turned into a traditional-looking dog food kibble. When compared to beef farming, Yora insects need just 2 per cent of the land and 4 per cent of the water to produce each kg of protein, meaning they cause 96 per cent less greenhouse emissions.

I was sent a pack to try out on Spud, our border terrier, who can be a fussy madam, but she loves it. It came packaged entirely plastic free, and the food pack itself is home compostable.

This really could be the world's most sustainable pet food.

MAKE YOUR OWN

The very dedicated may choose to make their own. Bear in mind, though, that pet food companies spend millions on nutritionists and on formulating pet food so that it has the right balance of all the things (technical term) your pet needs. Matching up to this with a homemade diet requires a lot of research, and while I think it's kind of doable to make your own dog food, I would never recommend trying it for cats (with my ex-vet's hat on) as they have a requirement for an amino acid called taurine that is only present in meat, and it can be tricky to get the balance right. Check out places like Pinterest for a wealth of homemade recipes, but as I say, do your research first, and maybe run it past your vet.

Poo

It's unavoidable. Pets make poo. And we have to deal with it. Here are some plastic-free(ish) options:

- If you've got rabbits/hamsters/guinea pigs etc, the straw/sawdust and poo can go in your compost heap quite safely. However, if you've got dogs and cats you shouldn't compost their poo, or if you do the compost shouldn't be used on food plants.
- Wood-based cat litters work well, and keep your eye out for cat litter in paper bags. If you use wood-based litter, you can add it and any poo to a wormery (as long as you don't then use the resulting compost on food plants). Otherwise the only thing you can safely do with cat poo and contaminated litter is bag it up and put it in your landfill bin – a good excuse to encourage your cat to go outside (although don't tell your neighbour with the prize flower beds that I said that!).

POO BAGS

There are lots of 'biodegradable' poo bags on the market, which on one hand are more sustainable, being made from plant-based plastics rather than oil, but as we've seen with nappies (page 147) and other plastics (page 63) they simply won't break down in landfill as they don't have the right conditions. So they sit there and act like any other plastic. Lily's Kitchen and Beco both now do home compostable poo bags, which look promising and can be used in dog wormeries and dog compost bins:

- Dog poo wormery – works like a wormery you might use for your food scraps, but this one is just for dog poo. Pop in your (dog's) poo and the worms will work their magic turning it into compost, which you can use in your garden. However you shouldn't compost your pet's poo if there is any chance the compost will be used on soil for food plants. You can buy one or make your own (hit the internet for instructions).
- Specific dog poo mini compost thing – these are sold at most pet shops and are kind of like a large sieve with a lid, which you sink down into the ground and pop the dog poo into, where it then rots down.

Although you shouldn't add dog poo to regular compost, you can still compost it as long as you don't spread it on land where food crops are grown or children play. You can sprinkle it around the base of fruit trees or bushes, or use it in your flower beds, hanging baskets or pots.

- 'Stick and flick' – using a stick to flick your dog's poo away from the path when in deeper woodland is a method advocated by the Forestry Commission. Be aware, the technique takes some practice…

At the moment it's difficult to dispose of your dog poo sustainably, but there are exciting developments happening, including a dog poo bin that can power street lights!

Treats

As with food, pet treats now seem to all come encased in plastic. Here are some alternatives:

- **CARDBOARD PACKAGING**
  See if you can find treats packaged in cardboard – our dog, Spud, loves the Lidl cat biscuits in a cardboard box so we use them as treats!

- **BUY LOOSE**
  We've got a great old-fashioned independent pet shop near us that has big boxes of treats that you can buy loose in your own bags. Some of the chains are also starting to sell 'pick and mix'-style dog treats.

- **MAKE YOUR OWN**
  If you've got a dehydrator you can dehydrate liver into little treats, or some dogs (and rabbits etc!) love nothing better than a carrot stick! If you've got a very foody dog, just 'treat' them with their regular biscuits taken out of their daily allowance so you don't end up with a fat pooch on your hands. Pinterest is overflowing with all kinds of recipes for homemade pet treats – you can even get bone-shaped cookie cutters to make biscuits…

Accessories

Hopefully, you can guess what I'm going to say next by now – yes, see what you can find secondhand. Bowls, beds, crates, even leads can be picked up secondhand – check out your local charity shops (the pet charity shops seem to do quite a good line in secondhand pet stuff, perhaps unsurprisingly!) or post a WANTED in your local Freecycle/Freegle group.

If you're buying new, buy to last. Metal and ceramic bowls will last longer and age better than plastic (as long as you don't drop them). You can also get 'eco bowls' made from bamboo and rice husks from Beco, which might be worth looking at.

And buy ethical; there are some amazing ethically made collars and leads out there. Check out the collars from Koko Collective (www. kokocollective.co.uk) – ethically made in India from old bike inner tubes and discarded saris!

BEDS

When it comes to beds, think about how often you might need to wash it. There are lots of beds and blankets now made from recycled plastic bottles, which sounds great, but as we now know, unfortunately each time you wash them, they will release microfibres of plastic (*see* page 127) into the waterways.

TOYS

Again, you can buy 'eco' toys', which are often stuffed with recycled plastic bottles, but these tend to pose less of a microfibre risk, although that depends on how fanatical you are about washing your pet toys (I am not). Remember with pets that less is often more. Cats love a good old ball of scrunched-up foil, or better yet, a scrunched-up ball of foil in a cardboard box! And for dogs you can make great pull toys by plaiting old bits of fabric together.

Grooming and parasites

I'm not a big fan of the excessively groomed look and have a suitably scruffy mutt as testament to this. However, she does love a good old roll in whatever poo she can find on walks – the smellier the better. Instead of reaching for the plastic bottles of designer-looking pet shampoos, see if you can find a bar soap. Yes, you can buy special pet shampoo bars, or just find a mild baby soap and use that.

Parasite-wise, I know that some people swear by the use of garlic or garlic powder as a flea treatment or deterrent, and if that works for you, then that's fab and an easy plastic-free solution, but bear in mind that in high doses garlic is toxic for dogs, and **garlic should never be fed to cats**! It can be hard to find a licensed flea and worm treatment plastic free – the best plastic-free(ish) option I've found so far is Bravecto, available as a tablet for dogs and a spot-on for cats. OK, so it's still packaged in plastic BUT it gives you 12 weeks' worth of treatment in one go versus only four weeks for other licensed alternatives.

5 QUICK SUSTAINABLE(ISH) FAMILY WINS

1 **Go for a toy embargo!** See how long you can go without buying any new toys – either brand new, or new to you. If you think your kids will struggle, take some of their current toys out of circulation, and then add them back in as and when they start to get bored with what's left.

2 **Have ONE conversation** Have one conversation with a friend or family member in the next week about the changes you're making. Tell them you're reading this book if you want a nice easy 'in'!

3 **Ban TV channels with ads on for younger kids!** Ours only tend to watch stuff we've recorded so they whizz through the adverts and it's really noticeable when we go to the cinema that they suddenly want ALL the new toys.

4 **Don't buy new for newborns** If you've got friends or family expecting a baby, don't buy them yet another babygro. Cook them a meal for the freezer, or offer to take the baby out for a walk so they can snatch a few precious moments' sleep.

5 **Experiment with a plastic-free version of your pet's food if you can find one** Just remember, though, to make any dietary changes slowly and to wean them on to the new food to prevent any stomach upsets.

MORE SUGGESTIONS:

- ☐ Go cold turkey on baby wipes – try using reusables at home at first
- ☐ Get together with a group of friends and have a toy swap
- ☐ Embrace hand-me-downs! Whether accepting or donating
- ☐ Watch a sustainable(ish) movie or documentary together (*see* page 140)
- ☐ Make it a family tradition to do a litter pick each time you visit the beach or go for a walk
- ☐ Ban glitter! Glitter is essentially a microplastic (*see* page 84) and when sparkly hands are washed it ends up in our waterways and heads on out to sea. If your little one (or you!) just can't do without it, look for eco-friendly plant-based glitters (www.ecoglitterfun.com)
- ☐ Have a family meeting and set some goals together
- ☐ Aim to have one car-free day out a month
- ☐ Switch to reusable nappies
- ☐ Take your own plastic-free snacks out with you – bananas and Tupperware pots of raisins are our go-to, or even a jam sandwich in a beeswax wrap

Over to you (aka now get up and do!)

List three or four ideas below for changes you could make for a more sustainable(ish) family life.

Action	Timeframe
1.	
2.	
3.	
4.	

Resources

- **CLIMATE FOR CHANGE (WWW.CLIMATEFORCHANGE.ORG.AU)**
An Australian organisation that works to support people to have effective conversations about climate change, and to take actions that will inspire others.

- **THE GREEN PARENT (WWW.THEGREENPARENT.CO.UK)**
Print magazine covering all aspects of 'green' parenting.

- *THIS BOOK IS NOT RUBBISH: 50 WAYS TO DITCH PLASTIC, REDUCE RUBBISH AND SAVE THE WORLD!* BY ISABEL THOMAS (WREN & ROOK, 2018)
Full of top tips for kids and families to help us to become 'eco-warriors not eco-worriers'.

- **WILD TRIBE HEROES (WWW.WILDTRIBEHEROES.COM)**
Children's book series on ocean plastic.

- **NATIONAL GEOGRAPHIC KIDS (WWW.NATGEOKIDS.COM)**
Website and print magazine for kids exploring all the planet has to offer, and touching on some of the big environmental issues in an age-appropriate way.

- **YOUNG CLIMATE WARRIORS (WWW.YOUNGCLIMATEWARRIORS.ORG)**
Sign up (free) for weekly emails with simple eco-challenges for kids to complete.

- *KIDS AGAINST PLASTIC: HOW TO BE A #2MINUTESUPERHERO* BY MARTIN DOREY (WALKER BOOKS, 2019)
A guide for children with 50 missions to complete to fight plastic at home, school and on days out.

7

Sustainable(ish) home

Home is where the heart is and it stands to reason that it's somewhere that should reflect our values. If we want to create a better world, we need to start right here, and we really can make a big difference with some more sustainable choices. From the amount of energy we use to the products we use for cleaning – it all has an impact, and therefore the potential for us to take action to reduce it.

Let's get started with all things energy.

First things first...

Switching to a renewable energy supplier

The definition of renewable energy is:

'Energy from a source that is not depleted when used'

It includes things like wind, solar, tidal and hydroelectric (water). Fossil fuels – things like coal, oil and natural gas (including that from fracking) – are a finite resource. Digging them up out of the ground is energy intensive and generally a fairly destructive process. Alongside which, when they're burned, they release the carbon stores from which they are made, and are a major contributor to climate change. Advances in technology mean that we're moving ever closer to the possibility of being able to supply all of our energy needs using renewables and at an ever-quickening pace. In 2011, renewable electricity contributed around 9 per cent to the National Grid. In 2018, this was 25 per cent. In 2017 there were more renewables added globally to the grid than fossil fuels, and the energy landscape globally is transforming rapidly.

I'm putting this first, before any energy-saving tips, because according to an article by the Institute of Physics, buying green energy is one of the six high impact actions that we can take as individuals to mitigate

Five reasons to switch to a renewable energy supplier

1 It's EASY! I would argue it's the single easiest thing we can all do to help protect the planet. There are even energy comparison sites such as Big Clean Switch (www.bigcleanswitch.org) that only list renewable tarriffs, meaning that the switching process takes minutes.

2 You will slash your personal carbon footprint.

3 You create a demand for more renewable energy being put into the National Grid. The higher the demand for renewable

WHAT TO LOOK FOR IN AN ENERGY SUPPLIER

Ethical Consumer has a whole section on gas and electricity on their website, and recommends looking for a company that supplies 100 per cent renewable energy (currently it's only possible to get 100 per cent electricity, not gas) AND crucially, that it is building new sources of green energy itself – so investing in things like wind and solar farms. They also recommend that you avoid tariffs that rely on coal and/or nuclear, and that fund fracking.

Energy suppliers Good Energy and Ecotricity both get the 'thumbs up' from Ethical Consumer, while EDF and British Gas get the thumbs down (EDF get most of their energy from nuclear, and British Gas has investments in fracking).

climate change. It has a higher impact than either switching to an electric car or going vegan. It's something we can ALL do, easily, painlessly, and, in all likelihood, it won't cost you a penny extra.

Seriously, if you do NOTHING ELSE after reading this book, please please please DO THIS **ONE** THING. I know that switching energy providers can be one of those things we put in the 'too hard' box as it feels like it will be super complicated and there's always that niggling concern that you might end up getting cut off. But that's totally not the case, it's easier now than it ever has been to switch – it literally takes a phone call.

energy, the more investment will be put into it, the quicker the tech will advance, the cheaper it will become, and the quicker we will transition to a lower carbon energy system.

4 It may not cost you any more than your existing tariff – renewable electricity is getting cheaper all the time with developments in solar, wind and hydro technology.

5 The more renewable energy we are using collectively, the more fossil fuels will stay in the ground, which is vital if we are to have any chance of keeping climate change below the crucial 1.5°C outlined by the 2018 IPCC (Inter-governmental Panel on Climate Change) report (*see* References on page 280).

WHY IS GREEN GAS SO MUCH HARDER?

In the UK we're getting pretty good at generating renewable electricity, but most of us rely on gas for our heating and some of us for our cooking. Even the greenest of green energy companies, Ecotricity and Good Energy, only supply 14 per cent and 6 per cent 'green gas' respectively, which is generated via a process called anaerobic digestion from grass (Ecotricity) or food and agricultural waste (Good Energy). Weaning ourselves off natural gas, switching to more efficient electric forms of heating and cooking and transitioning to green gas are all parts of the jigsaw that still need to fall into place.

Community energy

This is where local communities come together to create their own energy – often in the form of solar or hydroelectric projects.

Bath and West Community Energy (BWCE) is a brilliant example of a community energy project. Established in 2010, BWCE is a not-for-profit community enterprise that is owned and run by its members for the benefit of the community. Local people helped to crowdfund the capital needed for solar projects ranging from small arrays on the roofs of local schools and buildings through to a more traditional solar farm, by buying shares in the company. They then earn interest on those shares, and BWCE has been paying out an average of 6–7 per cent per annum to its community members.

What happens when you switch?

When you switch to a renewable tariff, there is no change at all to the gas and electricity that comes through the pipes into your home. It all comes from the National Grid. But what happens, broadly speaking, is that if you use 3000 units of energy in a year, 3000 units of renewable energy will be put into the Grid.

OK, have you switched yet?

If you haven't, PUT THE BOOK DOWN AND GO AND DO IT.

ENERGY SAVING

Be warned – switching to a renewable energy supplier doesn't give you carte blanche to happily use ALL the energy with a clear conscience. Using less energy is still really important. And if for any reason you can't switch suppliers, then don't feel like you can't do anything – energy saving is your secret super power.

I have to confess that saving energy and water feels like a pretty dull and grown-up thing to be thinking about, and it's easy to feel like it's all a bit like a drop in the ocean, especially when you walk down the road and see some of your neighbours' houses lit up like Christmas trees with every light blazing out of the windows. But no one said saving the world was going to be all glamour and fun…

I always thought we were pretty good at energy saving – we turned our lights off when we left the room (or at least *I* did) – but a few years ago we were invited to take part in a 'Great Energy Race' (effectively a competition with other households to see who could save the most energy over a couple of months) for the Observer Ethical Awards, and I spent some time geeking out on all kinds of energy facts and stats.

Here are five easy energy saves to get you started:

1 TURN OFF YOUR LIGHTS!

I know, I sound like your Dad here rampaging around the house screaming, 'Just who pays the bills around here?' But as lighting typically accounts for up to 15 per cent of our household energy bills, this is potentially a pretty good return for not much effort. There's an urban myth that it takes more energy for bulbs to heat up so you shouldn't keep turning them on and off. This might have been true in the 'old days' but doesn't apply to modern lighting and bulbs. So no excuses!

2 SWITCH YOUR LIGHTS

If you haven't already done it, switch your light bulbs to LEDs – you can even get LED bulbs now for your fridge and oven, as well as the obligatory fairy lights to brighten up your home in the winter. Replacing all the bulbs in a typical home with LEDs could save up to £230 a year on your bills. Not a fortune, but essentially free money. Another point in favour of LEDs is that they can be recycled at most local recycling centres, whereas even the old-fashioned glass bulbs are difficult to recycle due to the mix of glass and metal.

3 PUT ON A JUMPER

I know, I'm sounding like your Dad again. But seriously, I don't get these people who wander around their houses in T-shirts and shorts in the winter. Surely one compensation of the colder weather and the onset of winter each year is the chance to don all your favourite woollies?

4 PLUG THE LEAKS

If you've already paid for the heat, the last thing you want is for it to be escaping out of the house, and warming up your neighbour's garden. Get thermal linings for your curtains, check the insulation levels in your loft, and get a good old-fashioned sausage dog draught excluder. For draughty windows, you can buy special draught-proofing strips relatively cheaply from DIY stores to stick around the window that plug the gaps but still allow the windows to open and close.

5 DITCH THE TUMBLE DRYER

Line dry whenever you can, and if you do have to tumble-dry, make sure you spin as much water as possible out of the clothes first, and see if you can get away with part-drying them in the dryer, and then hanging out inside to finish off.

When energy companies and the government talk to us about saving energy, the main carrot dangled is usually the opportunity to save ourselves some cash. And that's awesome – a very visible (and very welcome) outcome of saving energy. BUT it's worth remembering that when we save a unit of energy at home, we've not only saved that unit of energy, but all the units of energy needed to create and transport it. I'd never really thought about it before, but it's obvious once you stop to consider it – it actually takes energy (electricity or gas) to create electricity. So the less we use in our homes, the less oil/gas/coal will need to be burned to create that energy overall. For me, that really helped me to overcome my lazy habits, and to actually get off my bum and switch things off at the mains, and to generally be more thoughtful about the amount of energy we're using. I mean, in the grand scheme of things if we save a few pounds each year turning the TV off standby that's not hugely life changing. But when I stopped to think about the energy that has been needed to create that wasted electricity, that for me is far more of an incentive.

Saving energy in the kitchen

1 CHOOSE YOUR COOKING APPLIANCE

- Slow cookers get a gold star for energy efficiency – they only require the energy of a light bulb to cook an entire meal.
- Microwaves use less energy than ovens.
- Fan-forced ovens with triple glazed doors and excellent insulation are the things to look for if you're in the market for a new oven.
- For the hob – electric induction hobs are more efficient than gas but cost more to run as gas is cheaper than electricity.
- And if you're buying new cooking appliances, look out for A-rated ones for maximum efficiency.

2 BATCH COOK

The oven is the most energy-guzzling cooking device and 'back in the day' people would have a baking day – the theory being that the oven has to work less hard as there is less heating up to be done, and less energy wasted when it cools down again. If time and your planning capabilities allow (confession: mine rarely do, especially the planning thing…), try and have things cooking on both shelves, such as one meal for now, and one to freeze for later.

3 TURN YOUR OVEN OFF 10 MINUTES BEFORE THE END OF COOKING

As long as you're not cooking a cake (and it might therefore sink), I reckon you can turn the oven off 10 minutes or so before the end of the cooking time, and the heat will stay pretty constant until you open the door to take your meal out (don't quote me on this, I have not scientifically assessed it, and the food safety types may very well be spitting out mouthfuls of tea in rage and indignation at such a suggestion).

Top Tips continues overleaf

4 SAVE ENERGY COOKING PASTA AND RICE

When cooking pasta and rice, just bring the water up to the boil, pop on a lid, turn off the heat and leave it to cook like this. Be warned, it adds an extra 10 minutes or so to the cooking time, so not one for those nights when you're hangry and need a meal in a hurry, but something to remember on less fraught occasions.

5 PUT LIDS ON SAUCEPANS (AND THEN DON'T FORGET TO TURN THE HEAT DOWN!)

If you remember your GCSE physics, it's something to do with trapping the heat/steam, meaning it needs less energy to keep the water simmering.

6 USE TIERED STEAMERS WHEN YOU'RE COOKING ON THE HOB

Potatoes on the bottom and veg on the top – all from one ring – genius!

7 WHEN YOU'VE FINISHED COOKING IN THE OVEN, LEAVE THE DOOR OPEN

The heat can disperse into the kitchen and warm it up (only in the winter, obviously).

8 USE THE TOASTER, NOT THE GRILL

The grill uses far more energy than the toaster as much of the energy escapes into warming up the surroundings.

9 BOIL ONLY THE WATER YOU NEED

Overfilling kettles costs British households £68 million on energy bills a year. Seriously, come on people. We can do this!! If you need some help getting into the swing of how much to use, keep a mug next to the kettle and fill this to tip into the kettle.

10 BOIL WATER IN THE KETTLE, NOT ON THE HOB

If you need boiling water for things like boiled eggs, or veg, boil it in the kettle rather than in the saucepan – it takes less energy.

(Relatively) low cost ways to cut your heating bills

- **TURN DOWN YOUR THERMOSTAT BY 1°C**

  I know, I know, we hear this advice all the time. But have you actually done it yet? This simple act can mean you use up to 10 per cent less energy heating your home.

- **MAKE SURE YOUR LOFT IS INSULATED**

  If it isn't, a significant proportion of the heat you're paying for is simply disappearing out of your roof and warming up the air around your house. The recommended depth of blanket-style insulation (glass or mineral wool) for a loft is 250–270mm. Even if you already have insulation, but it was put in some time ago, it's worth checking the depth, as the recommended depth has increased from 100–200mm to its current 250–270mm over the last few years. For extra sustainable(ish) points, you can now get 'eco-friendly' loft insulation made of either wool or plant-based materials. These are made in the UK and will compost down at the end of their life.

- **MAKE SURE YOUR BOILER IS INSULATED**

  Boilers made in the last 20 years or so have insulation on the inside, but older boilers will need a jacket to keep the heat in. NB If you have a boiler that is over 20 years old, chances are it will be hugely inefficient, and your energy bills would drop significantly if you were able to replace it.

- **PUT REFLECTIVE BACKING BEHIND YOUR RADIATORS**

  If you're feeling uber-keen then you can get special metallic cardboard things to go down behind your radiators, the idea being that they reflect the heat back into the room. Or DIY your own version with some foil and a cardboard box!

Bigger steps

Q Is your house/budget suitable for solar panels?

A We got ours fitted about six or seven years ago and I LOVE them – we've seen a really dramatic reduction in our electricity bills. In 2019 the UK government scrapped feed-in tariffs entirely (up until that point you would get paid for some of the energy your panels were putting into the National Grid) but it is still worth investigating the options – particularly when looked at from an environmental rather than a purely financial standpoint. At the time of writing, the government had just announced plans that would enable households with solar panels to sell their excess back to the grid. Battery technology is also coming on in leaps and bounds all the time, and it is now possible to get home storage batteries that will store any surplus energy produced on sunny days/when you're not using it, to use when the sun goes in. These are coming down in price (and the space they take up) all the time, and seem to have reached the point where they are a really viable option. (Take a look at the Tesla Powerwall.)

Q How about a heat pump?

A These work a bit like a fridge, but in reverse – they take the air from outside and by some kind of jiggery-pokery are able to convert it into warm air, and even work at temperatures as low as -15ºC (don't ask me how). They can be retrofitted to existing buildings, and are 300 per cent efficient – so for every unit of energy they take in, they put out three! You can find out more about home modifications for renewable heat generation from the Energy Saving Trust (www.energy savingtrust.org.uk).

Appliances

The general rule if you're in the market for new appliances is to go for the most energy-efficient one you can find/afford. The best energy rating is A or A+, and fridges and freezers have additional ratings that go up to A+++.

FRIDGES AND FREEZERS

Buy the size that suits your needs. As obvious as it might sound, I think it's worth me pointing out that the larger the fridge or freezer, the more energy it will use. As much as you might love a big American-style fridge in your kitchen, if it's just you and the cat it may well be overkill.

Clean the vents. This is the kind of pain-in-the-bum job that no one likes doing, so gets conveniently forgotten about. But dust and cobwebs can build up, meaning that the fridge has to work harder and uses more energy. If you can do this at least once a year, your fridge should last longer too (and you're a bona fide eco-hero).

WASHING MACHINES

Much of the advice to help cut down on microplastic pollution on page 127 applies to cutting the energy usage of your machine as well. Here's a quick recap of the biggest tips for saving energy:

* Wash at 30ºC – we all know this one by now, don't we?
* Only wash full loads.
* Wash less, that is, only when you really need to – my favourite!

TUMBLE DRYERS

Tumble dryers are hugely convenient but a pretty big energy suck. Cost per load varies according to the energy efficiency of your model – anywhere from 25–70p per load.

We've never had one, and we've coped OK with two kids in reusable nappies, and now with two older boys with a magnetic affinity to mud. In the summer, washing goes out on the line as long as it's not raining. And in the winter for a long time we made do with the merry-go-round of hanging on an airer for 24 hours and then finishing off in the airing cupboard. A year or two ago we invested in a heated airer to help speed the drying process up – it uses far less energy than a tumble dryer, and can accommodate at least one big load of washing at a time.

> *Confession: I still need to work out how to use the timer, and have been known to accidentally leave it on all night, which is NOT recommended for energy efficiency…*

Remember, this isn't about all or nothing, though – if you're in love with your tumble dryer, could you do just a couple of loads less in your tumble dryer each week? Or commit to not using it at all over the summer?

DISHWASHERS

For some reason it always seems to be a pretty contentious debate whenever the whole dishwasher versus handwashing issue comes up. According to uSwitch there's 'no absolute proof' as to which is better in terms of both energy and water usage, probably because there are so many variables.

If you already have a dishwasher (we do), use the eco setting if it has one – these use lower temperatures and less water, but are usually longer cycles, and only put it on when it's full. If you handwash, fill the washing-up bowl rather than use a running tap (I don't know anyone who does the running tap thing, but if you're one of them, stop it!).

STANDBY

DID YOU KNOW?

- Leaving items like the TV and computer on standby accounts for around 10 per cent of a typical household energy bill.
- Standby power use is responsible for roughly 1 per cent of global CO_2 emissions (which might not sound much, but it's 1 per cent we can easily save!).
- Devices left on standby mean that UK households waste £227 million a year.

The solution? Turn 'em off at the wall! It will be a pain at first, but after a couple of weeks it should be quickly becoming a new habit and part of your routine before going to bed.

> *Confession: I still really need to work on this – I am really bad at leaving the computer and the printer on overnight.*

Tech and gadgets

There are lots of gadgets out there that will help you to save energy. Here are a few of my favourites:

- **SMART METERS**

  These allow you to see how much energy you're using at any given point in the day, and although they were originally introduced to make billing simpler and more accurate, they can be a fairly powerful tool to help save energy too. Because you can see the spike when you boil the kettle, or as the lights start to go on in the evening, the idea is that you are then much more aware of the energy demands of different activities and appliances, and are more incentivised to reduce the energy-intensive ones.

- **SMART THERMOSTATS**

  A smart thermostat allows you to control your heating remotely via your smartphone or tablet (this totally blows my mind). This means that you can tell the smart thermostat what time you want your home to be warm, and it will use information such as the current external temperature alongside things it has 'learned' about your house, such as how long it takes to heat up, to ensure that when you walk in from work the house is toasty, using the minimum amount of energy. There are lots of different brands available, but the good news is that according to the Money Saving Expert website, whichever you choose they can save most households hundreds of pounds a year (and the energy savings that go along with that).

- **SMART PLUGS**

  This is another thing that I totally can't get my head around – you can connect up to 20 plugs/appliances to it and then control them via the app. So you can turn on lights at home if you're away, or to come on as you arrive home, and it also allows you to monitor your electricity usage.

Water saving

Water is a vital resource – not only for us to drink, but to enable us to grow crops and raise livestock. Access to clean, fresh water will become more and more of an issue as the global population continues to rise, and our waterways become ever more polluted.

UK households use an average of around 330 litres of water a day and saving water not only reduces your water bill, but it also reduces your energy bill too; if your water is heated via gas, it typically accounts for about 15 per cent of your heating bill to provide hot water for showers, baths and washing-up etc.

DID YOU KNOW?

- Since 1950, global water use has nearly tripled.
- One in five people globally don't have access to safe, affordable drinking water.
- Seventy per cent of the fresh water available for human use goes towards growing food and raising animals.
- The average UK diet takes 2757L of water A DAY to produce.
- Seventy per cent of industrial wastes are dumped untreated into the waterways, rendering it undrinkable.

If those facts don't serve as an incentive to save this most precious of resources, then I'm not sure what will. Here are some easy-to-implement tips:

STAYING CLEAN YET GREEN

Bathing, washing and teeth cleaning accounts for up to 21 per cent of our household water use, so is an area we can have a big impact on.

Baths

Baths have always got a bad rap, and the majority of advice is to take showers rather than baths. However, if you have a power shower, take long showers, or have kids, you might be better off having a bath.

Here are some tips for greener baths:

- Use less water! Not exactly cutting-edge surprising advice, but still valid nonetheless.
- Bath the kids together – if your kids are still little enough not to worry about it, chuck them in the bath at the same time. If they aren't keen, see if they can be persuaded to go in one after the other using the same water (maybe with a small top-up of hot if you're feeling kind).

Showers

With the advent of power showers, these are no longer the clear-cut water-saving winner. But they still can be:

- Take shorter showers. The average shower duration is apparently around seven and a half minutes. Taking a four-minute (or less) shower will nearly halve your water use.
- Stand a bucket in the shower to collect the water that would otherwise go down the drain when you're waiting for it to heat up. You can then use this to flush the loo.
- Use a water-saving shower head. When we took part in the Great Energy Race (page 169), this is one of the gadgets we invested in. We found one that claimed to use 50 per cent less water, and I was sceptical, so we put it to the (very scientific…) test, and it was true! It works brilliantly without any loss of water pressure by aerating the water as it comes out of the shower head.

Teeth cleaning

This one is simple – turn off the tap while you brush your teeth. A running tap wastes around 6L per minute, so if you're good and brush your teeth for the recommended two minutes, you could be sending 12L (or about 24 pints, if that's easier to visualise) straight down the sink.

OTHER WATER-SAVING TIPS

- Fit a water-saving device to your toilet cistern. Toilet flushing accounts for 30 per cent of household water use. You can get devices like a 'Hippo'(from www.hippo-the-watersaver.co.uk) that you can put into your toilet cistern that will save around 3L of water per flush. Alternatively, you can fill a large milk bottle with water and sink that in there.

- Get a water butt if you have access to outside space and a downpipe. Collect the rainwater that falls on your roof and use this to water your garden and plants. If you're feeling really keen, you can also use this water to flush your loo.

- Keep an old milk bottle or jug near the sink, and when you want hot water, let the tap run into this rather than down the sink. Tip this into your water butt, use it to boil the kettle, or use it to flush your loo.

- If it's yellow, let it mellow. If it's brown, flush it down... You may have heard this one before – the idea is not to flush the loo each time you just do a wee.

We may have gone a little too far with this with the kids, and failed to explain that when they are at someone else's house it's not considered polite to leave their wee sitting in someone else's loo. #parentingfail

- If you have a garden, in the summer tip any washing-up water on your plants. Avoid things like lettuces, though, unless you are partial to the taste of soapy water on your salad.

Cleaning

I am NOT one of nature's cleaners. I find it tedious and dull, and a bit like painting the Forth Road Bridge – as soon as you've finished, you need to start again. I am of the opinion that there is such a thing as too clean, and that a little bit of dirt is essential to build up a strong immune system (that's my excuse and I'm sticking to it). However, even hardened cleaning phobics like me must concede that it's a necessary evil. Cleaning is now easier than it has ever been, thanks to the plethora of dirt-busting products that are now available. Sadly, though, many of these products aren't good for either the environment or our own health (contributing to air pollution), so what are the other options?

What's wrong with my cleaning products?

There's a whole raft of chemicals that are used in conventional cleaning products that are detrimental to both our own health and that of the planet:

- Phosphates – these are water softeners that help to increase the efficacy of cleaning products, but that can contribute to algal blooms in waterways, resulting in the death of marine life. The EU severely reduced their use in household dishwasher detergents in 2017, meaning this is less of an issue now (although it's still worth finding a brand that doesn't contain phosphates – Bio-D fits that bill, see page 182).
- Palm oil – this stuff gets in everywhere (see page 107) and can be found in toilet cleaners as well as general household sprays.
- Bleach – we all know that bleach is pretty dangerous stuff and can damage eyes and skin if it gets splashed around. When it gets flushed down the loo it can become organochlorines, which are toxic and take hundreds of years to decompose.
- Parabens – these are compounds that are used in cleaning products for their antifungal and antimicrobial actions, as well as acting as preservatives. They are linked to hormone disruption and skin irritation, among other things.
- Triclosan – is used as an antimicrobial in cleaning products despite being classified as a pesticide, irritating to the skin and eyes and very toxic to aquatic animals.
- Phthalates – used to add fragrance to cleaning products; several have been banned in the EU due to their action as hormone disruptors.

'Green' products

I've used the quotation marks because, well… It's complicated and it's another area prone to greenwashing.

For a long time the forerunners in the eco-cleaning world were Ecover – the brand's 'raison d'être' was to create cleaning products that were phosphate free and they launched the first ever phosphate-free washing powder in 1979. However, along with sister company Method, they were recently acquired by SC Johnson, who have a poor record when it comes to things like animal testing, and many people are now choosing to avoid their products.

There are, however, lots of easily available alternatives:

- BIO-D (WWW.BIODEGRADABLE.BIZ)
  Available online and in some health food and zero waste stores, Bio-D has a wide range of cleaning products, from washing-up liquid to toilet cleaners and general cleaning sprays. They also do massive (up to 15L) bottles so you can use these to fill your own smaller bottles if you have the storage, reducing the number of plastic bottles you get through.

- GREENSCENTS (WWW.GREENSCENTS.CO.UK)
  They make organic and natural cleaning products, that have a 'no nasties' guarantee. They also supply their products in a range of sizes, from 500ml up to a whopping 20L!

- LIBBY CHAN (WWW.MYLIVINGWATERUK.COM)
  A totally different approach to cleaning, these products contain probiotics and 'helpful bacteria' and work by breaking down bacteria, grease and odour-causing microorganisms to leave even the stinkiest toilet smelling fresh. The product itself is concentrated and is diluted prior to use, and one product will apparently meet all of your cleaning needs!

  I've been trialling this and I have to say I'm impressed – it works particularly well at eliminating the aroma in the bathrooms that seems to come with two small boys with poor aim...

Homemade products

With homemade products, you know exactly what's gone into them, so there's no possibility of inadvertently using toxic chemicals, or anything that will provoke an allergy.

Confession: I tried. I really, really tried with homemade cleaning products for a long time. But, possibly because of my slightly slovenly attitude to cleaning, they just didn't work well for us. The toilets especially got super stinky (see previous page) and with some reluctance I was forced to concede defeat and search out the most eco alternatives that I could find. I do genuinely think that they can work really well for some people, so please don't give up before trying.

- **VINEGAR**

  White vinegar has a myriad of uses – you can use it diluted as an all-round cleaner, use it to clean your windows, add it to your washing machine instead of fabric softener and your dishwasher in place of rinse aid (we still do this and it works just fine). The fish and chip shop smell does dissipate after an hour or two, or you could use citrus peels and cloves to help to mask the smell. Simply chuck any old orange and lemon peel into a large glass jar and when it's full, add white vinegar and about 10 whole cloves. Leave to infuse for about a week, then drain and decant into a spray bottle.

- **BICARBONATE OF SODA**

  This is a brilliant deodoriser, and can be used to help with everything from whiffy fridges (pop an open jar with a couple of teaspoons of bicarb into the fridge and leave overnight) to trainers (sprinkle in and leave overnight) and sweaty sports stuff (sprinkle on before washing, or soak in a sinkful of cold water and bicarb).

- **LIQUID CASTILE SOAP**

  This can be used for all kinds of cleaning solutions. The most well-known brand is Dr Bronner's, which advertises its 18 in 1 liquid soap to use for washing dishes, people and pets, and for general cleaning. Dr Bronner's does contain palm oil (although it is apparently ethically sourced) so if palm oil is a no-no for you, then try the Greenscents version instead.

- **TEA TREE ESSENTIAL OIL**

  This has powerful antibacterial, antifungal and antiviral properties so is a good one to have in your arsenal. I add a drop or two to the softener compartment of the washing machine when washing the bath towels and bed sheets.

If you're keen to experiment with making your own natural cleaning products, Wendy Graham from the blog *Moral Fibres* (www.moralfibres.co.uk) has a brilliant book called *Fresh Clean Home* that has a plethora of fabulous sounding recipes that have almost got me thinking I might try again...

Money

I'm a big advocate of us all recognising the power of our money when it comes to the choices we make as consumers and am considering having a tattoo of one of my favourite quotes (I referenced it in Chapter 1, but I'm not going to apologise for repeating it here):

> 'Every time you spend money, you're casting a vote for the kind of world you want.'
>
> Anna Lappé

(Not really, I am not in any way cool enough or brave enough to get a tattoo, but I do love it!) But it took me a long time to realise that my money might not be casting the same vote that I would when it's in the bank or tucked away in any savings.

The big high-street banks have investments in things like fracking, the fossil fuel industry and nuclear weapons, which means that potentially if we bank or save our money with them, then our money is supporting things that personally I would never want to invest in.

Current accounts

For a long time the most ethical option for current accounts was a building society or the Co-operative Bank. Building societies tend to fare better than banks on the ethical stakes because they have strict regulations in place to limit the amount of money they are able to invest in certain industries. However, ethical bank Triodos launched a current account in April 2017, and promises to 'only lend to organisations that make a positive impact on people's lives, protect the planet, or build strong communities'. The debit card is also made from 100 per cent renewable resources, which is a really nice touch.

Switching bank account is a bit like switching energy supplier and something that very few of us do, fearing it will take up time, and will be a headache sorting out all of our direct debits and payments. However, most banks now sign up to the Current Account Switch Guarantee, which moves your money and all your regular payments for you, all within seven days.

Savings

It has long been assumed that there is an 'ethical premium' when it comes to savings and investments – meaning that the returns will be lower. However, I'm pleased to say that this is now no longer the case, with some ethical investments matching or even outperforming more traditional portfolios.

For cash ISAs, Ethical Consumer's top picks are Triodos Bank and Charity Bank. These two also score highly, along with Ecology Building Society, when it comes to savings accounts.

If you've got money to invest longer term, there is a list of fossil-free funds available at www.fossilfreefunds.org.

Pensions

The UK has around $3.1 **trillion** in retirement assets, which is a lot of money that has the potential power to bring about significant change depending on where it is invested. There has been a big push on both organisations and individuals to divest their pension funds from the fossil fuel industry in recent years. New York City announced its intention in January 2018 to divest $5 billion in fossil fuels from its pension funds and two London councils have done the same.

When it comes to your workplace pension, you may not have much say over where it is invested, but do remember that if you have a pension with a company, you are a stakeholder in it and as such you can use your voice to call on them to make more ethical investments. If you have a private pension, Ethical Consumer (*see* page 188) has a score table of pension providers, which is a useful guide.

5 QUICK WINS FOR A SUSTAINABLE(ISH) HOME

1 Switch your energy supplier to a renewable tariff.

2 Switch your lights to LEDs when your current bulbs expire.

3 Instigate a 'four-minute shower' rule.

4 Switch to eco-friendly cleaning products instead of reaching for your usual brand.

5 Consider switching your bank account or savings to ethical investments.

MORE SUGGESTIONS:

☐ Turn your thermostat down by 1°C

☐ Ditch the tumble dryer. Or at the very least challenge yourself to see how little you can use it

☐ Turn the tap off while you brush your teeth

☐ Put a 'water hippo' or water-filled milk bottle in your toilet cistern to save up to a litre of water per flush

☐ Get a water-saving shower head

☐ Ditch window and glass cleaners and have a go with white vinegar instead

☐ Replace your microfibre cleaning cloths (*see* page 129) with ones made of natural fibres (organic cotton or bamboo) or utilise old clothes that are beyond repair

- [ ] Cook one meal a week in the slow cooker (if you don't have one, post a WANTED on your local Freecycle/Freegle group, or keep your eye out in the charity shops near you)

- [ ] Always put the lids on saucepans

- [ ] Switch off standby – pick one appliance at a time and make it a new routine

- [ ] Only run the washing machine and dishwasher when they're full

Over to you (aka now get up and do!)

List three or four ideas below for changes you could make for a more sustainable(ish) home.

Action	Timeframe
1.	
2.	
3.	
4.	

Resources

- • ENERGY SAVING TRUST (WWW.ENERGYSAVINGTRUST.ORG.UK)
  The website provides independent and impartial advice to help home-owners lower emissions and cut energy bills.

- • COMMUNITY ENERGY COALITION (WWW.FORUMFORTHEFUTURE. ORG/COMMUNITY-ENERGY-COALITION)
  Information about community energy, how it works, and how to start your own.

- **WATER WISE (WWW.WATERWISE.ORG.UK)**
  Another great website, this time packed with resources to help us all save water in our homes.

- *FRESH CLEAN HOME: MAKE YOUR OWN CLEANING PRODUCTS* BY WENDY GRAHAM (PAVILLION, 2018)
  This is basically the bible for anyone wanting to have a go making their own cleaning products. It's a beautiful book, but Wendy also makes it all feel very do-able and practical.

- **ETHICAL CONSUMER (WWW.ETHICALCONSUMER.ORG)**
  Online resource profiling and ranking major brands, manufacturers and retailers for their 'ethical-ness'.

- **GOOD WITH MONEY (WWW.GOODWITHMONEY.COM)**
  A website designed to help you 'become good with money while doing good with money too'. There are sections on ethical current accounts, savings and investments, energy, insurance and more.

- **GO FOSSIL FREE (WWW.GOFOSSILFREE.ORG)**
  Information on why and how to divest from fossil fuels.

Sustainable(ish) work

M **ost of us** spend the majority of our waking hours during the week away from our homes, so it stands to reason that work is an area where we should be able to make a big difference. But changing our own habits, within the confines of our own houses is one thing – broaching all things sustainability with work colleagues, bosses and governing bodies might feel a little intimidating.

When I was working as a vet I used to cringe at the lack of recycling and the amount of rubbish headed to landfill every day but it took me a long time to feel empowered enough to speak to the practice manager about it. As it turns out, it was easy! Yes, I was the one who had to instigate the recycling bins and make sure they were labelled so people knew what was what, but overall it was a really positive move and colleagues commented that they couldn't understand why we hadn't done it sooner.

For some reason, in the work environment, it can feel like it's 'someone else's' responsibility for all the things that we might be doing routinely at home, like recycling, and shunning single-use plastic. But until someone steps up to be that 'someone', it's unlikely anything will change.

If you're like me and work from home, then obviously implementing the advice in Chapter 7 should see you polishing your 'green work' credentials. The winter months can, however, be tricky – trying to stay warm without heating up the whole house while you work only from one room. If your heating system has the capability, set it so that only your work room is heated during the day, or invest in a low-energy electric heater. Failing that, I have found that working wrapped in a sleeping bag keeps me toasty, although it is inconvenient when the postman knocks on the door...

If you work in a big firm, you should find that they have CSR (Corporate and Social Responsibility) strategies and policies in place to reduce their environmental impact. Ask your HR department to see them, and if they don't have any, let them know that it is something that matters to you; the more people that raise these issues, the more likely it is that big companies will take action.

If you work in a small/medium-sized firm where you might be able to have a bit more of an influence over policies and procedures, there are lots of easy changes you can suggest (do bear in mind, though, that you may well be the one who ends up being given the responsibility to implement these...!).

DID YOU KNOW?

- Leaving a computer on overnight for a year creates enough CO_2 to fill a double-decker bus.
- A PC monitor left on overnight can waste enough electricity to laser print over 500 pages.
- Leaving your photocopier on standby overnight wastes enough energy to make 30 cups of tea.
- Air conditioning an office for one extra hour a day uses enough energy in a month to power a TV for over a year.
- A 2 per cent increase in office temperature creates enough CO_2 in a year to fill a hot air balloon.

Reasons why it's good business to go green

1 It saves you money – cutting down on the amount of paper, ink and energy used is pretty much a no-brainer.

2 Some companies won't give you work unless you can prove your sustainability and community credentials, and it's becoming increasingly common to be asked to include information on environmental initiatives in tenders.

3 It helps with employee engagement – events such as 'eco weeks' or around World Earth Day can help engage staff with their work and its impact beyond that of the company.

4 More and more graduates are asking at interview about firms' CSR and environmental policies, and will actively seek out firms who are strong in this area. In fact, a 2019 study of 1000 office workers found that nearly a quarter of them would refuse a job at an organisation with a poor sustainability record.

5 It's the right thing to do. If we are to leave future generations with a planet they can peacefully live on, it needs action from ALL of us, and that includes businesses, both big and small.

Here are some ideas for getting started with all things sustainable(ish) at work:

START A 'SUSTAINABILITY TEAM'

Sound out work friends and colleagues to see if anyone would be keen to join you and become an office 'eco-champion'. It's always far easier and more fun doing these things with others, and you'll get more done.

REDUCE/REMOVE SINGLE-USE PLASTICS

Provide staff members with their own reusable coffee cups (these can be bog-standard mugs if that's easier) and water bottles, and let staff know that you won't be reordering single-use products (if you have the authority!).

SWITCH TO A GREEN TARIFF

In the same way that this is a hugely impactful move for our homes, this is one for offices and businesses too. Ecotricity and Good Energy both have a range of tariffs for different sized businesses. If you're in your own premises, this should be relatively straightforward; however, it can be more complicated if you are in a shared or rented building.

INVEST IN SOLAR PANELS

Installing solar panels on a suitable business building really does seem like a win-win to me. You will only be using energy during the day when the sun is shining, so there is a very good chance that your own panels can provide a significant proportion of the energy you use.

PRINTING

- Go paper free, or at the very least, paper-less. Send documents via email, and ask people to consider not printing them, but accessing them solely online if possible.

Confession: I struggle with the whole paper-free thing. I find it much easier to read things when printed out, but in my defence, everything then gets used as scrap paper before ultimately being recycled.

- Use FSC certified paper (which has been made from responsibly managed sources) or even better, 100 per cent recycled paper.
- Print double sided if your printer has the capacity.
- Use any scrap single-sided printing for note paper.
- Recycle scrap paper.
- Refill your printer cartridges – it is possible to have your old ink cartridges refilled to use again, either buying the ink and doing it yourself or taking them along to a specialist shop.

Confession: We tried this a few times without much success – the printer wouldn't recognise the refilled cartridges and we had some issues with the cartridges getting blocked. We may have just been unlucky, so please don't let this put you off trying.

- Recycle your cartridges – if you can't refill them, at least recycle them. Many local authorities now have collection points at their recycling centres, and some charities have schemes whereby you can send them your used cartridges and they are able to generate income from them.
- Use an eco-friendly printer – there is a whole range of eco-friendly printers available for both home and office use, which use less ink, less energy and can print on both sides of the paper. Printers with refillable tanks rather than cartridges are also becoming more widely available and are definitely an option worth exploring.
- Use an eco-friendly font – yes, there are such things available (*see* box below).
- Turn printers off overnight.

Three eco-friendly fonts

1 <u>**Ryman Eco**</u> Ryman Stationery have created a font called Ryman Eco that you can download for free and that uses 33 per cent less ink.

2 <u>**Courier**</u> Good old-fashioned Courier font was designed for typewriters and to use less ink.

3 <u>**Century Gothic**</u> Switching from Arial to Century Gothic uses up to 30 per cent less ink.

RECYCLED BUSINESS CARDS AND STATIONERY

- Moo (www.moo.com) do a brilliant range of business cards made from recycled T-shirt offcuts.
- There are a number of 'green printers' that will print your business literature on FSC certified and recycled paper with non-toxic vegetable inks. Or just avoid flyers altogether if you can!

WOODEN NAME BADGES

If you're a regular visitor to conferences, you may well have a (not so) little collection of plastic name badges, or those plastic mini wallet things that you slide in a piece of paper with your name on it. How much smarter and generally cooler would a wooden name badge with your company logo on it be? Seriously, I'm considering getting myself one of these even though it's just me and the dog at home in the office. Bough to Beauty Bespoke (www.b2b4b.co.uk) do a gorgeous range of badges made from sustainably sourced wood that are laser engraved in the UK with your choice of design.

COMPUTERS

- Reduce the brightness of your monitor or laptop – it's better for your eyes too.
- Check the 'sleep' settings of your computer and make sure it is set to go into sleep mode if you're away from your desk for any more than five minutes.
- Turn your computer off overnight.

LIGHTS

- LEDs are now available to replace old-fashioned, energy-hungry fluorescent strip lights.
- Label the light switches – if you have a lot of light switches in one place, chances are no one really know which does what, so they all get turned on at once. Label them, and then hopefully only the ones that are needed will get switched on!
- OR if you've got the budget, motion-activated lights are the way to go.
- Raise the blinds – on a sunny day, open the blinds and switch the lights off.

RECYCLING

- If your company currently recycles nothing, they stand to save themselves some cash by implementing a recycling scheme, as the costs for disposing of recycling are lower compared to sending rubbish to landfill. It doesn't have to be hugely complicated either – most of the big rubbish contractors have schemes that are designed to be as simple as possible and will usually collect all 'dry recycling' such as plastic bottles, paper, cardboard etc in one bin, saving the frustration of having people put the wrong stuff in the wrong bins. If you need to separate into different waste streams, make sure it's clearly labelled and as easy as possible for everyone.

- Compost your food waste. If you have a compost heap at home, and a relatively small work team, then one option is to provide a bin for people to put their food waste and teabags etc in, and for you to then take it home to pop in your compost bin (#hero).
- Workplace wormery – I will admit that you might have to work in a pretty dedicated office to make this work, but it's worth putting it out there... Install a wormery, either inside or outside (*see* page 54), for food scraps and teabags.

ECO FRIENDLY CLEANING PRODUCTS

Supply eco-friendly washing-up liquid and toilet cleaner to be used for washing up and keeping the loo fresh smelling.

DESK PLANTS

Bring some of the outside in. House/office plants are brilliant at brightening up what might otherwise be a fairly sterile environment, and are also great at 'cleaning the air' of toxins associated with indoor pollution (according to studies done by NASA, no less). Just make sure you assign someone reliable to keep them watered – it would be a very depressing sight to watch the office plant wither away from lack of TLC.

OFFICE FURNITURE

If you're having an office makeover or tech upgrade, donate your old furniture and PCs to charities that will pass them on to those in need. You can also source 'new' (to you) office furniture from companies that specialise in secondhand officeware.

THINK ABOUT FLEXIBLE AND REMOTE WORKING

Can you work from home at least some of the week, reducing commuting time and emissions?

Research from the Carbon Trust showed that working from home has the potential to save companies $5billion and 3 million tonnes of carbon emissions a year through reduced commuting. But it's not that clear cut (when is it ever?!). Working from home invariably means increased energy usage at home – the lights, computer, heating in the winter and all those cups of tea add up. The Carbon Trust report found that working from home will shrink an employee's carbon footprint if they usually drive more than 4 miles to work, take a bus for more than 7 miles, or travel by train for 16 miles or more. If journeys are shorter than that then the carbon saved from commuting is cancelled out by the increased energy demand of powering the employee's home.

Regardless of where you work, can you do conference calls rather than meet in person – especially when meetings require short-haul flights up and down the country? Climate scientist Katharine Hayhoe (@Khayhoe) is invited to give talks all around the globe and tweeted in January 2019:

'When I receive a speaking invite, my first Q is: could I do a low-carbon video talk? Thanks to people's willingness to give new-fangled tech a try, I now give about ¾ of my talks this way!'

CATERING

- If you're running events, and supplying food for participants, look to see if there are any food waste projects locally that can supply you. For example, the Real Junk Food Project (www.trjfp.com) is a national scheme that helps to redistribute uneaten food, and some of their groups cater for outside events.
- Source Fairtrade coffee, plastic-free teabags and organic milk (if you can get it in glass bottles, all the better) for those all-important tea breaks.

Gowling WLG, a UK law firm with 2000 employees based in Birmingham and London, was one of the first law firms in the country to get ISO 140001 and ISO 500001 accreditation (*see* page 200). Some of the measures they have implemented include:

- Override programmes for the lights in the building so they are automatically switched off between the hours of 10pm and 6am.
- Motion sensors on the lights.
- Implementing 'follow me printing', which means you have to be physically present and logged on to a printer to print documents, eliminating all those occasions when people send work to printers and then forget about it.
- Removing water coolers and plastic cups and replacing them with drinking taps in the kitchens on every floor.
- Providing reusable cups and glasses for employees and clients.
- Having bag holders in the kitchen areas where people can leave any carrier bags or reusable bags that they no longer want, which people can then take out if they are shopping in their lunch breaks.
- Standard positioning and type of recycling bins on each floor, with clear and comprehensive instructions for what needs to go where.
- Food waste bins on the worktops in each kitchen.
- Removing bins from people's desks so they have to get up to go to the recycling bins.
- Making the general waste bins smaller so that it's hard to fit much in and therefore becomes easier to separate it out into the recycling bins.
- Leftover food from the office canteen is donated to a local homeless charity.
- Top tips from Fiona Nicholls, Head of Assurance and Environment at Gowling WLG, include:
  - Be persistent!
  - Find people within your company who are genuinely passionate about sustainability and use them.
  - Engage employees with stories – positive messaging is vital.
  - Get your comms team on board if you have one.

I first met Simon Jakeman (BEM) at an awards ceremony organised by the World Wildlife Fund (WWF). Simon was a previous winner of the WWF's 'Hidden Heroes' workplace award and is a WWF Earth Hour ambassador and all round amazing guy. Here's his story:

'As a firefighter for more than 20 years, I've seen first-hand the effects of climate change and the devastating impact floods, storms and grass fires can have on people's lives. Having this experience inspired me to try and live a more sustainable life and encourage others to embrace environmentally friendly policies in the workplace.

My work has led to me being awarded the British Empire Medal for services to the Environment and I am London Fire Brigade's Green Champion Coordinator, which involves encouraging green living and coordinating our network of Green Champions. I became the Brigade's first Green Champion in 2011 and was made Super Green Champion in 2015. In that time I have carried out a number of initiatives, including creating the Brigade's first rooftop garden, which aimed to provide crews with local, sustainably sourced food.

I've given hundreds of presentations about what fire stations, Control and HQ staff can do to make their workplace more eco-friendly, including tips on energy saving and recycling and encouraging sustainable travel.

The Brigade embraces environmental initiatives. In 2018, London's Eltham fire station won the National Fire Services Energy Savers competition with an energy saving of 35 per cent by switching off lights and turning down radiators. There is a Ride to Work scheme and staff are also encouraged to cut back on single-use coffee cups, with reusable travel mugs offered to those who pledge to cut disposables.

The Brigade exceeded its CO_2 reduction target of 45 per cent from 1990 levels and has 57 electric vehicles – the first step towards its ultra low emission vehicles plan, which aims to move towards a zero emissions fleet by 2050.

People often think one person can't make a difference, but you can. I decided one day to grow some tomatoes on a fire station roof and I'm really proud of how far and wide my actions have spread. I hope to encourage more people to do the same in the future.'

YOU CAN FOLLOW SIMON ON TWITTER @SHYMAN33.

WHAT TO DO IF YOU MEET RESISTANCE

Don't give up! This might be something that you've been thinking about for a while, and you might have already 'normalised' a lot of the changes you've made at home, but for someone totally fresh to this way of thinking, it might be a bit of a shock!

Set out the case for making these changes – if people aren't really that bothered about the environment (I am told there are some people that aren't!) then arguing the case for the money saving might be a good way 'in'. Tell them you've been reading this book, and you've been thinking about some easy changes that could be made – offer to lend them your copy so they can read it for themselves.

Keep plugging away with little suggestions and tweaks here and there. If your boss realises you're serious about this, and that it's not going to be a whole load of extra work or money for them, they should eventually come round!

5 QUICK WINS FOR A MORE SUSTAINABLE(ISH) OFFICE

1 Implement a recycling policy if you don't already have one.

2 Think before you print – see how many of your daily documents you could simply email.

3 Replace any old fluorescent strip lighting with LEDs.

4 Switch to FSC certified or (even better) recycled paper for printing.

5 Provide reusable water bottles and cups for staff.

Over to you (aka now get up and do!)

List three or four ideas below for changes you could make to your work environment.

Action	Timeframe
1.	
2.	
3.	
4.	

Resources

- **THE CARBON TRUST (WWW.CARBONTRUST.COM)**
  Offers resources, guides and services for businesses to help them to function more sustainably.

- **INVESTORS IN THE ENVIRONMENT (WWW.IIE.UK.COM)**
  A national environmental accreditation scheme designed to help organisations save money, reduce their impact on the environment, and get promoted for their green credentials.

- **WANT DON'T WANT (WWW.WANTDONTWANT.COM)**
  A site to help you buy and sell used office equipment.

- **THE GREEN OFFICE (WWW.THEGREENOFFICE.CO.UK)**
  Online store stocking green stationery and office supplies.

- **RYMAN ECO FONT (WWW.RYMANECO.CO.UK)**

- **ISO ACCREDITATIONS**
  14001 – environmental management (www.iso.org/iso-14001-environmental-management.html)
  50001 – energy management (www.iso.org/iso-50001-energy-management.html)

9

Sustainable(ish) school

If you've got kids, unless you homeschool (in which case you have my utmost respect) your kids will spend a large proportion of their day at school. Teachers are under a massive amount of pressure to hit academic targets, most of which keep moving with frustrating and alarming frequency, so it's understandable why making sure the school is eco-friendly might not be high on the list of 'things that need doing'.

However, kids are often really passionate about the environment, especially when they see the damage that is being done. Teens especially are becoming increasingly aware that they are the ones who are going to inherit the mess our generation and those before us have created. There are lots of things that schools can easily implement that will help their pupils to have a voice, as well as reducing their own environmental impact.

But before we even get to what's happening at school itself, there's some stuff we can do at home to help reduce our children's school footprint.

Back to school

Before the summer holidays have even started, retailers are bombarding us with 'back to school' ads, insisting that we need new everything for the start of a new school year. Well, do you know what? We don't. They want us to think we do, so they can make more money from us, but we really really don't. Yes, I too remember the thrill of a new pencil case, and shiny new sharp coloured pencils all the same uniform size, and an unsullied eraser, but it's really about time we rethought this kind of mindless consumption – where we buy because we're told to, because it's a new school year.

SCHOOL UNIFORM

First and foremost, get your kids to try their uniform on. If it still fits, they don't need new uniform. It doesn't have to be pristine – let's face it, it's going to be worn to school and get nailed anyway, so the odd ink mark or slightly grey colour is genuinely neither here nor there.

TOP TIPS FOR GETTING WHITE SHIRTS WHITE

- Lemon juice is a brilliant natural whitener – rub it neat on to any grubby/grey patches and wash as normal.
- Sunshine is another great natural whitener – anyone who has had kids in reusable nappies will tell you that it works magic on washed-in baby poo stains, so get your whites out on the line on a sunny day and watch the magic happen.
- To remove marker pen stains (my kids' jumpers are always covered in these and they never seem to know how they got there…), use nail varnish remover, hairspray or methylated spirit – anything alcohol based. Thoroughly wet the area, leave to soak for 15 minutes, and then wash as normal.

If your kids have grown and do need new uniform, here are a couple of sustainable(ish) options:

- **SECONDHAND UNIFORM SERVICE**
  As I mentioned in Chapter 6 we have one of these at our school, and it is one of my very favourite things. I think I've managed to kit out both of our kids over the years they've been at primary school for under £20 (excluding shoes). It's a brilliant project for a PTA that doubles up as a fundraiser and a way to keep textiles out of landfill.

- **ECO-FRIENDLY UNIFORM**
  Most schools will have an arrangement with organisations to supply branded jumpers, T-shirts and blazers, and may not have

given much thought to the ethical credentials of these companies. Eco Outfitters (www.ecooutfitters.co.uk) are a UK company who stock organic cotton uniform basics as well as providing an embroidery service. Your school might be able to sign up with them alongside their existing provider, giving parents choice over where they spend their money.

- **M&S AND JOHN LEWIS**
Both these stores do plain white school shirts in organic cotton.

What's wrong with super cheap new uniform?

Each year the supermarkets try to outdo each other with their back-to-school offers, with prices that seem too good to be true. And they probably are. Fast fashion is as much of an issue for school uniform as it is for the choices we might make about our own clothes (see Chapter 5). The problem is that, despite their best efforts (or I suspect very little effort in some cases), the supermarkets simply cannot be sure who has made their clothes. The supply chains are so long and complex, with so much subcontracting out of orders at various points along the way, that it can be pretty much impossible to know for sure whether clothes have been made by people being paid a living wage and working in safe conditions, unless the supply chains have been specifically designed to be transparent (as is the case with 'ethical clothes').

The thought that my kids' uniform might have been made by someone else's child, who should be at their own school, not slaving over a sewing machine somewhere, doesn't sit well. So if I can avoid it, I do.

PENS, PENCILS AND PENCIL CASES

I love stationery as much as the next person. And there's nothing like the thrill and untold potential of a beautiful new notepad or finding that perfect pen. But it's a habit we need to curb, and above all not pass on to our kids. Look through their old stuff with them – chances are the pencil case at the very least will still be good to fight another year. If it isn't, look for ones made from recycled materials – pencil cases made from recycled tyres are widely available, as are ones made from recycled cotton.

If you can persuade them to forgo felt-tips in favour of colouring pencils, this is the better option. You can even get pencils made from recycled newspaper for double eco points.

SCHOOL BAGS

School bags work hard. They get stuffed to the gills with lunch boxes, water bottles and exercise books, slung around on the floor and generally bashed about. Here are three sustainable(ish) options that should go the distance and outlast the school year (and hopefully more):

1 PATAGONIA (WWW.EU.PATAGONIA.COM)
   Patagonia are a US brand with social and environmental responsibility at the heart of what they do. All of their kit is made to last, and they offer a repair service too.

2 MUDDY PUDDLES (WWW.MUDDYPUDDLES.COM)
   This UK brand are the recommended school backpack on the Buy Me Once website – meaning that the team at Buy Me Once believe it to be hard-wearing and robust. Muddy Puddles work hard to ensure all of their products are made to the highest ethical standards and visit their manufacturers every year, as well as supporting charities here in the UK that help children to make the most of the outdoors.

3 FJÄLLRÄVEN KÅNKEN BACKPACKS (WWW.FJALLRAVEN.COM)
   I assumed that these bags would be fast fashion given the number that I have seen around, so I was pleasantly surprised to check out the website and find out that they're made from recycled bottles (microplastics/microfibres aren't an issue here as they recommend you don't put them in the washing machine) AND they have a whole section on how to care for your bag so it lasts.

Greening your school

- Many primary and secondary schools now have 'eco clubs' or an 'eco council' where the children can learn about issues, communicate them to the rest of the school and then suggest/implement ideas to help the school become more sustainable.
- The Eco-Schools project (www.eco-schools.org.uk) is part of the Keep Britain Tidy charity and provides a seven-step framework for school and pupils to work through, along with inspections and certification for the schools that meet their criteria. So far there are more than 19,700 Eco-Schools registered in England alone.

ECO SCHOOLS

The Eco-Schools programme is the largest education programme in the world, with 52,000 schools in 67 countries taking part. It empowers pupils, raises environmental awareness, improves the school environment and also creates financial savings for schools. Registration (online) is free and is literally a matter of minutes – once you're logged in there is a portal for both pupils and teachers, giving you everything you need to get going for early years and primary schools, as well as secondary schools.

The whole idea of Eco-Schools is that it is student led (although it needs a member of the teaching staff to lead/assist) and schools are encouraged to set up a pupil eco-committee.

Lee Wray-Davies at Eco-Schools England has this advice for anyone wanting to get started:

- Stick with the existing school council you've got. That way there's no need for a whole new team, and extra time out of busy school days.
- Ask teachers to bring existing schemes of work to show you, and highlight the areas where environmental topics are already being covered – you are way more likely to get buy-in if they realise it's not going to create a whole heap of extra work.
- Look at the financial savings involved in energy, water and waste reductions, as well as the benefits associated with decreased litter and increased biodiversity in the school grounds.
- Don't ever think you're not doing enough to join the programme or apply for the first rung of accreditation – for new Eco-Schools, no action is too little.

Thomas A Becket Junior School in Worthing is featured in the Hall of Fame on the Eco-Schools website. I got in touch with their Eco Co-ordinator Michelle Mayes to find out more...

At Thomas A Becket Junior School we believe that all children should be aware of ever-changing environmental issues and we promote this within themes and topics, which contain clear, well-planned links to the Eco-Schools' ten areas and the National Curriculum. This is a key part of our school aims and ethos of "everyone works together to make a positive contribution to the world". Children embrace the activities undertaken, showing clear enjoyment and a developing understanding and commitment to knowledge and skills within these areas. We encourage all of our children to think of the "bigger picture" when discussing sustainability within our projects, such as "how does this affect our planet, what can we do to change, and how do our actions affect others?"

Since we started our "Energy Challenge" in September 2015 the school has managed to save on average £2500 a year. We are now one of the most energy-efficient schools in West Sussex. Our designated energy monitors ensure that electrical equipment (lights, projectors and computer monitors) are turned off when not required, especially when the room is empty. Our energy rangers keep the profile of efficient energy usage high within our school; leading various challenges among classes and year groups. They also undertake an energy check once a week and then at the end of every term they work with the eco-committee to calculate the score for each class, with the most energy-efficient class winning a certificate and prize which is presented during assembly.

Tegan is part of the eco-committee at the school and gives her perspective:

I love being part of my eco-committee as I feel very strongly about protecting our ecosystem and raising awareness among everyone at school. Being a part of the committee makes me feel really good because I know that I am doing something good for the world.

It is very hard to say what I enjoy the most about being on the committee because we do a lot of exciting things as a group and we all love taking part! If I had to choose, I would say it was our trip to the local Eco Summit event. I thoroughly enjoyed making a submission for the eco art competition. I loved looking for eco materials outside to add to a collage and also finding an eco-friendly way of creating a fully sustainable mini goblin go-kart. Going to the Eco Summit had a big impact on the way I look at cars, electricity and how we, as a whole civilisation, change the world.

Being on the committee has definitely helped my family look at the items we throw in the bin as the vast majority of our recyclable rubbish at home was going into the normal waste bin, but now we realise how important it is to recycle and reuse plastic, papers, tins etc. to help to save our environment.

EASY WAYS TO GO GREEN AT SCHOOL

Single-use plastic bans

In late 2018 the UK government issued a challenge to all schools to be plastic free by 2020. This sounds like it should be easy – with simply banning plastic bottles and disposable coffee cups from sale on the school premises. Yet how many of us have been confronted with our little darlings' beautiful artwork or technology designs that seem to largely consist of plastic straws, bubble wrap, sellotape and/or a liberal sprinkling of glitter.

Think about what reusable or recyclable alternatives could be used instead, for example, paper straws, paper tape, eco-friendly glitter. As with our own personal efforts to reduce plastic usage, start with ONE thing, maybe bottles or straws, and work on that rather than trying to do everything at once.

Refillable board pens

I had no idea these even existed until I was tipped off – what a brilliant idea! Lots of schools use Consortium for their supplies (www.educationsupplies.co.uk) and these are available there. They even do mini sizes for the kids to use!

Refillable glue

Instead of Pritt Stick, check out Pentel Roll'n Glue – they look a bit like deodorant roll-on bottles, can be refilled, and according to my eldest are 'a bit like Pritt Stick only better'. What better recommendation could you have?

Water fountains

Make sure that all pupils and staff have their own reusable bottle and access to a supply of clean drinking water to refill them.

Food waste

Talking to children about food waste and why it's important (*see* page 99) is one of the easiest ways to get them on board. Collect the food waste for a week, and use it as a very visual representation of how much is thrown away. One easy way to reduce food waste with hot meals is to think more carefully about portion control, or to let the children serve themselves.

Recycling

In the same way that businesses can save money by reducing the rubbish sent to landfill, schools can too. Many local authorities provide recycling collections for schools, and making it as easy as possible for pupils and staff to recycle can be achieved by having labelled recycling bins at various points around the site.

Terracycle (www.terracycle.co.uk) run pen recycling schemes that schools can sign up to and be paid money for recycling the hundreds of pens, felt-tips and board pens they must get through each year.

Litter picks

I remember having to do a weekly litter pick at secondary school and I think we all pretty much hated doing it, but I don't ever remember anyone explaining to us why we had to do it. Obviously, the subtext was that if we were going to have to pick it up, then it might be assumed that we would join the dots and be less inclined to drop it in the first place. However, backing this up with an assembly on the damage litter can do to wildlife (as well as making the site look messy) would be a much more powerful way to get pupil buy-in. Doing litter picks in the local community as well as the school grounds is a great way to bring the two together.

Energy saving

Turning off computers, monitors, smart boards and lights will all help to reduce energy usage. Schools with active eco-clubs will often appoint 'eco-monitors' who will check on these things (some have the power to hand out 'red cards' where appropriate!) as well as keep an audit of recycling and single-use plastic use.

Idling cars

This one drives me mad – I have lost count of the number of times I have walked up the road to school and passed parents sitting inside their cars with the engine running. It seems insane to me, actively polluting the air outside your little darlings' playground – the very air that they are going to be breathing as soon as they step outside the classroom door. I've never yet been brave enough to tap on the window and confront anyone about it (I do, however, tut and glare fiercely), but a letter home from school to that effect might be useful as an awareness raiser.

> Our school recently tied some posters to the school fence designed by one of the kids, saying something like 'Save our air, turn off your car'. I thought it was a really clever idea to use something done by one of the children, rather than being the finger-wagging school – hopefully less easy to ignore!

Think about the outdoor space

Is there room for an 'outside classroom' or an area to get the kids growing some veggies? How about a 'bug hotel' that pupils could help to design and build, or a designated area of the school field set aside for wildflowers to help encourage insects and natural pollinators.

Consider solar panels

Yes, I know this is potentially a massive investment, but as with office buildings, schools are using most of their energy when the sun is (or at least should be!) shining, so the potential energy savings are huge. Up until 2016, UK climate action organisation 10:10 ran a 'Solar Schools' project whereby they helped schools up and down the country to crowdfund from their local community for solar panels. Although the scheme has now finished, the idea remains sound (even with the loss of the feed-in tariff as you would be directly using most of the energy you create), and would be a brilliant project for PTAs to get their teeth into.

Getting the school on board

As I said at the beginning, schools are already massively under both time and financial constraints. The very last thing they will welcome would be a long list of their shortcomings and demands that they should pull their socks up. Try these options instead:

- Approaching the PTA or volunteering to join them – that way you can at least have some influence over some of the extra-curricular fundraising activities that go on and attempt to steer them away from glow sticks and plastic-wrapped sweets for the school disco. (I managed to successfully negotiate a glow stick ban at our school discos and I'm pretty sure the kids haven't even noticed. I also volunteered to bulk-buy penny sweets in large plastic jars and divvy them up into paper bags to sell.)

10 Easy plastic-free fundraisers

School fairs and stalls are pretty synonymous with plastic tat – whether the kids are paying to make a plastic bauble or Christmas decoration, or selling cheaply bought plastic trinkets that delight for about half an hour before being dropped on the floor. There are thankfully lots of easy ways to raise funds for the school that are more eco-friendly.

1 Secondhand school uniform stand.

2 Textile recycling – there are schemes like Bags 2 School (www.bags2school.com) that make this super easy. Simply ask parents/carers to donate any old/unwanted textiles; the company will arrange to pick it up, weigh it and write you a cheque on the spot.

3 Tin can alleys/skittles etc are popular stands at school fairs – give away paper bags of pick 'n' mix, or pencils as prizes.

4 Bottle tombolas – ask for donations of bottles of drink (you could stipulate glass bottles only if you were feeling especially virtuous) for a tombola stall.

- Sounding out a member of the governing body – find out who are the parent members of the school's governing body and engineer a chat with them about the school's environmental policies. Offer to help to review them, and suggest alternatives. You honestly don't need to be an expert – most of this stuff is common sense and just needs someone with the passion and willpower to make it happen.
- Offering to run an assembly for the school. The Eco-Schools website gives some good information on the curriculum tie-ins for various areas, which can be a good 'in'. Again, you don't need to be an expert – I did a 10-minute talk in my kids' primary school just covering the Big Four single-use plastics and alternatives (*see* page 64) and they were all buzzing about changes they could make by the end!

5 Jam jar tombola – ask the children to bring in old jam jars filled with something nice for a kids' tombola. Again stipulate non plastic – suggestions include packets of seeds, crayons, mini coloured pencils, hair bands, sweets etc.

6 Toy/game swap – everyone brings in their old toys, they get laid out nicely and then the children pay £1 entry (for example) to come and take x items away again.

7 Secondhand book sale – this always does well at our school. Just make sure you have a plan for the leftover books.

8 Cake sale – you can't beat a good cake sale. We have one every half-term and each class takes it in turn to bake for it and man it. It easily raises over £100 each time.

9 Sponsored walk/sing/silence.

10 Filling a tube of Smarties with 20ps – send each child home with a tube of Smarties, and ask them to return it at the end of term filled with 20ps!

5 QUICK WINS FOR A MORE SUSTAINABLE(ISH) SCHOOL

I'm not sure that actually any of these are quick – I'd be lying to suggest otherwise. They will all involve some degree of time commitment from you but if you decide to champion this cause then it will be time well spent!

1 Join your school's PTA. Don't go in with all guns blazing and a massive agenda, but once you're in use your position to gently suggest more eco-friendly alternatives to the way things have traditionally been done.

2 Volunteer to set up a secondhand uniform scheme.

3 Offer to get quotes for getting logos on organic cotton jumpers and T-shirts.

4 Help the school to look into options for recycling if they aren't currently doing any.

5 Offer your services to run an eco-council for the school with representatives from each class in each year; this doesn't have to be an onerous weekly commitment, it could just be one meeting a month/half-term (and don't forget you get the school holidays off).

Over to you (aka now get up and do!)

List three or four ideas below for changes you could make to your school environment.

Action	Timeframe
1.	
2.	
3.	
4.	

Resources

- **THE ECO SCHOOLS WEBSITE (WWW.ECO-SCHOOLS.ORG.UK)**
  Packed with information and resources, along with support to help you gain your school Eco-Schools status.

- **SUSTAINABILITY AND ENVIRONMENTAL EDUCATION (WWW.SS-ED. CO.UK)**
  A hub for bringing together, sharing and enhancing best practice in sustainability and environmental education.

- **ZERO WASTE SCOTLAND (WWW.ZEROWASTESCOTLAND.ORG.UK)**
  Has a section on how to save energy and reduce waste in schools.

- **SURFERS AGAINST SEWAGE, PLASTIC FREE SCHOOLS (WWW.SAS.ORG. UK/PLASTIC-FREE-SCHOOLS)**
  A pupil-led education programme from the marine protection charity, designed to equip pupils with tools and challenges that create positive, lasting environmental change.

- **BAGS2SCHOOL (WWW.BAG2SCHOOL.COM)**
  Textile recycling collections.

- **TERRACYCLE PEN RECYCLING SCHEME (WWW.TERRACYCLE.COM/ EN-GB/BRIGADES/THE-WRITING-INSTRUMENTS-BRIGADE-R)**
  At the time of writing, the website is saying the scheme is full and they aren't accepting new applications, but hopefully this will change!

10

Sustainable(ish) travel and transport

By and large we all need to travel – whether that's simply to do the weekly shop, commuting to work, or visiting far flung and exotic destinations for our annual holiday.

Now I am in no way any kind of expert on travel and transport and if I'm honest it's one of the main areas we really haven't done a huge amount of work on as a family. Having said that, since having the kids we've holidayed exclusively in the UK, cutting our carbon footprint by not flying. However, when it comes to everyday transport, convenience and time pressures mean that for us the car invariably wins.

So if travel is your Achilles heel, know that you're not alone. And that in writing this chapter I'm hoping to inspire myself as much as anyone else to get on and make some simple changes!

DID YOU KNOW?

- Transport is the biggest contributor to CO_2 emissions in the UK, accounting for 28 per cent of our total CO_2 output in 2017.
- Domestic transport is the most significant source of transport emissions, with cars accounting for 15 per cent of the total UK transport emissions.

Commuting

Travelling to work or school is a fact of life for most of us. It eats into our days, and depending on how you travel, it potentially adds to your carbon footprint too. The average daily commute in the UK adds up to 4343 miles a year. Over that distance a 4x4 or a sports car emits more CO_2 per passenger than an aeroplane (choose your car carefully! – *see* page 221).

So what are the options for greener commuting?

WALK OR BIKE

DID YOU KNOW?

- Thirty-eight per cent of journeys in Britain are under 2 miles – it would take around 30 minutes to walk this or around 10 minutes to bike.
- Just under half the population of England and Wales travel less than 3.1 miles to work – around a 45-minute walk, or a 15-minute bike ride.
- The average distance travelled to school in the UK is 2.5 miles – which would take less than 15 minutes to cycle.

Now you could, as many people do, cycle to work every day (over 760,000 people in the UK commute to work by bike) – or if you don't think you can face it, then even once or twice a week is going to help! Or during the summer, when the weather is (hopefully) better and the days are longer? I know that with kids the prospect of them whingeing at you all the way to town or school if you even *suggest* walking or biking can be off-putting right from the start, especially if there are hills involved; I've found that ours are far more amenable to scooting, which suits me as it means we make speedier progress, with less moaning.

If you can walk or bike, even just *some of the time*, you not only have the satisfaction of cutting your carbon emissions, you'll gain the mental and physical benefits of getting up and getting moving too.

Chris Bennett, Head of Behaviour Change at Sustrans (www.
sustrans.org.uk), the walking and cycling charity, has these tips:

'When you have a busy family life it can be tempting to jump in the
car to ferry everyone around. However, swapping just a few journeys
to travel by bike can be much easier than you think and is a big step
towards living more sustainably. And there's a wide range of bikes
out there to get you started, including box-bike-style cargo bikes
(which also come in an electric version if the thought of hauling
your kids around in a bike feels all a bit sweat inducing), which are
ideal for transporting young children around.

Despite this, 46 per cent of primary pupils are currently being driven
to school, with the danger of oncoming traffic being the biggest
concern among parents. Cycling with little ones in tow can seem
daunting at first but there are a number of ways parents can make
everyday cycling less stressful. For those concerned about safety, try
riding in a line with children in the middle of adults for maximum
protection and visibility. If there's only one adult, take up a position
at the back to ensure all children are in plain sight.

For those needing that extra confidence boost, there are courses
like Bikeability which teach valuable skills, such as good road
positioning, signalling and visibility and can help parents and
children feel at ease on busy streets.

Once your child is confident on their bike, getting them used to
riding on the roads will develop them in many ways, by helping
them gain a sense of freedom and independence while improving
their confidence and fitness.'

ELECTRIC BIKES AND CARGO BIKES

If you love the *idea* of riding your bike to work, but the reality leaves you
arriving hot, sweaty and red in the face, then how about an electric bike?

The range of an electric bike battery can be anywhere from 15 to 65
miles, depending on its size and capacity. Charging takes around 4–6
hours and costs between 5 and 10p per charge.

Although they are potentially more expensive than a conventional bike to buy, you might be able to take advantage of the government's 'cycle to work' scheme which allows you to spread the cost over 12 months and saves you between 25 and 37 per cent in tax, depending on which income tax bracket you're in.

If you need space to transport luggage, equipment or kids then an electric 'cargo bike' might be the answer. They come in different shapes and sizes and allow you to do your weekly shop, or the school run, by bike and in relative comfort.

You don't need to feel bad about being a 'slacker' either; research from a study in Sweden in 2018 found that the 'role of the e-bike in promoting health and fitness is comparable to that of a conventional bicycle'. Grab those bicycle clips and get ready to pedal!

PUBLIC TRANSPORT

If you live in a city or large town, public transport is a no-brainer – it's usually plentiful, good value, no parking hassles or costs, and you probably get where you're going quicker. For those of us in more rural locations, this sadly isn't the case, and it can therefore be an option that we forget about and so automatically plump for the car, regardless of the journey.

Coach or train travel for longer journeys can be a good option, and you get to sit back, read a book and drink a cuppa while you travel. If you book early, take advantage of travel cards and if you're able to travel outside of peak hours, then you might also hit lucky with some cheaper fares.

CAR CLUBS

If you only use a car infrequently and don't need it for your regular commute, then a 'car club' might be the answer. You join up and can then hire a car (many of them are electric or hybrids) for the time that you need it – whether that's an hour or a couple of days. You save money on the regular maintenance, insurance and upkeep of a car, but still have access to one when you need it. Some local communities have their own car clubs, or Co-Wheels Car Club (www.co-wheels.org.uk) has over 60 locations across the UK. According to Sustrans, if you're a low-mileage driver driving less than 6–8000 miles per year, you could save up to £3500 a year, and you'll be dramatically reducing your impact on the environment, too. Because car club cars are used more efficiently (they are in use and being driven for a much higher proportion of the day rather than sitting outside your place of work), they emit over 20 per cent less CO_2 per kilometre travelled when compared to 'normal' car use and one car club car can replace over 20 private cars.

CAR SHARING/POOLS

Car sharing can be another option to reduce your reliance on your own four wheels, and if Peter Kay's *Car Share* TV series was anything to go by, it could be a whole lot more fun than your regular solitary commute. Pairing up with someone from work who lives locally to you is possibly the easiest way to do it, although this is obviously only feasible if you work the same hours.

There's an app for everything now, which is good news if you're looking to car share as you can download the Liftshare app (www. liftshare.com), which allows you to find, and share, lifts with people near you quickly and easily. Liftshare have over 600,000 members and on average their members save around £1000 per year, as well as cutting congestion, pressure on car parking spaces, air pollution and their carbon footprints. It doesn't have to be just for your regular commute – you can find travelling companions to your next festival or football match, or even for doing the weekly shop.

Getting into a car with a complete stranger can feel a bit intimidating, so Liftshare has these top tips for safer sharing:

1 Avoid exchanging your full name or address before you've met someone.
2 Only agree to a lift if you're happy.
3 Some car sharers choose to show each other their IDs – e.g. passports, student cards or driving licences – so they know they're travelling with the right person.
4 You're never under obligation to take a lift. If you don't feel comfortable, don't go through with the lift – even if it's been agreed.
5 As with any activity that involves meeting new people, it's advisable to meet in a public place the first time. It's always a good idea to let friends and family know your plans too.

For many of us the car is sometimes the only option, but how you drive can have a significant impact on how much fuel you use. The AA ran an eco-driving trial for 50 of their staff a few years ago where they asked them to drive normally for a week, and then follow their eco-driving advice for a week. They saved an average 10 per cent on their weekly fuel bills. The best saved an impressive 33 per cent so here are some tips to help you to drive more economically, use less fuel and cut your **car**bon (get it?!) footprint.

- Size matters… as a general rule, the smaller your car and the smaller the engine size, the lower its fuel use will be. If you're in the market for a new car, do you really need a massive SUV or 4x4? Or even better, could you go electric (*see* page 221)?
- Try to drive smoothly – remember when you were taking your driving test and people would tell you about driving instructors putting cups of coffee on the dashboard and the idea was you didn't spill it? (Or was that just me?) That kind of thing. Avoid sudden accelerating and braking.
- Keep your car regularly serviced.
- Check your tyre pressures, especially before long journeys – apparently under-inflated tyres can mean you use more fuel – who knew?!
- If you're not using roof racks or roof boxes, **take them off** – they create a whole load of extra drag and resistance and will increase your fuel consumption.
- The same applies to all the crap you're lugging around in your boot – if you don't need it, take it out – it makes the car heavier, so it needs to use more energy (fuel) to move.
- Warm yourself up on cold mornings by using an ice scraper to defrost the windscreen rather than leaving the car to idle on your driveway belching out fumes and using up your fuel.

- Go easy on the air-con. And the heaters, the heated rear window, and anything else that might be sucking up electricity when you don't need it.
- Avoid the potential points on your licence and stick to the speed limit. According to the AA you can use up to 25 per cent more fuel driving at 80mph than you do at 70mph.
- Set yourself a challenge – make a note of your average miles per gallon (mpg) now, and see if you can better it over the coming month.

ELECTRIC CARS

We're told that these are the way forward for cleaner, greener driving, and in 2018 the UK government announced plans to ensure that all new cars will be effectively zero emissions by 2040. Personally, I love the idea of electric cars (EVs) and when replacing our car recently opted for a 'plug-in hybrid' (PHEV), meaning that I can do the school run and local journeys on electric, and we still have the capacity to tow the caravan and make longer journeys on petrol – a sustainable(ish) solution that seems to be working well for us. Dan Caesar from Fully Charged (www.fullycharged. show) helped me to compile some pros and cons:

PROS

- No exhaust, so no contribution to air pollution at a local level.
- If you sign up to a clean energy supplier (*see* page 165), you're effectively cutting your carbon emissions to zero.
- No gearbox, easier (and in my experience, nicer) to drive and requires less servicing.
- The cost of 'fuel' is a fraction of what you would pay for diesel or petrol.
- The UK government provides a £3500 EV grant towards purchases of new electric cars.
- The mechanical simplicity of EVs means that they have fewer moving components to fail, and when parts do eventually need to be replaced, it should be relatively straightforward.

CONS

- 'Range anxiety' – the fear of running out of electricity and being nowhere near a charging point. The range of a standard smaller electric car is around 150 miles (more than enough for most daily commutes and then you can plug in to charge up overnight), but newer ones are approaching 300 miles on a single charge. The charging infrastructure is only a few years old, so you do have to be organised when you are undertaking longer journeys.
- Cost – most EVs are still considerably more expensive than their regular counterparts (the cheapest is around £18,000 and most are in the £25–35,000 bracket), although prices are falling quickly and there are plenty available secondhand (starting from around £6000).
- Charging from a standard three-pin plug can take up to 12 hours, although there are government grants available to help EV owners install 'fast charger' points at home that cut charging times to around 4–5 hours for a full charge. There are 'rapid chargers' at service stations that can charge EVs up to 80 per cent in about half an hour (just enough time for a wee and a coffee while you wait).
- Ideally you need to have access to off-road parking (unless your workplace has a charging station) although the Office for Low Emission Vehicles (OLEV) have a residential on-street charge point grant, and companies like Ubitricity (www.ubitricity.co.uk) are able to retrofit charge points into street lamps.

Batteries

Batteries for EVs are what's called 'lithium-ion' batteries (similar to those found in laptops and mobile phones) and there is some concern around the sustainable sourcing and disposal of these elements. I spoke to Dr Euan McTurk, electrochemist and EV battery engineer, to find out more.

'Some people have expressed concerns about the sourcing of lithium and cobalt in lithium-ion batteries. Lithium is a surprisingly abundant element, with large reserves found all over the world; even Cornwall has lithium brines. Cobalt is mainly sourced from the Democratic Republic of Congo, which has ethical issues in some parts of its supply chain, but manufacturers are combating this in two ways. Firstly, they are signing supply deals with more ethical sources of cobalt, and secondly, they are significantly reducing the cobalt content of their lithium-ion cells.

Cobalt use in leading EV batteries has been cut by 90 per cent within the last decade – considerably more progress than has been made with the batteries in consumer electronics – and continues to fall, with Tesla stating that they could soon remove cobalt from their batteries altogether.

Lithium-ion EV batteries are already outlasting the expectations of many early-day armchair critics (most manufacturers offer an eight-year, or 100,000-mile warranty) but once they have eventually reached end of life in an EV (having lost about 20–30 per cent of their original capacity), they still have ample capacity left to allow them to be used in second life applications, such as grid storage, which will likely more than double their working lives. Once they have eventually lost most of their capacity, they can be recycled using one of the many increasingly efficient techniques that is under development as we speak; some firms claim that they can already recover up to 100 per cent of the components of lithium-ion batteries, which can then be processed into new, better batteries.'

So while it's not perfect, it sounds like significant progress is being made. It's also important to note that the lithium-ion batteries are used in laptops and mobiles – if we're reluctant to adopt electric cars because of ethical concerns over the batteries, are we also willing to give up our laptops and switch to Fairphones (where the metals used are conflict free and Fairtrade)?

Travel

Travel gets a bad rap when it comes to sustainability, largely because we associate travel with air travel, and the carbon footprint that comes with it. But it's not all bad news for those with wanderlust and a desire to make the most of all that our amazing and diverse planet has to offer.

UK TRAVEL

Granted, there's no guarantee of sunshine, and the palm trees are few and far between, but the UK has a wealth of wonderful destinations to check out. Whether you're a culture vulture wanting to check out the shows and museums of the big cities, or you're looking to escape the crowds and find your own secluded hideaway for walking and relaxing, or you want a full-on adrenaline-fuelled adventure, there will be something for you somewhere in the UK. We have some of the most stunning countryside and culture in the world, all on our doorstep, and it's really easy for us to forget that and take it for granted.

SLOW TRAVEL

Slow travel is like slow food and slow fashion. It's about making the journey as much a part of the holiday as the destination. Instead of travelling desperate to arrive at your destination so you can cram in as many activities as possible, tick off as many of the must-see sights as you can, and eat and drink as much as you can stuff into your face, it's about slowing down, quite literally. It's about experiences rather than purely seeing the sights so you can say you have and so you can take the obligatory #selfie. It's about connecting with local people and culture and taking the time to understand the place where you are, rather than experiencing the tourist trail. And it's often a more sustainable option.

You might choose to root out a local restaurant that serves traditional recipes using local and seasonal food, rather than the familiarity and security of a well-known big brand that ships its identikit ingredients halfway around the globe.

You might choose to 'let the train take the strain' and take a sleeper train rather than a short-haul flight. When you wake in the morning, you'll start to get a sense of the country you're in as you travel through the countryside rather than simply flying over it.

You might choose small, boutique-type B&Bs where the owners can share with you their recommendations and favourite secret spots to seek out over your morning coffee, instead of large anonymous chains with 'all you can eat' breakfast buffets.

Above all, it's a mindset rather than yet another list of 'things you must do or see'. Taking the time to stop, and breathe, and think. Making some different choices. Seeing travel as a whole experience, rather than a list of must-see destinations. (But remember, you've got the option of -ish. You don't have to go entirely fast, or entirely slow – go slow-ish if that's what works for you!)

FLYING

OK, let's address the elephant in the room – flying. Flying is bad for the planet, I think we all recognise that.

- Aviation makes up around 2-4 per cent of total greenhouse gas emissions.
- One return flight from London to Sydney will use about half the average person's annual carbon footprint.

So does this mean we can never set foot on board a plane ever again? No it doesn't. But what I think it **does** mean is that we need to start to travel, and fly, in a much more thoughtful way. Instead of hopping on a plane for a 24-hour business trip, or on a weekend stag do, we need to think first whether there are other ways we can achieve the same ends without the flight. So is Skype or video conferencing for business meetings an option? Could you have a stag do closer to home? Or travel by train if it's in Europe? We need to start to think about air travel as a luxury again, rather than as the norm. This is difficult when often air travel is so much cheaper than the train. But maybe we need to start factoring the cost to the planet at the same time as the financial cost to our bank accounts.

TOP TIPS FOR SUSTAINABLE(ISH) FLYING

- Fly economy – I'm sure that this is what 99 per cent of us do anyway, but just in case you're ever tempted to book a business class seat, remember it's not just your wallet that will be impacted. Business and first class seats take up a lot more room, meaning that your share of the emissions from the flight is greater.
- Fly direct – taking off and landing is energy intensive; fly the most direct route and limit stopovers.
- Travel light – reduce the amount of luggage you take, which will reduce the overall weight that the plane is carrying.

Top Tips continues overleaf

- Newer airlines will often have a more modern, and therefore more fuel-efficient, fleet.
- Take your own plastic-free food. When you book your ticket, let them know you don't want a meal and reduce your plastic footprint.
- Take your water bottle on board – you'll have to empty it to get through security, but you can then refill it on the other side.

WHAT ABOUT CARBON OFFSETTING?

One option to potentially negate the negative impact of flying is simply to carbon offset our flights. A quick click of a button and a fiver later and we can fly with a clear conscience. Right?

A 2016 EU study found that 85 per cent of carbon offsets failed to reduce emissions. Bummer. One of the big problems with carbon offsetting is that it does exactly what we want it to do and makes us feel less guilty. We then feel like we've been given some kind of 'get out of jail free' card and can continue to fly willy-nilly, when actually it would be far more effective to fly less and more thoughtfully.

Also, a lot of schemes focus on planting trees – replanting new forests to replace areas of deforested ancient rainforests is like putting a sticking plaster on a gaping wound. Existing and established rainforests act as massive carbon sinks (trapping CO_2 and preventing it from entering the atmosphere), as well as providing vital habitats and ecosystems that can't be easily replaced by simply planting an equivalent number of new trees.

If you are going to carbon offset, then make sure that you research the scheme thoroughly; the World Land Trust (www.worldlandtrust. org) and Cool Earth (www.coolearth.org) are both endorsed by David Attenborough and work to protect existing carbon sinks and rainforests rather than replace them.

What is carbon offsetting?

Carbon offsetting is a way to compensate for your emissions by funding an equivalent carbon dioxide saving elsewhere. Our everyday actions, at home and at work, consume energy and produce carbon emissions, such as driving, flying and heating buildings. Carbon offsetting is used to balance out these emissions by helping to pay for emission savings in other parts of the world.

CAN TRAVEL AND TOURISM EVER BE SUSTAINABLE?

I have to confess that until recently my whole thought process around travelling for holiday went something like this: 'We would need to fly. Flying is bad (for the planet). Therefore, holidaying abroad is bad.' I figured that the only things we could do would be to try and make our travels have a *less negative* effect, and had never really considered that it has the potential to have a *net positive* impact on both people and planet until I spoke to Vicky Smith, founder of sustainable travel company Earth Changers (www.earth-changers.com) for my Sustainable(ish) podcast.

Tourism itself isn't a bad thing. In fact, it accounts for 10 per cent of both the world's jobs and of global GDP. It is possibly the only industry that has infiltrated pretty much every corner of the globe, and therefore its potential for either a negative OR a positive effect is huge.

Sustainable tourism is defined by the UN World Tourism Organisation as:

'Tourism that takes full account of its current and future economic, social and environmental impacts, addressing the needs of visitors, the industry, the environment and host communities.'

Which sounds kind of dry, and not a huge amount of holiday fun if we're honest, doesn't it? But Vicky talks about how tourism is a bit like a recipe for a cake. Flying is one ingredient, but there are lots of other ingredients that are needed to make up the whole experience and each of those has the potential to have a positive impact on either the people in the local area, or the planet, or ideally both. So your choice of accommodation, for example, can have a big impact on the overall sustainability of your trip. What are their recycling policies? Do they save/recycle water? Do they source food and drink locally and seasonally? What steps are they taking to reduce their energy usage? How are they supporting the local community and economy?

These aren't questions that we automatically think about when we start shopping around to book a holiday, but a little bit more digging and research can make our holiday much green-er and probably also a more authentic experience.

Booking your holiday through dedicated sustainable tourism sites means that everything is researched and rigorously checked by an expert, but it's getting easier and easier to find eco-friendly holidays. TripAdvisor, for example, has a Green Leaders Programme that 'showcases a variety of eco-friendly hotels and B&Bs, from budget to luxury – and they're all committed to green practices like recycling, local and organic food, and electric car charging stations'. (NB This is, however, self-proclaimed by the accommodation providers, so always do a spot of research yourself too.)

Greenwashing and tourism

Like many other sectors, tourism has been quick to recognise that there is a growing demand from customers for more ethical and sustainable options, and unfortunately opportunities for 'greenwashing' (see page 13) are rife. Companies will make claims of green and sustainable practices that look good from the outside but really don't stand up to closer scrutiny. So as an average consumer looking to book a holiday, how can we try and pick the most sustainable options?

Unfortunately, there's no consistent accreditation process that can be applied across the board to help us, but doing a bit of digging via the web can be a helpful place to start:

- If sustainability is high on the agenda for a travel company, resort or hotel, then it should feature pretty strongly on their website.
- Look for inconsistencies – do they proudly proclaim to have recycling bins, yet fly in all their food from around the globe, for example?
- Ask questions – don't be afraid to fire off an email and ask. People and companies who are genuinely trying to do better should be pretty open to questions, and be able to back up their claims with data and evidence.

With thanks to Vicky Smith at Earth Changers for compiling this list.

1 Take the train instead of flying – travelling by train instead of plane within Europe can result in up to a 90 per cent reduction in carbon emissions.

2 Take other public transport – coaches and buses emit less carbon than planes, where trains aren't available.

3 Once you're at your destination, walk or cycle if you can.

4 Think about your accommodation – for example, their energy source and use, water use, food sourcing etc. Also be aware of issues like staff employment, pay and conditions, support for the local community, and conservation.

5 Eat local and seasonal if you can – buying local organic food supports the local staff and economy and environment.

6 Choose your experiences and activities carefully. Jet skiing sounds like a lot of fun, but uses a lot of fuel in a short space of time. Look for 'lower carbon' activities and shop local – if you're looking for souvenirs and gifts, look out for local artisan craftspeople to buy from rather than a novelty hat or T-shirt.

7 Reduce your plastic use – just because you're on holiday doesn't mean you can take your eco-hero cape off.

- Take a reusable water bottle with you. If you're travelling somewhere where the water might not be safe to drink, check out water-to-go (www.watertogo.eu), which is a portable water filtration system in a reusable bottle that 'eliminates over 99.9 per cent of all microbiological contaminants including viruses, bacteria, chemicals and heavy metals from any non-salt water source'.

- Take your reusable shopping bags with you and look out for loose fruit and veg if you're food shopping.

- Remember to say 'no straw please' if you're sipping cocktails by the pool.

5 QUICK WINS FOR SUSTAINABLE(ISH) TRAVEL

1 Walk or bike any journey under 2 miles.

2 Holiday in the UK.

3 See if you can commute by public transport or bike once a week.

4 If/when you're in the market for a new car, investigate options for either a full electric or a plug-in hybrid, whether it's new or secondhand.

5 Give your car a sustainable(ish) once-over – check the tyre pressures, and take off that roof box you're still lugging around six months after your holiday.

MORE SUGGESTIONS:

☐ Consider an electric bike to help you commute to work

☐ Sign up for Liftshare and get sharing your car

☐ Stick to the speed limit!

☐ Have a car-free day a week – you can always do this at the weekend if that's easier

☐ Have a car-free day out once a month

☐ Suggest video-conferencing for work meetings rather than in person

☐ Replace one flight with the train (especially short haul)

☐ Travel light – if you can fly with hand luggage only, the plane will be carrying less weight. Yes, it's only marginal, but what if everyone did it?

☐ Get a water-to-go filtration bottle if you're travelling somewhere with questionable water hygiene (www.watertogo.eu)

☐ Shop independent and local when you do travel and you reach your destination

☐ Eat local. If you're in a strange city, the temptation can be to head for the familiar chains. Take the time to research and try out some local options and some seasonal delicacies

Over to you (aka now get up and do!)

List three or four ideas below for changes you could make to how you travel.

Action	Timeframe
1.	
2.	
3.	
4.	

Resources

• SUSTRANS (WWW.SUSTRANS.ORG.UK)

Walking and cycling charity with a website packed with helpful suggestions to help make walking and cycling easier and more doable. They also support a whole network of cycle routes around the country.

- **CYCLE TO WORK SCHEME (WWW.GOV.UK/GOVERNMENT/ PUBLICATIONS/CYCLE-TO-WORK-SCHEME-IMPLEMENTATION- GUIDANCE)**

    These are quite dull government documents – the vast majority of bike shops and retailers are now signed up to the scheme and should be able to provide you with the information you need.

- **LIFTSHARE (WWW.LIFTSHARE.COM)**

    The easy way to share your car journeys.

- **FULLY CHARGED (WWW.FULLYCHARGED.SHOW)**

    The world's no.1 clean energy and electric vehicle channel. With more than 380 free episodes on YouTube, it has everything you need to know about driving electric.

- **SLOW TRAVEL EUROPE (WWW.SLOWTRAVELEUROPE.EU)**

    Website offering thoughts that might appeal to those interested in exploring slow travel options as they explore Europe.

- **EARTH CHANGERS (WWW.EARTH-CHANGERS.ORG)**

    Not only can you book inspirational and transformative positive impact holidays on the site, Vicky's blog is a wealth of well-researched and balanced information on all aspects of sustainable travel.

- **FLIGHT FREE UK (WWW.FLIGHTFREE.CO.UK)**

    A campaign asking people to give up flying in 2020, with a goal of 100,000 making the pledge. The site is packed with ideas and incentives for alternative flight-free holidays. And you can sign up while you're there – I have!

11

Sustainable(ish) celebrations

Celebrations seem to have become synonymous with consumerism. Retailers are quick to jump on the bandwagon of any 'special day' and to cleverly market all manner of gifts just for the occasion – Father's Day craft ales or golf ball markers; specially made Easter bonnets and baskets for collecting the myriad of eggs and bunny-themed paraphernalia; and it seems that no child's birthday is now complete without age-appropriate helium balloons and a whole class party, which inevitably generates 30 or so gifts (and the ensuing tantrums and meltdowns).

Maybe it's time we started to question a little bit our need to celebrate with 'stuff'.

More and more stuff. To buy, to wrap, to squeeze into our already cluttered and overcrowded homes. It has become a societal expectation and a pressure that we put on ourselves and others to give new things – because it's Christmas, because it's your birthday, because how else will people know that we care?

All of this stuff, the gifts, the decorations, the paper plates, the food – it all comes from somewhere. It has used up precious resources, and someone somewhere may have been working for a pittance in some godforsaken factory on the other side of the world to make it. And it has to go somewhere when we're done with it – some of it might only be used for a matter of minutes or hours before being casually tossed 'away' (and if you've been paying attention so far, we all know now that there is no such place as 'away').

While we all want our gifts to be loved, cherished and used, the reality is that the best-case scenario for some of them is that they end up in the charity shop, but our charity shops are already overflowing with well-meaning, lovingly given gifts. And the worst-case scenario is they go straight to landfill. To sit and rot.

But it's hard, isn't it?

It's *really* hard to push back against all that without feeling mean, or worrying about being judged. There is a real pleasure that comes with giving, and I am by no means suggesting we should ever stop giving – time, love, attention – all can be gifted with abandon. However, the vast majority of us are lucky enough to already have pretty much everything we want or need, and may well be feeling overwhelmed with the sheer volume of stuff in our houses, our garages, our sheds and our lofts.

To **not** give a present to someone else can feel so very, very wrong. Especially at times like Christmas, when everyone is giving presents, and it's all so jolly and lovely, and to not give a present would seem to cast some kind of Scrooge-like dampener on the whole celebration of excess. So how do we celebrate, how do we show our love, our affection, without trashing the planet?

GIVE LESS

Could you cull your Christmas present list?

Do the grown-ups really need gifts? Or stockings? (My mum used to make up stockings for me and my brother well into our late 20s...)

As nerve-racking as it might feel to be the one who makes the first move, you may well find that suggestions of 'kids' presents only' for Christmas, or even a Secret Santa type thing for the wider family, may actually be greeted with relief from the rest of the family who had also been feeling the pressures of time and money during the festive period.

Does your little darling really need 10 presents from you on top of all the ones from Auntie Cath, cousin Jim, and other relatives you barely see yet still feel obliged to send a present to. Will your kids really notice if the tower of presents is fractionally smaller?

Will they feel any less loved or cherished?

If all else fails, tell yourself it's character building for them.

GIVE SECONDHAND

I struggled with this one for a little while during our year buying nothing new – is it 'OK' to buy gifts from charity shops? I once found three brilliant books for my Dad for the princely total of about £2.50, and really had to resist the urge to make up the rest of the usual 'present budget' with other things. He got some books he loved, and was none the wiser about the origin or the price (I made sure I rubbed out the pencil price from the inside cover), and I got to do my little bit to save the planet – #smug.

Our kids are now pretty well used to the fact that Lego doesn't always come in boxes, and are genuinely as pleased with presents that are 'new to them' rather than brand new. Keep your eyes out in the charity shops and car boot sales and you will be surprised at what you might find. eBay is also a great place to look if your kids (or in fact anyone else) want something really specific.

RE-GIFTING

This one is always a little controversial, but I come firmly down on the side of 'Yes, it's OK to re-gift'. Especially with kids' gifts from birthday parties – they can end up overwhelmed with the sheer number of presents, and as parents we can get overwhelmed with figuring out exactly where it's all going to go. I've heard some people argue that it's rude, or ungrateful, but with a few provisos it's a strategy that can work really well.

- Squirrel the gifts away before your kids have a chance to play with them. Or if you're braver than me, you can just let them know what you're doing and why.
- Make a note of who has given what so you don't commit the cardinal sin of re-gifting a present back to the very person who bought it in the first place.
- Try and wrap the present up away from the prying eyes of your kids, who are otherwise bound to suddenly remember being given it, and that inevitably it was their favourite present ever.

Re-gifting is also totally acceptable for adult gifts – keeping them for the school tombola/raffle, or simply passing them on to someone who you think will love them more than you do is OK.

MAKING

During our year of buying nothing new I spent many an hour slaving over first Pinterest for ideas, and then my sewing machine, trying desperately to recreate that perfect Pinterest vision using only materials I already had. Needless to say, more often than not I failed, and if I'm totally honest there may be a teeny possibility that some of my homemade creations were more than a little ~~crap~~ underwhelming. If you're a dab hand with the sewing machine, or an amazing knitter, then knock yourself out with handmade gifts, but it's probably a good idea to give some thought to where your 'raw materials' have come from (*see* page 124), and whether the gift will actually be cherished and used in relation to the time and energy you put into it. I'm sure we all have memories of those knitted jumpers or cardigans from well-meaning maiden aunts that we were obliged to wear for a photo and then never saw the light of day again.

It took me longer than it perhaps should have done to face up to the crapness of my painstakingly home-sewn gifts, and that maybe I needed to look for another skill set I could use.

So I turned to baking. Which has many advantages:

- Edible gifts are nearly always appreciated and will very rarely end up in landfill.
- Recipes can be adapted pretty easily according to what ingredients can be sourced sustainably (*see* Chapter 4).
- Batch cooking means you can spend an afternoon in the kitchen and whip up several presents all at the same time.
- They can often be portioned up in old jam jars, eliminating the need for wrapping paper.
- I'm much better at baking than I am at sewing.

So play to your strengths and skills. And if your skills/lifestyle/energy levels don't match up to a handmade Christmas, please don't sweat it.

BUY LOCAL

Once upon a time local craft markets were full of knitted loo roll dollies and acrylic baby cardis, but now if you choose your market well you will be very pleasantly surprised at the loveliness on offer. All of which has been lovingly crafted by an independent artisan who will do a delighted happy dance when you buy from them.

BUY ETHICAL

I talked about this way back in Chapter 1, but it bears repeating. When you spend money, you're effectively casting a vote for the kind of world you want. Think about that when you're buying gifts. Don't vote for mass-produced tat from China. Vote for local, Fairtrade, organic, handmade, sustainably sourced.

Sustainable(ish) gift wrapping

> **DID YOU KNOW?**
>
> Each year in the UK alone we throw away the equivalent of 108 million rolls of wrapping paper, and that's just at Christmas!

That is a bonkers amount.

And when you consider that most of it can't or won't be recycled, much of this is going to landfill, and with so many shiny or glittery gift wraps now, these can sit for years contributing to the microplastics issue. And then there's sellotape, so even if your paper can be recycled, the sellotape is probably going to contaminate the recycling.

All in all, not good.

> **TOP TIP**
>
> If your wrapping paper stays in a ball when you scrunch it up, it can be recycled (providing it's not covered in glitter). If it unfurls itself, it can't.

PRE-LOVED WRAPPING PAPER

Yes, I am that person sitting in the corner of the room visibly wincing as the kids rip away at the wrapping paper, and who squirrels it all away to smooth out and keep it to use again. I have even been known to take a tip from my Nana and iron it – a good press with the iron not only removes the creases, but can make the sellotape easier to remove.

Embrace your inner Nana and ignore the sniggers/rolling of eyes.

MAKE YOUR OWN WRAPPING PAPER

Old newspapers and magazines can make really effective wrapping paper and can be prettied up if needed with the addition of some reusable ribbon.

If you're feeling especially clever you could even get appropriate papers/mags for the person in question (ask on Freegle if anyone local has finished with the publication you're looking for) – the *Financial Times* for your accountant sister, or *Vogue* for your fashion-mad nephew.

Another option is to use plain brown kraft paper – this can be 'tastefully decorated' by the kids using paint or stamps if you want a personalised touch/aren't too precious about how nice your wrapping paper looks.

GLASS JARS

My love for the humble jam jar knows no bounds, and I never ever throw one out (or even recycle it). I also keep my eye out in charity shops for pretty glass jars and snap them up whenever I spot one to add to my hoard. My only issue is that I can sometimes be loath to gift my favourite jars in case I never see them again.

Drop heavy hints to your friends about how much you love it when people give you the jars back to use again.

FUROSHIKI

This Japanese style of using fabric for wrapping is rapidly becoming all the rage, with the likes of Lush stores offering it as one of their gift-wrapping options. The bonus of this method is that the fabric can count as part of the gift – use fabric from your stash if you have one, or have a look in charity shops for old sheets and duvets. They give you lots of fabric for very little money, and if you are lucky you might find some funky 70s' florals. Things like vintage head scarves also work well, and can often be found for pennies in charity shops. Search online for instructions – there are some great videos on YouTube.

REUSABLE WRAPPING PAPER

There are companies that make and sell reusable fabric wrapping paper, cleverly designed to be used without the need of any kind of sticking together. You can even get some that 'crinkle' when you excitedly poke the present to try and work out what's inside. My only concern with this is making sure that the recipient reuses it themselves, or gives it back!

GIFT TAGS

Cut up old birthday and Christmas cards to use for gift tags – I can't remember the last time we bought any!

PAPER-BASED STICKY TAPE

Washi tape is all the rage, and a great option for anyone who likes their gift wrap to be as enticing as their gift. There is also a paper-based packing tape, which is compostable (*see* page 259), and you can find it online in a variety of widths.

> We use this ALL the time now and it also means I wince less when my youngest goes on a random 'creative spree', which essentially means raiding the recycling box and sticking loads of bits together randomly with sticky tape. Previously I would have had to laboriously pick all the tape off (or I'd have given up and consigned it all to the bin, the shame). Now I can still chuck the cardboard back in the cardboard recycling with a clear conscience.

(Kids') birthday parties (lots of these tips will apply equally to grown-up celebrations)

I can't be alone in finding throwing children's birthday parties hugely stressful. I am in awe of those mothers (because it is usually the mothers) who manage to colour match the plates with the theme, and effortlessly wrangle 20 overexcited children through intricate games, only to top off the whole thing with a homemade cake that looks like Jane Asher has spent the week at their house.

A desire to host a 'sustainable' party might then seem to be adding yet another layer of pressure to an already fraught occasion. But there are some really easy hacks to make your party more eco-friendly.

INVITES

- Go paper free and create a Facebook invite, or email/text the parents.
- Make your own invites using the fronts from old birthday cards.
- Rope in your child to make some using recycled paper or card if you're fine with the fact that they will almost inevitably ~~look a bit crap~~ have that rustic charm to them.

PRESENTS

Unsurprisingly, I've still not been able to persuade my kids to go for letting me add 'no presents please' (if you're a grown-up having a party, do this!) to the invites. But there are ways to manage the influx:

- Invite fewer kids! A whole class party means 20–30 presents (depending on how posh/popular your kid's school is) to shoehorn into your house at the very least. One useful suggestion I remember reading was to allow your child to invite the same number of children as their age, plus one – so a five-year-old could invite six friends, an eight-year-old nine etc. And then hopefully you'll find that once they get much older they'll naturally go for more select gatherings anyway.

- Be prepared – parents may well come and ask you what your little darling wants. Have a list of reasonably priced suggestions so that at least they end up with something they actually want.
- Books are a great idea – ask your kids for a list of books they want to read and circulate that.
- 'Fiver parties' hit the news a while back and caused a bit of a storm in a teacup. The idea is that you ask guests to contribute £5 to a bigger present that the birthday boy or girl is saving up for. I think it's a great idea!

DECORATIONS

- AVOID THE BALLOONS

  Regardless of what they're made of, balloons are single use, and end up in landfill. Go for reusable options like bunting instead (bonus points if you make it yourself from secondhand fabric…). Pom pom garlands are another good option – you can buy them readily online, but there is a certain satisfaction to be gained from making your own (and remember, all of this can be done well in advance, and once the hard work is done, you get to benefit from it again and again in subsequent years).

- PAPER CHAINS AND STREAMERS

  Good old paper chains work really well and can be saved for reuse (if you're super careful!) or simply recycled once the party is over. You can rope the kids into making them too – use old magazines or newspapers for bonus eco points. Another thing that you can get the kids to 'help' with is paper snowflakes – you can make them using coloured paper so they aren't too overtly 'snowflake-y' for a spring or summer party.

- TABLECLOTHS

  Again, avoid single use if at all possible. Can you use the one you already have? Or can you borrow one from a friend or put a shout out on Freecycle? Fabric tablecloths are the best option as they are relatively absorbent and can simply be chucked in the washing machine once you're done.

FOOD

Keep it simple and don't over-cater (applies for grown-up parties too). Most of the children will be far too excited to eat much at all (possibly doesn't apply to grown-up parties – depends on how excitable you/your friends are…). I think one of the best kids' party food ideas I've ever seen was hot dogs, followed by massive bowls of strawberries and blueberries. That was it. No endless bowls of lurid party rings and bright orange crisps, no token gestures of carrot sticks that we all know they are never going to eat but that make us feel better about the massive amount of sugar laid out on the table.

- If you're going with the crisps option, buy a big bag and dish it out into bowls on the table, rather than lots of individual packets.
- Use reusable plates and cups – another great reason for keeping numbers down! If you don't have enough of your own, ask friends if you can borrow theirs for the afternoon, or ask on your local Freecycle site if anyone has any you could borrow.
- If you are lucky enough to have a 'Share Shop' near you, there may well be a set you can borrow, and you can hire glasses for big grown-up bashes (*see* page 21).
- Kids' partyware hire is becoming increasingly popular – a mum local to me has started one up where you can hire the plates etc and a percentage of the fee goes to your school's PTA. Alternatively, some school PTAs are starting their own schemes as fundraisers. Check out the Reusable Party Kit Network (www.partykitnetwork.uk).

CAKE

Let's face it, a birthday party isn't a birthday party without a cake. Cupcakes are a great option – I use reusable cases and simply peel them off before icing. You can get home-compostable cake cases from If You Care, although they only come in brown.

Again, keep it simple if you possibly can, saving yourself hours of your life fiddling with sugar paste, and all of the plastic bags that said sugar paste comes in. Butter icing is my go-to plastic-free option, decorated with sweets or sprinkles.

PARTY BAGS

Gah! Party bags – every parent's nightmare, and every kid's dream.

> *Confession: My youngest LOVES a party bag – the tackier and plastic-ier (may have just made up a word there) the better. My heart sinks when he comes home proudly bearing his plastic bag full of landfill in transit and sugar.*

While I can't do anything about the party bags he brings home, I can certainly make sure that the party bags we hand out are more eco-friendly.

Here are some ideas for sustainable(ish) party bags:

- Use plain brown or white paper bags – the kids can decorate them as part of the party if you want, or you can set your own kids to work beforehand.
- Piece of cake or a cupcake – avoid clingfilm if you can – a paper napkin can be composted, or foil can be reused or recycled.
- Colouring pencils – one year our eldest had a forest school party and I managed to find some pencils made from coppiced wood sticks. They all got one of those and a cupcake – happy days!
- Little packets of seeds, maybe with a mini pot and instructions for planting them?
- Books – you can often get big multipacks of books from places like the Book People that work out at less than £1 a book.
- Little pots or jam jars of homemade play dough – a great idea for little-er ones.
- Chocolate coins.
- Pick 'n' mix sweets in paper bags.

If all else fails, you can order plastic-free party bags online (another genius idea I wish I'd thought of...) at www.plasticfreepartybags.com.

Five sustainable(ish) gifts to give to kids

If your kid's excitement level at another party invite isn't quite matched by yours and you just can't face buying any more plastic crap to foist on other people's children, here are some ideas:

1 **A book** If possible, ask the parent what books/authors they like, and what they've already read. Or see if your child has something they think their friend would love that they've read and/or have sitting on their bookcase.

2 **A book token** If you're really not sure, this is a brilliant option – you will look like the sort of highbrow parent who really values reading and all things bookish and they can get something they actually might sit and read.

3 **Giant chocolate buttons** These are my all-time favourite ever party gift and can be whipped up on the morning of the party when I've forgotten all about it. Simply take 100g bar of chocolate (Fairtrade and plastic free, obvs) and melt it in the microwave. Then use a teaspoon to splodge and smoosh teaspoons of chocolate on to a lined baking tray and into vaguely round giant button shapes. Add sprinkles if you're feeling crazy/have some in the cupboard, and then leave to set before packaging up in a clean jam jar. All the kids we've given these to have loved them.

> Confession: I've not been brave enough to ask the parents if they think we're weird, or maybe just a bit mean, but I tell myself that they love them too.

4 **Club together** Join together with the other parents to buy them one big thing they actually want. Admittedly, this involves a little liaison with the other parents, and probably some kind of parental WhatsApp group, but if you all chuck in a fiver they could get something decent rather than lots of plastic tat.

5 **Money** If all else fails, give them some money. I know it feels wrong, and not in the spirit of things, but at least they can put it towards something they (or their parents) really want, rather than something they'll play with for five minutes and then forget about (see 'Fiver Parties' on page 241).

Christmas

Christmas seems to have become the most commercialised and consumer focused of our celebrations, with the pressure to provide the biggest, the best, the most presents mounting year on year. My mum would go a bit bonkers at Christmas, especially as money became less tight, and as a child my Christmas memories are of huge stockings bulging with presents, and a mountain of presents under the tree come Christmas morning. And I can't deny that there is something magical, and oh so exciting about the gaudily wrapped piles of presents just waiting to be ripped open. But I also now know the terrible impact that our rabid overconsumption is having on the planet, and each Christmas find myself torn between wanting to create that magic and joy for my own kids, and wanting them to learn that more stuff, more toys, more presents do not equate to happiness. I want our Christmases to be about experiences, time together playing board games and watching crap TV, watching the local pantomime and boo-ing the villain. Not about how many presents they got.

But it's a work in progress, and I think a difficult time of year for many of us.

> *Confession: Last Christmas I was running a 'Crap-free Christmas' course online and my youngest saw me posting about not buying so many presents. He promptly started shouting at me and telling me that 'Presents are the whole point of Christmas. They bring the joy!' I clearly have work to do.*

Ultimately, I guess it comes back to the premise of 'conscious consumption' that I talked about way back in Chapter 1 – taking some time to step back and to think about what we are buying, and why. Where it has come from, and what will happen to it once the kids are bored with it and have moved on to the next thing.

Here are some tips for a more planet-friendly Christmas.

ADVENT CALENDARS

Is it just me or have Advent calendars gone a bit bonkers? Gone are the days of the simple excitement of peeling back the window to see what picture lay beneath (and quite possibly reusing the same calendar year on year until the doors fall off), and the jealousy of friends whose parents let them have chocolate Advent calendars!

Now it seems the sky's the limit for what you can find behind each door (miniature bottles of whisky, different cheese, dog treats), and for the price tag too! In a (possibly vain) attempt to 'de-commercialise' the Christmas countdown we have an 'Advent lorry', which has a small drawer to open each day, each containing a scrap of paper listing an activity. Some will be things that would have happened anyway, like 'star in your school nativity' or 'school/pre-school carol concert'. Others will be a cunning way of getting them to do the things they need to do like make or write Christmas cards, or maybe decorate some wrapping paper. I also rope them in with helping to make mince pies and decorate the Christmas cake. And some will be 'proper' treats like going to the pantomime, or visiting Father Christmas.

Five ideas for alternative Advent calendars

1 **Photos** Scroll through your photos from the year, print out your favourite 24 and pop each one into a numbered envelope.

2 **Reverse Advent calendar** Put one item of non-perishable food into a box each day during Advent and then donate to the Foodbank.

3 **Random acts of kindness** There are loads of templates/ ideas for these online – the idea is that you do a 'random act of kindness' each day – they can be as big or as small as you like.

4 **Reusable Advent calendar** Buy one or make one (if you're that way inclined) and pop a sweet/note/activity into each pocket. I am told this is what the Germans do and the calendars become family heirlooms that get passed down.

5 **Books** Keep your eye out for Christmas books in the charity shops (or simply use the ones you already have if you have enough), then unwrap one each day to snuggle up and read a (short!) story together. Then simply donate the books back to the charity shop. Or keep them and shuffle them up each year so the stories become family traditions and the excitement is in which story they will get each day.

DECORATIONS

We have never been one of those families who buy a new set of Christmas decorations every year, or even have anything resembling a colour scheme. Our box of Christmas decorations comes down from the loft each year, and goes back up pretty much unchanged after the festivities are over, perhaps with the addition of a homemade offering or two from the kids (think assorted loo roll angels and paper snowflakes).

- Good old-fashioned paper chains can be made from newspapers, or if you are feeling the need to be slightly more 'on trend', vintage (or just plain old secondhand) sheet music can look really effective.
- Paper snowflakes are a good one to make with the kids, and can either be stuck to windows or strung together like bunting.
- If you can resist eating them, making gingerbread baubles for the tree is a traditional way of decorating it, but it always seems such a waste to me that they just sit there and go stale. I'd much rather eat them!
- Keep your eyes out on Freecycle and your local charity shops in the run-up to Christmas for people having a sort-out of their Christmas decorations, and you can often pick up all sorts – fairy lights, baubles, artificial trees.

THE TREE

The debate over which is better for the planet – artificial trees that can be used again and again, or real trees that are used only the once – is one that 'rages' each Christmas. If you already have an artificial tree, then stick with it. Cherish it and look after it and keep it going for as long as you can. For a real tree, I think the best option is one with roots that can be planted out and reused each year, but not everyone has the space for that. OR there are more and more places popping up around the country where you can rent a tree for Christmas and return it to them to look after the rest of the year!

If you have the time, energy or inclination, check out Pinterest for some great ideas for 'upcycled' Christmas trees – we made one from egg boxes during our year buying nothing new (it was awful) but since then have done a little better with a pallet tree that my hubby made with the kids and a pom-pom tree that now takes pride of place each year.

STOCKINGS

The temptation can be to fill these with cheap plastic that delights our little darlings for a few minutes, and then gets scooped up into a black bag come Boxing Day. Edible things are a good option – gold coins, fudge rolled into balls of 'reindeer poo', cardboard tubes of sweets, foil-wrapped chocolate Santas. I start to scour the charity shops from about September, squirrelling away finds – books, colouring books (check that none have been done first), small toy cars, maybe a soft toy. Colouring pencils, rubbers and pencil sharpeners are things that we always seem to be losing in our house, so replacements are always needed. You can also find wooden and 'eco-friendly' stocking fillers with a quick search of online shops if you're struggling.

GIFTS

Can you 'cull' your present list at all?

Do the grown-ups really need gifts? Could you make them some chutney or fudge instead? Or offer up your babysitting services for an evening? Or do an office Secret Santa?

Experiences

I love the idea of gifting experiences rather than things. In the past we've bought the kids an 'Owl Experience' at the Hawk Conservancy, where they've been able to fly all kinds of different owls, and dissect an owl pellet – they still talk about it now!

We've also agreed with friends to not buy gifts and to all meet up for a day out at the pantomime over the festive period. Some of these might be more expensive than your budget allows, but teaming up with other family members can help to overcome this. In the past I have had some brilliant 'experience' gifts, ranging from a day's bread-making at River Cottage HQ to a knicker-making workshop!

Secondhand books

In the past we have hit lucky in local charity shops with some great books in fabulous condition. Or get on eBay – one year we bought my cricket-loving brother a copy of the *Cricketer* magazine from the month and year of his birth.

Have a swap evening with friends in the run-up to Christmas

Ask everyone to have a sort-out, and bring along anything they no longer want or need. You can then swap. This works really well with kids' toys and books etc for stocking fillers.

Give your time

If you know people who have young kids, give a babysitting voucher; if you have a friend who wants to learn to sew or knit, and you already can, offer to teach them in the New Year; if you have an older relative with a large garden, give them a couple of hours of gardening time.

Audio gifts

If you have family who live overseas, spend an evening recording you and the kids reading bedtime stories, and burn it on to a CD/create an audio file. Even the thought of doing this makes me a bit weepy, and I have to admit to feeling a little bit cheated of the opportunity to do it by not having any far-flung relations…!

FOOD

- Don't over-cater! It's only a Sunday roast after all, with a few extra trimmings (if you choose to do them). Do a meal plan for Christmas week, factoring in visitors and any staying guests.
- If you can, make some meals in advance and stash them in the freezer.
- Buy local – visit your local butcher for your turkey. Buy free range and organic if you can afford it.
- Factor in leftovers to your meal plan. I always order a bigger turkey than we need, and deliberately cook too much veg, so we can have bubble and squeak and a turkey pie!

CRACKERS

More often than not made from shiny paper, decorated with glitter, filled with plastic tat, and shipped from China, crackers are not the planet's friend. Making your own is simpler than it might sound (think empty loo rolls and wrapping paper) – there are loads of tutorials online and you can buy cracker snaps pretty easily. There are also reusable crackers (we have some of these from www.keepthiscracker.com) that slot together and can be used year after year. To fill them, I'll often get the kids roped into making paper hats, then pop in a chocolate coin and a scratch card (obviously if you're more inventive/generous than me, you can put in something more exciting).

Dealing with friends and family

While gift-giving seems like a pretty simple transaction, we all know that it's not. It's fraught with emotional subtext, and for many (especially my parents' generation, it seems in my experience), giving = love. To not give a gift would be mean, and rude, and would drain the joy from the occasion. Or at least that's how they see it. Trying to explain to friends and family that you want to try and do things a little differently (especially anything that might buck the family traditions) is going to be tricky.

Here's some suggestions for getting started:

1 **Don't try and do it all at once** This applies to all things sustainable(ish) – the 'ish' is there for a reason! Think of any changes you make as a diet – if you crash diet and go at it hell for leather, you'll end up miserable, cranky and resenting the choices you've made. Plus the family will think you've lost the plot and you're unlikely to be able to bring them along with you if you suddenly go all evangelical and start berating them for their choice of cracker. Slow and steady (as dull as it sounds) wins the race. Go for the 'low-hanging fruit' (i.e. the easiest changes!) first, and pick your battles, for example wrapping paper, or choosing to only buy books as gifts.

2 **Be brave** Be the one who makes 'that phone call' (or sends that WhatsApp message) suggesting that maybe only the kids get pressies this year. Or that the grown-ups do a Secret Santa. Or that you do a Secret Santa for the kids if you have lots to buy for – they get one present they really want, everyone saves time, money and stress, you save the planet (#winwinwin).

3 **Make it easy for people** If your house is already full to bursting and you hold your head in your hands and weep when you peek into the kids' bedrooms, your inside voice may well be screaming 'NOTHING!!!' when you get asked by anxious relatives what the kids want this year. Have some suggestions ready for them. EITHER for stuff the kids genuinely do want and you know they'll love and play with for a long time
OR for days out/experiences you can all do together – I always think National Trust membership is 'the gift that keeps on giving' for families.

4 **Show don't tell** Families are complicated beasts at the best of times, and even more so at Christmas. As much as you might be visibly wincing as you see that Aunt Mildred has wrapped up the gifts in glittery metallic paper (a total no-no, it can't be recycled), don't berate her. But make sure that your gifts are wrapped up in reusable or recyclable options – e.g. brown kraft paper, 'upcycled' newspapers, magazines or old maps, fabric wraps. And if anyone comments or asks, just have a sentence or two at the ready, like 'Yes, I'm really pleased with them – we've been looking at how to make our Christmas a little bit greener this year' (and try not to look too smug).

5 **Enjoy it** Christmas is stressful enough for lots of people. Do what you can. Focus on the positive changes and the different choices you HAVE been able to make, and don't feel guilty about the things you might not have got around to. The last thing Christmas needs is more guilt attached!

Easter

I know this will make me sound an old curmudgeon, but back in my day, Easter meant little more than a hot cross bun and a couple of Easter eggs (and school assemblies about the resurrection of Jesus, obvs). Now it seems, like so many things, to have grown, and expanded into yet another opportunity to buy stuff we don't need.

I have no objection to Easter eggs. I welcome the influx of chocolate with open arms, especially now lots of the manufacturers make boxes entirely out of cardboard, which are therefore recyclable. And even more so when my children forget about them, and it becomes my moral duty to use them up (eat them) before they go past their sell-by date (not that I pay any attention to best-before dates, unless they are providing me with an opportunity to 'have' to eat chocolate).

- **SEEK OUT FAIRTRADE EASTER EGGS**
  They are pretty mainstream now, and can be found in most
  supermarkets, so no excuses!

- **RECYCLABLE PACKAGING**
  Try and buy the eggs that come in boxes without plastic
  windows or those plastic shells that are supposed to stop them
  from breaking.

- **AVOID SINGLE-USE EASTER TAT**
  I'm thinking flimsy plastic baskets, 'Easter egg hunt kits', crappy
  plastic bonnets etc etc.

- **PUT THE CHOCOLATE TO 'GOOD USE'**
  If you do end up with too much chocolate (is there such a
  thing?), then I find that for some reason it is more acceptable
  to me to eat it in the form of brownies than it is just to stuff
  it into my face. Or Rice Krispie cakes, if your culinary talents
  are limited.

Valentine's

There is a part of me now that rebels against Valentine's Day – the fact
that, like so many of our celebrations, it has become just another way for
manufacturers and retailers to sell us more stuff. We all know that love
isn't about one day a year, a bunch of flowers and a Hallmark card – the
love is in the cups of tea, in the folded laundry, in biting our tongues
when the other one says something stupid. We've given up on Valentine's
Day but I can still see the romance of it, especially if you're in the first

flush of love! Here are some ideas that help you to love the planet as well as your beloved.

SAY IT WITH FLOWERS

February is not a great time of year for home-grown flowers here in the northern hemisphere, but there are ways to source your flowers without the associated carbon footprint of either flying them in from warmer climes, or them being grown in heated polytunnels. Anemones, hellebores, alstroemeria, daffodils, narcissi, ranunculus and tulips can all be grown in the UK and be available for Valentine's Day without the need for additional heating. Bulbs of snowdrops are a lovely alternative, or something like a heart-shaped willow wreath.

SAY IT WITH FOOD

Treat each other to a lovely meal in, with locally sourced ingredients. Get out the candles, turn off the TV, lay the table and talk to each other!

SAY IT WITH FAIRTRADE CHOCOLATE

If you're going down the chocolate route (always a sure-fire winner in my book), look out for a Fairtrade option, and recyclable packaging (not the most romantic, I know…).

Wedding gifts

I will hold my hands up and confess that when we got married, it was pre *My Make Do and Mend Year*, and my hubby and I embarked with glee on a trip round our nearest John Lewis, armed with one of those barcode zappers, happily and, it has to be said, fairly indiscriminately adding all manner of homewares to our wedding list. I look back now and feel more than a little ashamed. We had no real need for anything. We had already been living together for a couple of years, and had functioned perfectly well with the mishmash of things we had acquired. I struggle now to remember how we justified what seems in hindsight to be such a thoughtless act of consumerism.

I can see the logic of how it started – years ago, when people didn't live together first, and were embarking on their married life together without plates, spoons and kettles, it made sense that their friends and family would want to help them on their way, with a gift that would be genuinely useful and that would help the newlyweds to make a home together. But by and large, this isn't the case any more, yet we still feel this need to give, and most of the time we are just facilitating our friends' desires to upgrade the things they are bored of. I have no problem with celebrating the coming together of two people who love each other, however they choose to do it. But I do now recoil a little from celebrating that by buying the happy couple a toaster when they already have one that works perfectly well.

So is there another solution? Another way to say, 'Yay, you got married, I'm so happy for you!' without resorting to buying your friends the steak knife set of their dreams? How about some of these?

GIVE YOUR SKILLS

Offer to contribute to the wedding in some way: for example, you could offer to make the cake, or do the bride's hair, or make some bunting for the wedding reception. Hubby once drove one of his friends to their wedding in his 1970s' Dolomite (not at all eco-friendly, I know).

BUY THEM AN EXPERIENCE

If the newlyweds are going on honeymoon, ask them if there's anything special they were hoping to do while on it, like a hot air balloon ride, or a posh meal out, and then club together with some other friends and book it for them.

DONATE TO A CHARITY ON THEIR BEHALF

This probably sounds really lofty and worthy, but I can't help think how much more meaningful it would have been if we had asked our guests to collectively donate to a charity building wells so that communities in developing countries could have access to clean, safe water, or provide education for a year for a kid who couldn't go to school, rather than acquiring yet more stuff the day we got married.

New baby gifts

The safe arrival of a new baby is always a cause for celebration, and the temptation is to plump for bright shiny toys, or beautiful teeny-tiny outfits. For first babies, it can actually be useful sometimes to get clothes, but the baby clothes that are gifted often end up getting saved for 'best' and then never getting worn because babies grow so quickly. And for subsequent children, most already have the things that they need in the form of hand-me-downs from their siblings. Here are some alternative ideas that I think any new parent would love to receive.

SLEEP!

I know you can't really gift this, but you can offer to take the baby out even for just an hour, so that the new mum can sit down and maybe even close her eyes for a moment. And if you make her a hot cup of tea before you go, she will be eternally grateful.

MEALS

Making some 'ready meals' that can be stashed in the freezer and pulled out and chucked in the oven for those days when the baby just refuses to be put down will be a godsend.

ANYTHING ESPECIALLY SWEET AND YUMMY TO EAT

I have taken to visiting friends with new babies armed with a tin of flapjack, or brownies, or cookies. Even if they don't need the sugar fix themselves (although I struggle to foresee a scenario where they wouldn't – even the most hardened sugar-free warrior must weaken in the aftermath of childbirth, surely), they can offer them round to the small army of visitors that will descend on them in the coming weeks.

BABYSITTING

While the baby is new and fresh, and so very very tiny, it is unlikely that any new parents are going to even contemplate the thought of stepping more than three metres away from them, but as the baby gets older, an evening out for a spot of grown-up time will probably be welcomed with open arms. The bonus of this is that you are pretty much guaranteed an early night, as the new parents will be so tired they will be unable to stay out late.

TODDLER ENTERTAINING

If the new baby is a sibling to an older child, offering to take the toddler out for an afternoon, or even to the park for an hour, will be a welcome break for all concerned.

5 QUICK SUSTAINABLE(ISH) CELEBRATION WINS

1 Make chocolate buttons as a present the next time your child is invited to a birthday party. Feel the fear and give them anyway!

2 Review your present list and start crossing off some names...

3 Start saving jam jars to use as receptacles for edible gifts.

4 Make your own bunting or pom-pom strings, or source some that are ethically made, ready for the next party!

5 Save your old Christmas cards to use as gift tags next year.

MORE SUGGESTIONS:

- ☐ Try an alternative Advent calendar
- ☐ Buy one present secondhand
- ☐ Ditch the sellotape – get yourself some paper-based sticky tape (*see page 259*)
- ☐ Aim for plastic-free party bags
- ☐ Buy Fairtrade flowers or chocolate (bonus points for plastic-free packaging)
- ☐ Could you give up Christmas cards and send emails or a WhatsApp message instead?
- ☐ Refuse the temptation to buy any new Christmas decorations
- ☐ Have a 'no-presents' Valentine's Day pact with your other half
- ☐ Give a charity gift
- ☐ Have a 'zero waste' party

Over to you (aka now get up and do!)

List three or four ideas below for changes you could make to celebrate more sustainably.

Action	Timeframe
1.	
2.	
3.	
4.	

Resources

- LOVE A CHRISTMAS TREE (WWW.LOVEACHRISTMASTREE.CO.UK)
  Christmas tree rental.

- WRAG WRAP (WWW.WRAGWRAP.COM)
  Reusable fabric wrapping paper.

- KEEP THIS CRACKER (WWW.KEEPTHISCRACKER.COM)
  Reusable crackers.

- ECO-CRAFT (WWW.ECO-CRAFT.CO.UK)
  Paper compostable sticky tape, as well as a wide variety of recycled card blanks and envelopes if you want to make your own cards.

- THE BRITISH FLOWER COLLECTIVE (WWW.THEBRITISHFLOWER COLLECTIVE.COM)
  Site championing British flowers with information about what flowers are in season during different times of the year, and where to find florists that stock them.

12

Activism(ish)

Activism: The policy or action of using vigorous campaigning to bring about political or social change.

I don't know about you but the phrase 'vigorous campaigning' leaves me feeling a little lacking, and wanting to retreat under the duvet. I speak and write a lot about sustainable living, but do I 'campaign vigorously'? I'm not so sure. It sounds a bit intimidating. A bit 'shouty'. I'm genuinely not sure if I have the time, energy or confidence to campaign vigorously. Does this make me a bad person? Does it mean I don't care 'enough' if I'm not prepared to take placards on to the streets and chant angry slogans? Does this make me a pretty poor advocate for our planet?

I'm sure there are people out there who would say 'yes it does'. That now is when we all need to step up, no matter how uncomfortable it might make us. Because the discomfort we feel now is nothing compared to what we'll feel if nothing changes and we continue on our current trajectory. But I also know that there are lots of people like me out there who care very deeply, but who just don't feel that traditional forms of activism are for them. Maybe what we're talking about is 'activism(ish)' – doing what we can, when we can, to raise awareness not just about the problems, but about the solutions too (and to make all those small but important changes!).

I'm talking about creating change, speaking up about issues, making your voice heard, all without necessarily needing to go on a march (although if you can in any way pluck up the courage, I would really

really encourage you to step up and swell the numbers – it's such a powerful and visible way to show our governments how many of us care and want urgent action).

So if we're not natural activists and campaigners, where does that leave us? Never fear, there are plenty of options for activism(ish).

> The global Youth Climate Strikes (sparked by the amazing Greta Thunberg), along with the Extinction Rebellion protests in spring 2019, eventually forced me out of my introvert's comfort zone and I have now taken part in a climate strike! I went along to the first Mother's Rise Up climate strike in London in May 2019. I'm not going to lie, I felt a little bit uncomfortable for most of the day: I hid my homemade placard on the train journey, and may have moved away discreetly from the shouty/chanting types for fear of being expected to join in – but I'm really glad I went. As much as I am an advocate of 'ish' and 'doing what we can', it is starting to feel to me like it's time I stepped up, and made my voice a little louder. That's not to pressure you into marching and getting shouty if it's not your thing, but just to let you know that it can be done and it's not too hideous an experience.

Greta Thunberg

I couldn't have a chapter on activism (ish or otherwise) without referencing one of the most prominent climate activists of recent years. Greta is a Swedish school student who, on learning about the climate crisis at the age of 15, decided to take action in the form of a weekly strike from school every Friday to protest outside the Swedish parliament. What started as a lonely and solitary action in August 2018 then caught the imagination and hearts of a whole generation of young people and inspired the School Strike for the Climate movement which, most recently at the time of writing, saw over 4 million people take to the streets in September 2019 calling for action on the climate emergency.

If you haven't had the chance to listen to any of her speeches, check them out on YouTube. She pulls no punches. She calls out global politicians and leaders (many of whom are sitting in the room hearing her speak) for their failure to act. She is a remarkable young woman, and has certainly inspired me to be a little bit braver, a little bit more outspoken.

'No one is too small to make a difference, everyone can do something. If everyone did something then huge differences can happen.'

BECOME AN EVERYDAY RADICAL

A few years ago I did a TEDx talk (my first ever public-speaking gig – yes, it was terrifying) and the theme of the event was 'Everyday Radicals'. I was kind of shocked to be asked to apply – I had never in a million years thought of myself as a radical, or that our year of buying nothing new was a radical act. But the more I thought about it, the more I realised quite how radical, how countercultural it is, to push back and to talk about buying *less*. About making do. And mending. And not just to talk about it, to actually do it as well! Depending on which reports you read, we are apparently exposed to up to 5000 ads a day. Now obviously this all depends on where you live, how you travel, how much time you spend on social media, and how much TV you watch, but sadly that's quite a believable number. We are constantly being bombarded with images of the perfect family/couple/life, all made possible by particular products. The subliminal message that is pumped out day in and day out is that new is better. More is better. So in that context, not buying, or buying less and buying better, actually **is** a pretty radical act. Who would have thought it?

And I have to say that now I have embraced my inner rebel, I love it! I see these kinds of acts as a sort of gentle rebellion against the status quo. Every time I patch my jeans and wear my visible mends with pride. Every time I choose secondhand first. Every time I reuse and resist single use. It truly is an act of activism. And you too can be an everyday radical. Simply and easily. Without even getting out of bed if you don't fancy it. **Just say 'No'**. Question the status quo. Question yourself and your motivation. Did you already want that new dress, or that latest upgrade? Or did someone (an ad company paid a lot of money to get you to buy) tell you that you do?

So let's get radical. This is possibly the laziest call to arms ever. Be radical. Buy less.

VOTE WITH YOUR MONEY

I know I've banged on a lot about this already, but that doesn't mean I'm not going to do it again, because it bears repeating. When we spend money, when we give our money to businesses and retailers, when we support certain brands, we are letting the world know that this is what we like. It's our endorsement of their business, and their practices. We're saying that this is what we want more of.

> *My husband and I used to have something of an ongoing battle when we used to buy our milk from the supermarket (before we discovered the excitement and joy of being able to refill glass bottles from a milk-vending machine near us). If he was doing the shopping he would buy the cheaper 'normal' milk, and if I was doing the shopping I would buy organic. His argument was that the normal milk was cheaper and that he didn't really think organic milk was better for the kids. And I would argue that I didn't really care whether it was better for the kids or not (does that make me a bad mother?) but that I wanted to show my support for the organic system, which by and large is a gentler, more sustainable way to farm.*

If we buy fast fashion, we contribute to the demand for it. If we buy fracked gas, we're saying that we think it's OK. I know it's not always that black and white and sometimes our choices are dictated by our finances rather than our values, but on the occasions where you can afford to, vote with your money.

LET RETAILERS KNOW

If you don't like something a brand or a retailer is doing, let them know. The typical British reaction is to tut, maybe to seethe a little inwardly, but to smile through gritted teeth, nod politely and carry on as before.

Let them know. If you love their product but hate the plastic packaging it comes in, email them. If you think your favourite coffee chain should ban disposable cups, tweet them. If you've stopped shopping at what was once your favourite high street store after learning about fast fashion, send them a message on Facebook. Let them know.

Do online petitions work?

Natalie Fee, founder of City to Sea (www.citytosea.org.uk), a non-profit organisation running campaigns to prevent marine plastic pollution at source, shares her experience of their successful 'Switch the Stick' campaign – an online petition calling for supermarkets to switch from plastic cotton buds to cardboard, which is stopping over 400 tonnes of non-recyclable, single-use plastic at source every year!

Q Why did you decide to focus on cotton buds for the Switch the Stick campaign?

A It was during beach cleans (or river cleans in my case!) when I became aware of the cotton bud problem – I was literally picking up hundreds of plastic sticks along a 500-metre stretch of riverbank! Asking retailers to switch to paper stems seemed like such a no-brainer – it wouldn't affect the product, but it could bring about a massive reduction in the 6.2 per cent of plastic on our beaches coming from our toilets!

Q How long did it take to get to 150,000 signatures?

A We started with our own petition, and as a new organisation at the time, we were pleased with the 6000 signatures we managed to collect in a month. But I felt we needed more numbers, so when 38 Degrees approached us to see if we wanted to run it on their platform, I naturally said yes! Which was a great move, as a month later we had another 150,000 signatures on top of ours!

For most businesses, the financial bottom line is king. If enough people let them know that they don't like what they're doing and are willing to take their money elsewhere, that's a pretty strong incentive for them to change.

Q Was there a 'critical number' or event that caused the supermarkets to really sit up and start to take notice?

A Once the petition pushed past the 100,000 mark, I realised we had a serious proposition for the supermarkets. We could demonstrate that these people were their customers and they would no longer be buying plastic cotton buds – so they needed to switch the stick... or lose customers!

Q People sometimes talk a little cynically about 'clicktivism' – how powerful do you believe things like online signature campaigns are in terms of creating real, impactful change?

A Well, 'Switch the Stick' is hard evidence that online petitions can, and do, bring about lasting change. Of course, its success depends on lots of factors, for example the nature of the ask, how popular that subject is with the media or the public, or how powerful the story is that goes with it.

Q What advice would you give to anyone wanting to start their own campaign?

A Do your research. See which campaigning organisations are already working on the thing you want to change, and talk to them so you don't duplicate. You may even be able to do it in collaboration with them, with all their connections, media contacts and supporters ready to support you. If there's no one doing it, or working together isn't an option, then go for it. Be clear, realistic and use great images and video footage to help make your mission stand out from the rest.

WRITE TO YOUR MP

This sounds like the dullest, most grown-up thing a person could do. And I totally acknowledge that it can sometimes feel futile too. But a 2018 report by Green Alliance found that although MPs recognise the need for action on climate change, 'they report limited interest from their constituents'. They don't see it as an issue that they might lose their seats over (although it genuinely feels as I'm sitting writing this that we are on the cusp of change – 2019 saw David Attenborough's *Climate Change – The Facts* air on prime time, and the efforts of Extinction Rebellion and the Youth Climate Strikes are making it more and more difficult for politicians to ignore the issue). And to some extent that's our fault. Because we haven't let them know how much climate change concerns us, how much the government's lack of action frustrates and terrifies us, how scared we are for the future if change doesn't happen at every level.

If you don't already know who your MP is, you can find out here: www.theyworkforyou.com. The next thing is to write them a letter. And more than that, to write them a letter that will actually get read and have an impact.

TOP TIPS FROM THE CLIMATE COUNCIL FOR WRITING EFFECTIVE LETTERS TO MPS

1 INTRODUCE YOURSELF AND YOUR ISSUE

Start the letter by telling your MP who you are and why you are writing to them – make sure you have a specific and focused purpose. Maybe you want to let them know how concerned you are about climate change, or to ask them about renewable energy, or plastic pollution, or fast fashion. Be concise, not vague. In your opening sentence, mention that you are a constituent (aka a voter!). MPs tend to care more about the people they represent. Remember, they are there to represent you.

2 STATE THE FACTS

Recognise and thank your MP for the positive steps that have already been taken in this area (for example, signing up to the Paris climate agreement). Then articulate the fact that the action being taken is insufficient. Clearly state the facts that highlight the need for urgent further action. Why should they act? Be brief and objective, utilising scientific data to persuade rather than hyperbole or embellishment. You need to tell them what needs to change and why.

3 ADD A PERSONAL TOUCH

Explain why the issue is important to you. Include a relevant personal anecdote or experience. This will help make the issue real and tangible for your MP. Storytelling used in conjunction with statistics is crucial in advocacy as it connects the head and the heart of your MP – helping them understand the need for change both rationally and emotionally. Inform them that their stance on this issue affects the way you vote. Also express that others within your electorate care about this issue.

4 TELL THE MP WHAT YOU WOULD LIKE THEM TO DO

To bring about change, you need facts and anecdotes about the issue, but ultimately, you need action. Be clear on what action you want your MP to take. This could include actions such as making a speech in parliament, raising the issue at a meeting, voting for or against something in parliament, or attending a local event.

5 FOLLOW UP

Finish the letter by saying that you look forward to receiving their reply. Provide your contact details so the MP can respond. Be patient as you wait for a reply – politicians lead busy lives! Wait one month, then call your MP's office to remind them of your letter and ask when you may expect a response. If you still don't hear back from them for another two weeks, try again. Be both persistent and polite. (And I would add to this advice. Don't be fobbed off with a standard 'pat on the head, thanks for getting in touch, your concerns have been noted' reply. Write again, ask for a meeting and make sure they know you are serious about this.)

WRITE TO YOUR LOCAL COUNCIL

Once you've gone to the hard work of crafting an effective letter to send to your MP, you may as well rattle one off to your local town and/or county council. It might seem like something of a scattergun approach, but I think this is one of those occasions where more is definitely more. The more people you can let know about your concerns, the better.

VOTE!

While we're on the subject of politics and politicians, let's get this one out there.

Vote.

Your vote counts. Personally, I don't vote strategically. I vote for the party whose values most closely reflect my own, and whose policies are prioritising the things I care about. It's not my place to tell anyone who to vote for, but get informed, and vote for the party you would love to see in power, even if you think it will never happen.

USING SOCIAL MEDIA

Activism on social media is another thing that has a bad rap and is referred to by some as 'slacktivism':

> 'Actions performed via the internet in support of a political or social cause but regarded as requiring little time or involvement, e.g. signing an online petition or joining a campaign group on a social media website or application.'

And I can see the point in some respects – signing a petition to supermarkets claiming outrage at the overpackaging of our food while doing nothing to make a reduction in our own personal consumption may in some circumstances be a little ill thought out. But what if that's all you can do? What if you don't have the financial or physical capabilities to do any more, to shop anywhere differently, or to make different choices? Does this mean you're a slacker?

No, it certainly doesn't. As with all things, the black and white, the 'right way' and the 'wrong way' are interspersed with a myriad of shades of grey. We can only do what we can do. And yes, the more we can do the better, but don't let accusations of slacktivism or not being a 'good enough' activist stop you. So go ahead, sign that petition – at the very least it will do no harm. And if it gets enough support, it will gain some

PR, shine some light on the situation, let retailers know that a lot of people care about these issues, and maybe even end up being debated in parliament, which sends a message to our MPs.

Obviously, I hugely advocate and encourage making positive personal changes around these issues at the same time, but if that's all too much for where you are right now, pick your battles, and there is no harm at all in going with the low-hanging fruit.

If you're on social media, use it. Contact brands and retailers to complain, or to let them know your feelings (politely, obviously). Take a picture of excessively packaged items in the supermarket, share it on Twitter or Facebook tagging the supermarket and the brand. Take a picture of litter, and tag the brand – I've seen some great tweets along the lines of 'Ermmmm, [insert brand name], I just found this, is it yours?' with an accompanying picture of a littered packet of crisps or dropped soft drinks bottle or fast food packaging.

#Whomademyclothes?

This brilliant campaign is run by Fashion Revolution (www. fashionrevolution.org), a charity campaigning to: '…unite people and organisations to work together towards radically changing the way our clothes are sourced, produced and consumed, so that our clothing is made in a safe, clean and fair way.'

Every April, Fashion Revolution Day marks the anniversary of the Rana Plaza factory collapse in Bangladesh, which killed 1138 garment workers in 2013, and throughout the whole week, consumers are encouraged to ask the question, 'Who made my clothes?' on social media using the #whomademyclothes hashtag along with a picture of themselves wearing an item with the brand name or label visible, and tagging in that brand. In 2017 the hashtag reached nearly 150 million accounts, and over 2000 brands and retailers responded with real information about their suppliers and workers.

I love the idea of doing a similar thing with our banks, and asking #whereismymoney to find out what it's funding, or the Big 6 energy companies asking #wheredoesmyenergycomefrom (not quite as snappy, I will agree…).

DONATE

If there's an issue that you care deeply about, and you want to support those on the front line doing the 'vigorous campaigning' that you might not have the time, energy or stomach for, make a donation if you can afford to. Many environmental campaigns are run on a shoestring and rely heavily on volunteer time. Making a donation helps them to print materials, pay for website costs, even buy the odd cuppa or two to keep morale up.

CRAFTIVISM

The term craftivism was first coined by American Betsy Greer, who defines it as:

> 'a way of looking at life where voicing opinions through creativity makes your voice stronger, your compassion deeper and your quest for justice more infinite.'

One of the most effective and passionate proponents of craftivism is the fabulous Sarah Corbett, who is an award-winning activist, author, 'craftivist' and founder of Craftivist Collective (www.craftivist-collective.co.uk). I'm a massive fan. Sarah has worked on projects both on her own and with larger charities and organisations to help change hearts, minds, cultures, systems and structures causing oppression of people and harm to our planet.

Mini Fashion Statements

One of my favourite of Sarah's projects is her *Mini Fashion Statements*, which she talks about here:

'Our pocket-sized scrolls are powerful and poignant little reminders of the role we can play as consumers. They're designed to make us think about how the clothes we buy and wear are made, and how we might be able to help tackle problems like poor conditions for workers or the use of materials that are damaging to the environment.'

Sarah writes on her website, www.craftivist-collective.com:

'Your covert mission, should you choose to accept it, is to pop a little inspiration – your scroll – into the pockets of clothes you feel represent the issue you're addressing. This undercover "shop-dropping" mission will mean your message is delivered with the added spice of surprise once found. Give some thought to where you will hide it. A friend or

> colleague's pocket, perhaps? Or inside a garment hanging up in a shop you think should improve their practices.'
>
> The finished scrolls, tied with a pretty bow and featuring an invitation to 'please open me', neatly written in lowercase in the maker's neatest handwriting, a smiley face and a kiss, can then be 'shop-dropped' into the pockets of garments in fashion stores, or clothes worn by family, friends and colleagues.

This deliberately non-confrontational form of 'guerrilla activism' using handcrafts is designed as an alternative to some of the more traditional aggressive or quick types of activism. It's a form of slow activism using your hands, heart and head together to reflect and think critically and strategically. To engage audiences who might not see themselves as activists and positively encourage people to take action. The project has been made into a DIY kit that can be used anywhere in the world; it has been delivered as workshops to hundreds of people in places such as the Barbican and the British Museum, in support of Fashion Revolution, and has been featured in mainstream media including the BBC News homepage, a double page spread in the *Guardian* newspaper, *Huffington Post* as well as the Business of Fashion.

HAVE CONVERSATIONS

Confession: For someone who is very vocal online and in print, who makes regular appearances on the radio, takes part in panel discussions, gives talks, and has even made the odd TV appearance or two, I find it really difficult to have conversations with friends and family about what I do and why.

I'm a people pleaser at heart. I want people to like me, and I don't want them to feel like I'm constantly judging them on what they wear, what they buy, and their use of clingfilm (obviously I am judging them, I'm just using my inside voice). I don't want to be 'that person' that people try to avoid making eye contact with in case they're in for another lecture on the perils of their lifestyle. I don't want to cause family arguments at Christmas about what temperature the thermostat is set at, or whether the fairy lights are LEDs. But I probably go too far the other way. There has to be a sweet spot somewhere, but I will be honest and say that I'm still struggling to find it.

Probably the easiest way to broach these conversations is simply by living your values. In your everyday 'radical' acts of activism. My very visibly mended jeans were a brilliant example of this – whenever I wore them, they pretty much never failed to strike up a conversation about repair, and fast fashion, and lost skills. In a really non-preachy, non-judgemental way. Even simply remembering to take your reusable coffee cup to the next work conference you go to, and standing there slightly sheepishly holding it in the queue for drinks, will probably get a conversation going with the person next to you about how they forgot theirs/wish they'd brought one with them. And then you have the perfect 'in' to a little chat about how a particular statistic, or social media post, or TV documentary really shocked you into action, and maybe share a couple of the other simple changes you've made. The more normal we make these acts, the more confident we feel talking about the changes we're making and why we're making them, the more people will be inspired and empowered to change too.

BE PREPARED TO FEEL A BIT UNCOMFORTABLE

For lots of us, stepping out against the flow, and away from the accepted 'norms' of society, can feel a little bit scary. Even if we're not going to be marching and waving banners around, doing new things outside of our comfort zone to stand up for what we believe in can feel uncomfortable, and maybe even cause a few butterflies. That's totally normal and totally OK. But I would urge you to push on through that discomfort and take action regardless. Get some moral support, break it down into the smallest steps you can. But take action. It's how we grow. And it's how change happens.

5 QUICK WINS FOR YOUR INNER ENVIRON-MENTAL ACTIVIST

1 Tweet a picture to a brand or retailer and ask them what they are doing to help combat plastic pollution, or fast fashion, or climate change etc.

2 Switch ONE purchase to a more sustainable option.

3 Challenge yourself to have one conversation with a friend or family member about environmental issues this week. For this first conversation, pick someone who you think is probably already pretty on board. Maybe ask them why they think we (as a general population) don't talk more about environmental issues as a starter?

4 Write to your MP – we need to let the people in charge of policy know that this stuff matters.

5 Donate. Find a cause or charity that resonates and whose environmental work you support, and make a one-off donation, no matter how small.

MORE SUGGESTIONS:

☐ Resist impulse buys and being manipulated by clever ads (*see* page 16)

☐ Get clear on your values and think about how you can bring your purchases more in line with them

☐ Join in with Fashion Revolution every April and ask the question #whomademyclothes

- [ ] Engage in a spot of craftivism – there are projects on the Craftivist Collective website (www.craftivist-collective.co.uk) that you can do yourself, and you can also find out when Sarah is hosting workshops

- [ ] Wear a visible mend, badge or T-shirt with a sustainable(ish) slogan on (I've got one that says 'Climate Optimist') – it's an easy way to start conversations

- [ ] Buy less! It's a radical act

- [ ] Share some of your favourite ethical brands or purchases on social media – thank them for the great stuff they're doing and invite friends to check them out

- [ ] Talk about the changes you're making – whether that's on your personal FB page, or in person. The more people seen to be making changes, the more everyday these 'radical' acts become

- [ ] If you want to get a bit more vocal and 'march-y', check out all the amazing stuff Extinction Rebellion (www.rebellion.earth) are doing

Over to you (aka now get up and do!)

List three or four ideas below for changes you could make to up your activism game.

Action	Timeframe
1.	
2.	
3.	
4.	

Resources

- **THE CLIMATE COUNCIL (WWW.CLIMATECOUNCIL.ORG.AU)**
  An Australian site but packed full of relevant information and authoritative expert advice on climate change and solutions.

- **THEY WORK FOR YOU (WWW.THEYWORKFORYOU.COM)**
  Find out who your MP is, how they voted on various legislation, and how to contact them.

- **CITY TO SEA (WWW.CITYTOSEA.ORG.UK)**
  A great example of how online campaigns and petitions can bring about real world change.

- **38 DEGREES (WWW.HOME.38DEGREES.ORG.UK)**
  Online campaigning site that enables you to start a petition about issues you care about.

- **CRAFTIVIST COLLECTIVE (WWW.CRAFTIVIST-COLLECTIVE.CO.UK)**
  Find out about the latest Craftivist campaigns and how you can take part.

- **FASHION REVOLUTION (WWW.FASHIONREVOLUTION.ORG)**
  Annual campaign to create positive change for a more sustainable fashion industry.

- **MOTHERS RISE UP (WWW.MOTHERSRISEUP.ORG.UK)**
  A fast-growing group of ordinary mums who are worried sick about the climate crisis.

- **EXTINCTION REBELLION (WWW.REBELLION.EARTH)**
  An international movement that uses non-violent civil disobedience to achieve radical change in order to minimise the risk of human extinction and ecological collapse.

- YOUTH STRIKE FOR CLIMATE (WWW.UKSCN.ORG)

  Inspired by climate activist Greta Thunberg's Fridays for the Future school strikes, a youth climate action network has sprung up around the globe, calling on students to strike from school once a month and take to the streets demanding climate action.

Conclusion

I'm not entirely sure how to end this book. You'll probably have gathered from reading it that there are no nice simple solutions. No one size fits all answers. The climate crisis is complex, and there's no reason to think that the solutions will be any less so.

A phrase I often find myself saying to people when trying to help them find solutions that will work for them, their family, their unique set of circumstances, is that there is no 'black and white'. There's very rarely a 'right' and a 'wrong' way of doing something when it comes to trying to reduce our impact. In fact, there is no 'green and white'. There's a whole myriad of shades of green in between, and that shade of green will vary in different areas of our lives, and even from day to day.

Without wanting to make you vomit by using a cliché, 'it's a journey'. We're all on it. We're all going to have to make changes over the coming years, whether we do so willingly or we're forced to do so by legislation. As individuals and families, we're not going to go from where we are now to uber-green perfection (whatever that looks like) in the course of a couple of weeks. But that shouldn't stop us from starting. That shouldn't stop us from moving from one shade of green to the next. One step at a time.

I hope in this book that I've shown you that. And that I've given you options – ideas to help you to make better choices. What you choose might not be the 'perfectly green' option, but it will be something that works for you, that you can keep up, and that **does** make a difference.

I would love for you to keep this book by your bedside, to make one change in one area, then check back in to see what the next change you can make is. And failing that, I would love you to pass this book on to someone else, to help them to get started.

Thank you for reading. Thank you for the actions you've already taken, and the actions you will take. We're all in this together. Sink or swim. Let's grab our armbands, our buoyancy aids, and do what we can to keep the ship afloat.

Acknowledgements

First and foremost I need to thank my agent Kate Johnson at MacKenzie Wolf, without whom this book would have remained half-formed in my head, and I would never have been brave enough to make it a reality. Thank you Kate for 'getting it' straightaway, and for holding my hand through the whole process.

Thanks also to the wonderful team at Green Tree and Bloomsbury, especially to Charlotte Croft for editing some of my ramblings into salient points, and to Holly for so efficiently keeping me up to speed with every step of the process.

The saying about it taking a village to raise a child is also apparently true for writing a book. I said in the introduction that I'm not an environmental scientist, or an 'expert', so I am hugely grateful to all the actual experts who answered my questions, provided quotes, insights and the benefit of their far superior knowledge and experience – thank you to all of you for contributing, and any errors are mine!

A big thank you to my brilliant friend Michelle, for her unswerving support of both me and all things sustainable(ish), for the endless Skype messenger chats, and the kicks up the butt.

To William and Samuel – the sheer terror of what might be lying ahead for them stops me regularly from throwing in the towel and keeps me going when it all feels a bit too hard and I start to feel overwhelmed at the enormity of the task ahead for humanity.

And of course, thanks to my amazing husband, Ben – who has always believed in me, especially when I didn't or couldn't.

Lastly, my thanks to each and every person who reads this book. To misquote Anne-Marie Bonneau, aka the Zero Waste Chef: 'We don't need a handful of people doing sustainable living perfectly, we need millions of people doing it imperfectly.' Here's to your imperfect journey.

References

Introduction

- Simon Sinek, Start with Why TED talk: https://www.ted.com/talks/simon_sinek_how_great_leaders_inspire_action?language=en

Chapter 1: Conscious consumption

- Household consumption is responsible for more than 60 per cent of global greenhouse gas emissions: *Journal of Industrial Ecology*, https://onlinelibrary.wiley.com/doi/abs/10.1111/jiec.12371 (accessed 6 January, 2019)
- Better educated households have generally higher consumption levels, and therefore emissions: Mapping the carbon footprint of EU regions, Ivanova, D., Vita, G., Steen-Olsen, K., *et al.*, 2017, *Environmental Research Letters*, 12 :(5): 054013
- Buyerarchy of Needs: http://longliveirony.com

Chapter 2: Zero waste(ish)

- 20,000 historic landfill sites: https://www.qmul.ac.uk/geog/research/research-projects/historiclandfill/ (accessed 12 January, 2019)
- Each year we bury 18 million tonnes of waste in landfill: https://www.recyclingbins.co.uk/recycling-facts/ (accessed 12 January, 2019)
- The average person in the UK will throw away their own body weight in rubbish every seven weeks: https://www.recyclingbins.co.uk/recycling-facts/ (accessed 12 January, 2019)
- We recycle less than 50 per cent of our waste in the UK: https://assets.publishing.service.gov.uk/government/uploads/system/uploads/attachment_data/file/746642/UK_Statistics_on_Waste_statistical_notice_October_2018_FINAL.pdf (accessed 12 January, 2019)
- Landfill sites are a major source of methane: *An estimate of methane emissions from UK landfill sites based on direct flux measurements at representative sites*, Milton, M J T, Goody, B A, Partridge, R H, Andrews, A, NPL Report QM 134, June 1997

- More than 50 per cent of the world's population don't have access to regular rubbish collections: http://www.worldbank.org/en/news/feature/2016/03/03/waste-not-want-not---solid-waste-at-the-heart-of-sustainable-development (accessed 17 January, 2019)
- Energy from waste: https://assets.publishing.service.gov.uk/government/uploads/system/uploads/attachment_data/file/284612/pb14130-energy-waste-201402.pdf

Chapter 3: Plastic free(ish)

- Over the last 10 years we have produced more plastic than during the whole of the 20th century: Ellen MacArthur Foundation report – *The New Plastics Economy: Rethinking the future of plastics*, https://www.ellenmacarthurfoundation.org/publications/the-new-plastics-economy-rethinking-the-future-of-plastics
- Almost half of all the plastic produced is used just once: https://plasticoceans.org/the-facts/ (accessed 6 January, 2019)
- Unless it's been incinerated, every piece of plastic ever made is still in existence: https://www.plantingpeace.org/2015/05/plastic-footprint (accessed 17 January, 2019)
- Only around 10 per cent of plastic made has ever been recycled: http://advances.sciencemag.org/content/3/7/e1700782 (accessed 6 January, 2019)
- One in three fish caught contain plastic: https://www.sciencedirect.com/science/article/pii/S0025326X12005668?via%3Dihub (accessed 6 January, 2019)
- More plastic in the ocean than fish: Ellen MacArthur Foundation report – *The New Plastics Economy: Rethinking the future of plastics*, https://www.ellenmacarthurfoundation.org/publications/the-new-plastics-economy-rethinking-the-future-of-plastics
- Plastic microfibres have been found in human poo: Schwabl, P. *et al.* (2018), *Assessment of microplastic concentrations in human stool* - Preliminary results of a prospective study, Presented at UEG Week 2018 Vienna, 24 October, 2018.
- Two million tonnes of plastic waste: https://www.bbc.co.uk/news/business-42456584 (accessed 17 January, 2019)
- China's plastic ban and where our plastic is going now: https://www.nationalgeographic.co.uk/environment-and-conservation/2018/11/where-does-your-plastic-waste-end (accessed 6th January 2019)
- Malaysia returning thousands of tonnes of plastic waste: https://www.bbc.co.uk/news/av/world-asia-48438364/malaysia-orders-tonnes-of-imported-waste-to-be-returned (accessed 7 June, 2019)
- Carbon footprint of plastic bags vs cotton reusables: http://www.niassembly.gov.uk/globalassets/documents/raise/publications/2011/environment/3611.pdf (accessed 7 June, 2019)
- Glass vs plastic vs tetrapacks: https://friendsoftheearth.uk/plastics/plastic-or-glass-milk-bottles-crate-expectations (accessed 7 June, 2019)

- Only 14 per cent of the plastic produced is recycled: https://www.ellenmacarthur foundation.org/publications/the-new-plastics-economy-rethinking-the-future-of-plastics (accessed 6 January, 2019)
- We won't save the earth with a better kind of disposable coffee cup: https://www.theguardian.com/commentisfree/2018/sep/06/save-earth-disposable-coffee-cup-green (accessed 13 January, 2019)
- One million plastic bottles produced every minute: https://www.theguardian.com/environment/2017/jun/28/a-million-a-minute-worlds-plastic-bottle-binge-as-dangerous-as-climate-change (accessed 6 January, 2019)
- Plastic periods facts: https://www.wen.org.uk/environmenstrual-in-numbers (accessed 6 January, 2019)
- Lil-Lets period plastic: https://www.lil-lets.co.uk/period-plastic (accessed 6 January, 2019)
- *Cosmo* magazine review of period pants: https://www.cosmopolitan.com/uk/body/a19591494/period-proof-underwear-modibodi/ (accessed 6 January, 2019)

Chapter 4: Sustainable(ish) food

- Food production is responsible for a quarter of all global greenhouse gas emissions: More than half of food emissions comes from animal products, https://ora.ox.ac.uk/objects/uuid:b0b53649-5e93-4415-bf07-6b0b1227172f
- Approximately 30 per cent of the food produced never reaches the table: http://www.fao.org/save-food/resources/keyfindings/en/ (accessed 17 January, 2019)
- Livestock farming accounts for 14 per cent of GHG: https://www.sciencedirect.com/science/article/pii/S221209631730027X (accessed 12 January, 2019)
- Beef production emits five times more greenhouse gases, compared with the production of chicken and pork: Meyer N, Reguant-Closa A, 'Eat as If You Could Save the Planet and Win!' Sustainability Integration into Nutrition for Exercise and Sport, *Nutrients*. 2017;9(4):412, published 21 April, 2017, doi:10.3390/nu9040412
- If food waste were a country it would be the third biggest emitter: http://www.fao.org/docrep/018/i3347e/i3347e.pdf
- Around 50 per cent of food waste in the UK occurs in the home: Not wasting good food and drink, http://www.wrap.org.uk/content/food-overview (accessed 12 January, 2019)
- 4.2 million tonnes of avoidable food and drink annually: http://www.wrap.org.uk/content/household-food-and-drink-waste-uk-2012 (accessed 12 January, 2019)
- 5.8 million potatoes, 24 million slices of bread, 5.8 million glasses of milk: https://www.ukharvest.org.uk/news-and-media/the-most-commonly-wasted-foods-in-british-households-and-how-to-rescue-them (accessed 12 January, 2019)
- The Planetary Diet: https://eatforum.org/eat-lancet-commission/ (accessed 17 January, 2019)

- Ethical Consumer – palm oil and consumers: https://www.ethicalconsumer.org/food-drink/palm-oil-and-consumers (accessed 7 June, 2019)
- Palm oil list of worst offenders from Greenpeace: https://www.greenpeace.org.uk/faqs-palm-oil-answered/ (accessed 7 June, 2019)

Chapter 5: Sustainable(ish) fashion

- Clothing production doubled: Ellen MacArthur Foundation, *A new textiles economy: Redesigning fashion's future*, 2017, http://www.ellenmacarthurfoundation.org/publications
- 80 billion pieces of clothing a year: https://truecostmovie.com/learn-more/environmental-impact (accessed 12 January, 2019)
- Fast fashion disposed of in under a year: Ellen MacArthur Foundation, *A new textiles economy: Redesigning fashion's future*, 2017, http://www.ellenmacarthurfoundation.org/publications
- 2720L of water to make a T-shirt: https://www.worldwildlife.org/stories/the-impact-of-a-cotton-t-shirt (accessed 12 January, 2019)
- Garment workers earn 1–3 per cent of the retail price: http://labourbehindthe label.org/campaigns/living-wage/ (accessed 12 January, 2019)
- Beading and sequins can be an indication of child labour: *To Die For – Is fashion wearing out the world?*: Lucy Siegle, Harper Collins, 2011
- 10–30 per cent of donated clothing is sold in charity shops: https://www.bbc.co.uk/news/magazine-30227025 (accessed 12 January, 2019)
- RiverBlue film: http://riverbluethemovie.eco
- Eighty per cent of garment workers are women aged between 18 and 35: http://www.worldbank.org/en/news/feature/2017/02/07/in-bangladesh-empowering-and-employing-women-in-the-garments-sector (accessed 12 January, 2019)
- Living wage in Asia: http://labourbehindthelabel.org/campaigns/living-wage/ (accessed 12 January, 2019)
- Cotton farmer suicide: https://www.independent.co.uk/life-style/fashion/fashion-revolution-2016-the-true-cost-of-fast-fashion-a6991201.html (accessed 12 January, 2019)
- Average British woman hoards £285 of clothes: https://www.huffingtonpost.co.uk/entry/235-million-items-of-clothing-landfill-sites-in-the-uk-this-year_uk_58e62581e4b0917d34776259 (accessed 17 January, 2019)
- Twenty per cent of our clothes 80 per cent of the time: https://www.businessinsider.com/people-dont-wear-most-of-their-clothes-2013-4?r=US&IR=T (accessed 17 January, 2019)
- Extending the life of clothes by nine months: http://www.wrap.org.uk/sites/files/wrap/VoC%20FINAL%20online%202012%2007%2011.pdf (accessed 12 January, 2019)

- 70,000 microfibres per wash: https://www.theguardian.com/science/2016/sep/27/washing-clothes-releases-water-polluting-fibres-study-finds (accessed 17 January, 2019)
- *Clothing Poverty: the hidden world of fast fashion and secondhand clothes*, Andrew Brooks, Zed Books, 2015

Chapter 6: Sustainable(ish) family

- Mattresses for babies: https://www.lullabytrust.org.uk/safer-sleep-advice/mattresses-and-bedding (accessed 13 January, 2019)
- Secondhand car seats: https://www.childcarseats.org.uk/choosing-using/second-hand-child-seats (accessed 13 January, 2019)
- 5000 disposable nappies per child: http://www.wrap.org.uk/content/real-nappies-overview (accessed 13 January, 2019)
- Three billion nappies per year in the UK: http://www.wrap.org.uk/content/real-nappies-overview (accessed 13 January, 2019)
- Three per cent of household waste: http://www.wrap.org.uk/content/real-nappies-overview (accessed 13 January, 2019)
- Households using cloth nappies reduce landfill waste by half: http://www.wrap.org.uk/content/real-nappies-overview (accessed 13 January, 2019)
- Disposable nappies use up to three and a half times more energy to make compared to cloth nappies: https://www.veolia.co.uk/westberkshire/waste-minimisation/real-nappies-facts (accessed 13 January, 2019); https://www.theguardian.com/environment/2014/jun/22/wrong-to-use-disposable-nappies (accessed 13 January, 2019)
- Wet wipes cause 93 per cent of sewer blockages: https://www.theguardian.com/environment/2017/dec/12/baby-wipes-93-percent-matter-causing-uk-sewer-blockages (accessed 13 January, 2019)
- Dog, cats and climate change: https://www.forbes.com/sites/jeffmcmahon/2017/08/02/whats-your-dogs-carbon-pawprint/#53eaa00813a6 (accessed 13 January, 2019)
- Impact of pet ownership on carbon footprint: Seth Wynes and Kimberly A Nicholas, 2017, *Environ. Res. Lett.* 12 074024 http://iopscience.iop.org/article/10.1088/1748-9326/aa7541
- Environmental impacts of food consumption by dogs and cats: Okin GS, 2017, Environmental impacts of food consumption by dogs and cats, PLoS ONE 12(8): e0181301. https://doi.org/10.1371/journal.pone.0181301
- Yora pet food: https://www.yorapetfoods.com/yora-pet-foods (accessed 13 January, 2019)
- 'Stick and flick' dog poo: https://www.telegraph.co.uk/news/2017/03/14/dog-owners-urged-use-stick-flick-method-instead-poo-bags (accessed 17 January, 2019)

- Dog poo-powered street light: https://www.theguardian.com/environment/2018/jan/01/stools-to-fuels-street-lamp-runs-on-dog-poo-bio-energy-waste- (accessed 13 January, 2019)

Chapter 7: Sustainable(ish) home

- Energy statistics: https://assets.publishing.service.gov.uk/government/uploads/system/uploads/attachment_data/file/729317/Energy_Consumption_in_the_UK__ECUK__2018.pdf
- Impact of switching to renewable energy: The Climate Mitigation Gap: Education and Government Recommendations vs. Effective Individual Actions, Wynes S and Nicholas K, 2017, *Environ. Res. Lett.*, 12 074024, http://iopscience.iop.org/article/10.1088/1748-9326/aa7541 (accessed 14 January, 2019)
- Contribution of renewables to the National Grid: https://www.theguardian.com/business/2017/dec/21/nuclear-power-renewables-low-carbon-provide-record-share-uk-electricity (accessed 16 January, 2019)
- Renewable tariffs set to become cheaper than standard tariffs: https://theswitch.co.uk/blog/cheapest-green-supplier (accessed 14 January, 2019)
- 2018 IPCC report https://www.ipcc.ch/sr15/
- Lighting accounts for 15 per cent of a typical household's energy bill: http://www.energysavingtrust.org.uk/home-energy-efficiency/lighting (accessed 14 January, 2019)
- Savings from switching to LED bulbs: https://www.which.co.uk/news/2017/11/could-you-save-232-on-your-energy-bill-by-switching-to-led-bulbs/ (accessed 16 January, 2019)
- Overfilling the kettle: http://www.energysavingtrust.org.uk/sites/default/files/reports/AtHomewithWater%287%29.pdf (accessed 14 January, 2019)
- Turning down your thermostat: https://assets.publishing.service.gov.uk/government/uploads/system/uploads/attachment_data/file/128720/6923-how-much-energy-could-be-saved-by-making-small-cha.pdf (accessed 14 January, 2019)
- Air source heat pumps: http://www.energysavingtrust.org.uk/renewable-energy/heat/air-source-heat-pumps (accessed 14 January, 2019)
- Standby accounts for 10 per cent of household electricity bills and 1 per cent of global CO_2 emissions: https://ec.europa.eu/energy/intelligent/projects/sites/iee-projects/files/projects/documents/selina_consumer_guide_en.pdf
- Devices left on standby mean that UK households waste £227 million a year: https://www.uswitch.com/media-centre/2014/08/households-waste-227-million-a-year-leaving-appliances-on-standby/ (accessed 17 January, 2019)
- Since 1950 global water use has nearly tripled: *Sustainable Resource Development: Policy, Problem & Prescription*, Udai Prakash Sinha, Concept Publishing (2011)
- 1 in 5 people don't have access to safe, affordable drinking water: Half the world's people do not have access to sanitation, http://www.worldwatercouncil.org/fileadmin/wwc/Library/WWVision/Chapter2.pdf (accessed 15 January, 2019)

- Water needed to produce the average UK diet per day: https://www.timesofmalta.com/articles/view/20180911/health-fitness/over-3000-litres-of-water-required-to-produce-daily-diet.688889 (accessed 15 January, 2019)
- Bathing, washing and teeth cleaning accounts for up to 21 per cent of our household water use: http://www.energysavingtrust.org.uk/sites/default/files/reports/AtHomewithWater%287%29.pdf
- A running tap wastes 6L of water a minute: https://www.water.org.uk/news-item/the-quick-fix-way-to-cut-water-waste-at-home/ (accessed 17 January, 2019)
- One third of the water we use at home is flushed down the toilet: https://www.anglianwater.co.uk/_assets/media/Fact_File_5_-_Using_water_at_home.pdf (accessed 15 January, 2019)
- $3.1trillion in retirement assets: https://www.consultancy.uk/news/16104/pension-funding-across-top-22-markets-hits-41-trillion (accessed 17 January, 2019)

Chapter 8: Sustainable(ish) work

- Leaving a computer on overnight for a year creates enough CO_2 to fill a double-decker bus, PC monitor left on overnight, Leaving your photocopier on standby, Air conditioning, Two per cent increase in office temperature: https://www.environment.admin.cam.ac.uk/facts-figures (accessed 13 January, 2019)
- Nearly 1 quarter of office workers would refuse a job in an organisation with a poor sustainability record: http://hrnews.co.uk/a-quarter-of-office-workers-would-turn-down-a-job-over-sustainability/ (accessed 11 June 2019)
- Houseplants and air pollution: https://archive.org/details/nasa_techdoc_19930072988/page/n11 (accessed 14 January, 2019)
- Energy savings of working from home: https://www.carbontrust.com/media/507270/ctc830-homeworking.pdf (accessed 14 January, 2019)

Chapter 9: Sustainable(ish) school

- Schools challenged to go plastic free by 2020: https://www.gov.uk/government/news/schools-challenged-to-go-single-use-plastic-free-by-2022 (accessed 17 January, 2019)

Chapter 10: Sustainable(ish) travel and transport

- Twenty-eight per cent of GHG emissions from transport: https://www.theccc.org.uk/wp-content/uploads/2018/06/CCC-2018-Progress-Report-to-Parliament.pdf (accessed 15 January, 2019)
- Cars account for 15 per cent of UK transport emissions: https://www.theccc.org.uk/wp-content/uploads/2018/06/CCC-2018-Progress-Report-to-Parliament.pdf (accessed 15 January, 2019)

- Average miles travelled commuting per year: Carbon emissions of plane vs car over that distance, http://www.bbc.co.uk/guides/zxjy6fr (accessed 15 January, 2019) `
- Thirty-eight per cent of journeys in Britain are under 2 miles, Just under half the population of England and Wales travel less than 3.1 miles to work – around a 45-minute walk, or a 15-minute bike ride, the average distance travelled to school in the UK is 2.5 miles – which would take less than 15 minutes to cycle: https://www.cycling-embassy.org.uk/wiki/cycling-is-not-practical-for-the-transportation-or-commuting-needs-of-most-people (accessed 16 January, 2019)
- 760,000 people commute to work by bike: https://www.thetimes.co.uk/article/commuting-by-bike-soars-by-nearly-a-fifth-c0p2780x6p2 (accessed 16 January, 2019)
- Forty-six per cent of primary pupils are currently driven to school: Department for Transport, National Travel Survey 2014
- Swedish study into health impacts of electric cycling: https://www.sciencedaily.com/releases/2018/07/180726161118.htm
- If you're a low-mileage driver driving less than 6–8000 miles per year (a car club) could save up to £3500 a year: https://www.sustrans.org.uk/what-you-can-do/use-your-car-less/car-clubs-and-car-sharing
- The AA – eco-driving advice: http://www.theaa.com/driving-advice/fuels-environment/drive-smart (accessed 9 January, 2019)
- Liftshare: https://liftshare.com/uk/about/safetytips#Help (accessed 16 January, 2019)
- Aviation accounts for 2–4 per cent of total greenhouse gas emissions: https://www.icao.int/environmental-protection/Documents/EnvironmentReport-2010/ICAO_EnvReport10-Ch1_en.pdf
- One return flight from London to Sydney: https://www.wanderlust.co.uk/content/to-fly-or-not-to-fly/ (accessed 16 January, 2019)
- Eighty-five per cent of carbon offsets fail to reduce emissions: https://ec.europa.eu/clima/sites/clima/files/ets/docs/clean_dev_mechanism_en.pdf
- Carbon footprint of train versus plane: https://www.seat61.com/CO2flights.htm (accessed 16 January, 2019)
- Tourism accounts for 10 per cent of the world's jobs and global GDP: https://www.wttc.org/-/media/files/reports/economic-impact-research/regions-2018/world2018.pdf

Chapter 11: Sustainable(ish) celebrations

- 108 million rolls of wrapping paper: https://www.independent.co.uk/life-style/christmas/christmas-waste-total-wrapping-paper-food-scraps-packaging-sticky-tape-study-a8119821.html (accessed 15 January, 2019)
- Christmas waste statistics: https://www.biffa.co.uk/biffablog/2017/12/18/tis-the-season-to-reycle (accessed 15 January, 2019)

- 500 tonnes of fairy lights are thrown away: https://ciwm-journal.co.uk/364700km-of-wrapping-paper-and-other-facts-figures (accessed 15 January, 2019)
- One in 10 unwanted Christmas presents end up in landfill: https://www.ziffit.com/en-gb/blog/blogitems/great-british-christmas-declutter (accessed 15 January, 2019)
- We waste around 250,000 tonnes of food each Christmas: https://www.theguardian.com/environment/2016/dec/20/brits-christmas-dinner-turkey-sprouts-bin (accessed 15 January, 2019)
- 81 million unwanted presents are received each year: https://www.ziffit.com/en-gb/blog/blogitems/great-british-christmas-declutter (accessed 15 January, 2019)
- The UK generates the weight of 3.3 million emperor penguins in plastic waste: https://www.wcl.org.uk/uk-christmas-gift-to-the-environment.asp (accessed 15 January, 2019)

Chapter 12: Armchair activism (or how to be an everyday radical)

- 6.2 per cent of plastic waste on beaches comes from toilets: https://www.mcsuk.org/media/gbbc-2018-report.pdf
- MPs and action on climate change: https://www.green-alliance.org.uk/resources/Building_a_political_mandate_for_climate_action.pdf

Index